W9-AAB-660

Winning the Reputation Game

Winning the Reputation Game

Grahame R. Dowling

The MIT Press
Cambridge, Massachusetts
London, England

This book was set in Sabon by Toppan Best-set Premedia Limited. Printed and bound in the United States of America.

Library of Congress Cataloging-in-Publication Data

Names: Dowling, Grahame R. (Grahame Robert) author.
Title: Winning the reputation game : creating stakeholder value and competitive advantage / Dowling, Grahame R.
Description: Cambridge, MA : The MIT Press, 2016. | Includes bibliographical references and index.
Identifiers: LCCN 2015039867 | ISBN 9780262034463 (hardcover : alk. paper)
Subjects: LCSH: Corporate image. | Social responsibility of business. | Organizational effectiveness.
Classification: LCC HD59.2 .D696 2016 | DDC 659.2—dc23 LC record available at http://lccn.loc.gov/2015039867

10 9 8 7 6 5 4 3 2 1

Contents

Preface

One thing that makes the study of corporate reputations interesting is why some companies become admired and respected for their achievements while others in their industry go largely unheralded. Across the world there are now more than 100 annual opinion polls that document these effects.[1] Why does a company like *Apple* have a better reputation than *Samsung*? It has been voted as the World's Most Admired Company in the annual *Fortune* survey every year from 2008 to 2015. Why does *Harvard University* have a better reputation than its cross-town rivals *Boston College, Lesley University, MIT, Northeastern University, Suffolk University, Tufts University,* and the *University of Massachusetts*? Academics, consultants, and commentators in the business media each have their own favorite theory. Here I will outline mine.

The theory described in this book seeks to explain companies with three broad types of reputation. One group has weak reputations. They really don't register on the radar of the people who buy their brands or most members of the general public. Then there are organizations that have strong reputations. Some have a generally good reputation such as the *Red Cross* or a generally poor reputation such as Rupert Murdoch's News Corp. Finally, there are companies with a mixed reputation, either across different groups of people or where the same people consider the company has some good and some bad aspects. These are an interesting group of companies. They appeal to some people and are repulsed by others. And they don't fit easily into any of the current theories of corporate reputation.

My theory is grounded primarily in the field of strategic marketing. The strategy part focuses on how companies use their capabilities to create superior products and services. The marketing part focuses on how they attain and retain their target customers. Success at these endeavors is at the heart of why a company like *Apple* and a university like *Harvard* have strong reputations that have helped them achieve leadership in their industries. They offer superior value to their employees and target customers than most of their competitors. From this success comes the authority to tell an engaging story about the character and market leadership of the organization. These stories contextualize the reputations of each organization for employees, customers, business partners, media, and investors.

To describe how companies with strong reputations attain their status, I use the metaphor of a game, defined in my Webster's dictionary as "a procedure or strategy for gaining an end." The strategy is to build and maintain a strong corporate reputation, and the end is to gain a sustainable competitive advantage. Hence the title of this book—*Winning the Reputation Game*. The goals, rules, language, and scoring of this game are described in chapter 2. Scholars should note that this book does not follow the precepts of game theory or economics that discuss reputation. While the reputation games formalized in these disciplines provide insights for some of the ideas discussed here, they are too limited to describe the behavior of organizations with complex reputations like *Apple* and *Harvard University*.

Throughout the book I use a number of case examples to illustrate the points being made. Their role is to complement the more scientific studies referred to and to highlight the peculiarity, complexity, and differences between organizations. For example, some of these companies have good reputations that stand up to repeated attacks by their critics. Others like tobacco and alcohol companies, called "sin" stocks, have bad reputations but make handsome financial returns.[2] And some companies are admired and respected far beyond what their fundamentals would suggest. As Bill Starbuck explains, when scientists use statistical techniques to uncover relationships between large numbers of companies they often lose sight of the commonsense content of the data.[3] To help avoid this, he suggests that the observations (companies) studied should also include the exceptional and the mundane as these require explanation about the unique ways in which companies exploit their environments.

Over the last twenty years my professional interest in corporate reputations has focused on answering two questions. What does a company need to do in order to be admired and respected? What are the payoffs from having such a good reputation? An economist might paraphrase these questions as—is there a market for reputation? And a strategist might ask: How does a good reputation provide a competitive advantage to a company?

While a considerable amount of research has focused on these questions, a recent summary of this scholarship in *The Oxford Handbook of Corporate Reputations* revealed that there is little consensus about the answers to them.[4] There are many competing theories about how corporate reputations are formed and how they work to provide one company with an advantage over its rivals. While some of these theories have received support from piecemeal research findings about the effects of good and bad corporate reputations on the company's stakeholders, others are speculative in nature. Notwithstanding this patchy support, at face value most of these theories seem sensible. They are based on the simple proposition that companies that behave well will be admired and respected for this behavior. And this will help them attract the custom they need to survive and prosper.

However, what is disconcerting about this field of scholarship is that there are some high-profile companies that seem to ignore the advice of scholars and consultants about how to create a reputation of distinction. And there are some other companies that deliberately do the opposite to what is suggested. For example, many scholars and business commentators suggest that companies will be admired and respected more if they become more transparent about their operations and their dealings with outsiders. The logic behind this proposition is that transparency allows outsiders to make better judgments about the company's prospects.[5] But transparency is abhorrent to many companies. The last thing they want is members of the general public, or nosy journalists, or competitors scrutinizing their operations. The most likely outcome here is a public relations nightmare.

Corporate practice that does not reflect scholarly advice can be the result of three factors. One is that the companies that don't conform are anomalies. For some specific reason it is not in their best interest to follow the lead of their peers. A second reason is that these companies are not aware of, or are unable to follow, the advice proffered. The final explanation is that the academic advice is outdated or simply wrong. In this case practice is leading theory. However, regardless of the reasons for nonconformity, these different behaviors of companies are worth investigating. They can provide insight into the field of corporate reputations that traditional scholarship might have missed. So throughout this book I will identify some such "odd" companies and identify what seems to make them admired and respected.

This book is a scholar's reflection on a field of research and practice. Hence it is not written as a dissertation or a practice manual but rather as a monologue with you the reader. It is written for academics, consultants, managers, and other people who are curious about corporate reputations. The motivation for writing the book is captured in the following quote:

:

I set out to discover the why of it, and to transform my pleasure into knowledge.

Charles Baudelaire (a Parisian art critic).

I am certainly not the first person to offer much of the advice in the following chapters about how to create a better corporate reputation. Decades ago scholars like the late Peter Drucker suggested that companies focus on creating superior value for their customers as the principal way to achieve success. And academics who teach business unit strategy to MBAs and executives offer similar advice on a regular basis. Why the focus on creating better value for stakeholders is again relevant is because a variety of approaches to creating good corporate reputations have crowded out this back-to-basics approach. So what follows is my attempt to reclaim lost ground. You will judge if I am successful.

Last, I must alert you to a potential shortcoming of the evidence used in this treatise. Despite the growing economic power of the emerging countries of the world, most of the companies discussed in the book are of Australian, American, and European origin. The reason for this is that there is more accessible research and discussion of these companies than for African, Asian, Indian, Middle Eastern, Russian, and South American companies. The problem with this mindset, however, is that what follows is based on what has been termed WEIRD companies and managers—Western, Educated, Industrialized, Rich, and Democratic.[6] While this focus is somewhat lamentable, it may not be too distorting because many companies in developing markets look to US and European businesses for their leadership.[7]And, as they compete in international markets, they are likely to be assessed against the standards set by their WEIRD peers.

A second warning is about the choice of companies used to illustrate the issues. While they all are noteworthy, not all should be considered exemplary. By this I mean, these companies had a good corporate reputation at the time of writing this book, but this does not guarantee their future if their strategic choices are poor. As we have seen with companies like *Nokia*, *Research in Motion / Blackberry,* and *Nortel Networks*, a poor strategy can quickly destroy the company's fortunes and its good name.

1

The Value of a Winning Corporate Reputation

Many years ago I gave a talk to a group of CEOs about corporate reputations. I opened my discussion with the results of an opinion poll among members of the general public of the reputations of various companies, some of whom were represented in the room. At this point I paused and asked for their reaction to the list of reputation scores. One person quickly summed up the position of all the CEOs in the room—"irrelevant!" Another then took pity on me and suggested that while this information might be nice to know, it was not necessary to know. It told them nothing about the competitive standing of their company. For example, because *American Express* and *Qantas* did not compete with each other for suppliers, employees, or customers their relative reputations as assessed by the general public told neither CEO anything important about their future prospects. In essence, the CEOs were asking "show me the money" or at least tell me why creating a reputation that was better than their direct competitors was a sensible investment. So here is my updated answer and a good reason for reading the rest of the book. Much of the theory and empirical evidence to support each claim can be found in two sources, namely the journal *Corporate Reputation Review* and *The Oxford Handbook of Corporate Reputations,* as was noted in the preface.

The Payoffs of a Good Corporate Reputation

As described more formally in chapter 3, a corporate reputation is the evaluation of a company by its stakeholders. This evaluation is generally expressed in terms of the admiration and respect in which the company is held. Both such assessments are emotional. And consequently they are influential. Psychologists have discovered that many if not most people make judgments and decisions by consulting their emotions.[1] It is these emotions that turn a good corporate reputation into money. When people admire and respect a company, research indicates that this can have some powerful effects:

- Current employees are more engaged, more likely to recommend their employer to potential employees, and less likely to bad-mouth the company.
- More potential employees will consider working for the organization and seriously consider its job offer.
- Current customers give the company a higher share of their spending, are more tolerant when they experience an isolated episode of bad customer service, believe and like the company's advertising, and provide a positive recommendation if asked.
- Potential customers are more likely to notice the company's advertising, believe what other people tell them is good about the company, and consider its products and services.
- Business partners are more likely to offer more opportunities and be willing to engage with the company on favorable terms.
- Unions are less likely to encourage damaging action by their members.
- Shareholders are more likely to be longer term investors and believe what the company tells them.
- Politicians are less likely to be hostile to the company.
- Regulators are less likely to make an example of the company when they have the choice.
- Media are more likely to give the company unwarranted praise. Remember how *Enron* was lauded by the business press when it was the darling of the US corporate scene.
- Community members are more likely to tolerate the company's presence or praise its contribution.

While all these effects are quite intuitive, their occurrence is not definitive. Hence they are expressed as being more or less likely. There will always be some exceptions.

Each of these effects can be thought of as a form of corporate reputation currency. They help monetize a good corporate reputation. For example, from a corporate point of view, they can increase cash flow, reduce expenses, and/or help mitigate the risks of doing business with the company. While each effect is important, in combination they make a formidable set of reasons to invest in creating a good corporate reputation. And if one competitor's reputation is better than its rivals, then it may capture the benefits of this advantage if it can promote its good name. Chapters 6 and 7 focus on these issues.

How a Good Corporate Reputation Drives Share Price

The answer to whether a good corporate reputation drives the share price of a company seems to be a guarded yes. That is to say, anything to do with modeling the stock market is complex. To establish that there is a positive relationship between a good corporate reputation and a better share price is the Holy Grail of the corporate reputation industry. And as you would expect from tales about the Holy Grail, there is a tendency to exaggerate claims that a better corporate reputation helps companies have better (stronger and/or higher) share prices. When it does, CFOs take notice, and CEOs may consider funding specific reputation-enhancing programs. When it does not, corporate reputation might be consigned to the public affairs group and only get board room attention if a crisis occurs. Thus the stakes are high for reputation managers and consultants.

The search for a better reputation has proceeded along two adjoining paths. The first is to establish that a good reputation helps a company attain and retain superior financial performance. More than a decade ago Peter Roberts and I did a study that showed that companies with relatively good reputations are better able to sustain superior profit outcomes over time.[2] We also found that good reputations help poor performing companies return to profitability. Reputation disciples were thrilled. At the time of writing this chapter, our paper has been cited by other scholars more than 1,300 times—which is a lot in this field.

What we found was that there was a statistically significant positive affect of better reputations on better financial performance for very large, mainly US companies. We also found that this effect was small. Given the complexity of theories like net present valuethat explain how a good corporate reputation can raise the profit performance of a company and the limitations of the data we used to estimate these effects, this small effect was expected by us but has sometimes been overinterpreted by disciples. Thus our advice is to proceed cautiously to the second path.

The second path is to link this small reputation-based profit effect to share price. This is a big challenge that has so far eluded good scholarship because it involves modeling how past profit performance, expectations, and a host of other factors drive share price valuation and stock market behavior. This intellectual challenge, however, has not deterred some consultants from plotting a selected group of company reputation scores against their share prices and claiming that because a positive relationship is obvious, reputation drives share prices. The fallacy of this argument is discussed in the case of *BP* and the Gulf of Mexico oil spill below.

There is an old saying in science that to truly understand a phenomenon, you need to be able to predict what will happen when you reverse the effect. Thus we should also look at what happens to a public company when it suddenly develops a bad corporate reputation. Here there is plenty of interesting ad hoc evidence. Every time a big public company is involved in a major crisis, there is ample opportunity for its stakeholders to punish it on the share market. Rather than merely publicly berate the company, customers can buy from competitors, business partners can stop dealing the company, regulators can fine the company or might even seek to close it down, and key employees can leave. Any combination of these effects will affect the underlying drivers of the company's profitability. This should reduce its share price.

A study by the UK law firm *Freshfields Bruckhaus Deringer* found that of 78 crises between 2007 and 2012 involving large international businesses 40 percent of these companies suffered no fall in their share price.[3] When a fall did occur, its timing (immediate or delayed), severity (zero to +50 percent), and longevity (it lasted a few days or up to 6 months or more) were determined by the type of crisis. For example, crises triggered by reports of illegal or questionable conduct triggered the largest one-day falls. These falls were modest (<30 percent) but lasted longest (on average the shares were still down 15 percent after 6 months). In contrast, crises involving a company's IT or data systems almost went unnoticed by the share market. And to completely confound the situation when the settlement of the *Barclays Bank* LIBOR scandal was announced in 2012, the share price rose on that day and continued to rise for the next six months. All this happened on the back of a £290 million fine.[4]

When a major crisis decreases the share price of the company the efficient markets theory suggests that the new information revealed during the crisis has resulted in people lowering their expectations about its future prospects. This effect will be incorporated into its share price almost immediately. Now the interesting issue here is what role corporate reputation plays in this company revaluation? Jonathan Karpoff and his colleagues propose that companies that engage in misconduct that directly affects their counterparties (suppliers, shareholders, customers, etc.) experience a loss in share market value greater than that associated merely with the financial losses associated with the misconduct. This extra loss is due to the devaluing of the company's reputation.[5] This is triggered by a perception that the company has lax internal controls and/or a dysfunctional organizational culture. Here reputation acts as a proxy for how well the company is run, and thus what are its prospects for recovery.

A complementary explanation of the role corporate reputation plays in a postcrisis share market reaction is revealed by the case of *BP* and the Gulf of Mexico oil spill. The extensive commentary after the crisis suggested that many of *BP*'s deep water oil exploration operations were riskier than they should be. Thus we should expect that the company's operational reputation was tarnished and its share price fell because of this. However, the financial commentary suggested that most of the fall in the company's share price was due to the estimated size of financial reparations, the sale of assets, reduced cash flow, and the temporary suspension of the company's dividend. The usual nervousness displayed by the share market when a company is involved in a big crisis was likely an added effect.[6] And the trashing of the company's reputation in the media might also have had some effect. Thus the drop in *BP*'s share price was caused by many factors, with its media reputation probably playing only a secondary role. One reason that supports this conclusion is that while most of the negative publicity occurred in America, most customers and shareholders were located overseas. So much of the potential damaging effects of the media were "out of sight and out of mind" for investors. Hence people who plot a company's media reputation against its share price would do well to also show the plots of these other contributing factors against the share price.

The evidence from *BP* and many other such corporate crises is that the affects of reputation on share price are contingent on the circumstances of the incident. It also suggests that a company's reputation among different groups should be the focus of attention, not simply that of the general public. Following Karpoff, if the company's counterparties are directly affected, then they will downgrade the reputation of the company, and this will flow into their expectations of future performance. If these groups are not affected, then the financial loss will likely be contained mostly to the loss of production and reparation. In many cases the primary role of negative media coverage is to alert regulators and lawyers that there might be sufficient public interest to prosecute the company. A secondary role is to highlight the crisis handling and public relations skills of the company. And from the media's perspective a good crisis is always newsworthy.

Most large crises provide a window into management's ability to manage the various types of risk to which their company is exposed. Though the public's reputation of the company may remain depressed, when investors believe that the crisis has resulted in an improvement in the company's risk management protocols, they will not adversely reverse their expectations. What happens is that during a crisis most people outside the professional investment community will look at the crisis and the way that the company is responding to it. Most professional investors, however, will look through the crisis at the fundamentals of the company to determine if the crisis can weaken any of these fundamentals or result in an overhaul of poorly designed or performing capabilities. It is this evaluation that sends shares up or down more than the amount of noise made by the media. For example, a few years after the Murdoch phone-hacking affair (described in more detail in chapter 4), Mr. Murdoch and his family have more than doubled their wealth. The crisis forced Mr. Murdoch to make some difficult corporate restructures that vastly improved the *News Corporation* share price. Before the crisis and the vast amount of negative media publicity that accompanied this, he was unwilling to make these changes that had been called for by his shareholders.[7]

What the search for the corporate reputation Holy Grail alters us to is the contingent nature of corporate reputations. Sometimes reputations seem to have a big impact on performance and share price and sometimes not so much impact. So we need to establish the circumstances that would provoke a company to invest in creating a reputation of distinction.

Circumstances When a Company Should Invest in Creating a Good Corporate Reputation

A company needs a good corporate reputation for a number of reasons:

- When the institutional frameworks in a society do not provide adequate protection for people who interact with companies. Many emerging economies are burdened with such conditions. Here the rule of law and the institutions that should protect people are either corrupted or insufficient. In these circumstances a good corporate reputation signals trustworthiness, and it is used as a performance bond offered to the other party in each transaction. Poor performance depreciates the value of this bond.[8]
- When unobserved properties of an organization that are thought to be especially important to stakeholders. For example, a company may be a very good place to work, but it can't say that it is—this is "cheap talk." A good reputation will signal this fact to potential employees. Moreover a good reputation will signal that a company is well managed (important to investors), honest (important to business partners), concerned about quality (important to customers), and concerned about the environment (important to the community).
- When people use reputation to enhance their self-images. For example, many business schools aspire to be ranked in the top 10 or 20 places by the various reputation opinion pollsters because their faculty, students, and alumni bathe in this prestige. It helps cement their identification with their business school.
- When an intense level of customer complaints is unavoidable. For example, an airline will typically have millions of service encounters each year. Even if their service quality is outstanding (e.g., 99.9 percent satisfaction), they will still have 1,000 bad customer episodes per million service encounters. Often a very good corporate reputation will get the customer to tone down their criticism and sometimes even blame themselves.

- When reputation is a necessary condition for people to deal with a company. For example, some customers, investors, employees, and businesses will only deal with the most reputable companies. Many years ago when *IBM* was tops in computing, there was a saying among many of the managers who were responsible for buying a mainframe computer and operational systems that "nobody ever got fired for buying IBM." Similarly, when *McKinsey & Company* was perceived to be tops in management consulting, board members felt safe when engaging "the firm" as they call themselves.
- When the quality of a product or service can't be determined prior to purchase or from its consumption. Examples of such "credence goods," as they are called, are vitamin supplements, many forms of medical services, and education. Here buyers rely on the reputation of the company that produced the product to reduce any cognitive dissonance associated with the purchase.
- When a company needs to bridge across areas of operation or product lines. For example, the old reputation of *Rolls Royce* cars helped it sell the quality of its aircraft engines. More recently *Apple*'s reputation for design helped it bridge across from personal computers into personal lifestyle products. However, the dark side to this phenomenon is that as soon as a company demonstrates that it is weak in one area, most people will assume that it is weak in other areas it ventures into.
- When a market is characterized by continual product innovation as occurs in many technology markets. A good reputation provides confidence for consumers that upgrades are simply better than previous versions. For example, *Microsoft*'s reputation has not been strong enough to play this role for many of its users who skip versions of its Windows operating system. In contrast, *Apple*'s reputation has helped many people justify needing to have the latest version of the iPhone.
- When a company is compelled to divert attention away from the risky parts of the business. This is why many of *Enron*'s dodgy business practices were ignored for so long before its ultimate demise.
- When the company needs a "benefit of the doubt" in times of crisis. The company will be given more time and scope to present its case

and rectify the underlying problem. This will help it recover from the crisis with dignity.

- When a company needs to combat an attack by an outsider such as a hostile NGO. For example, if the company has a better reputation than the attacker, then it is granted more scope to fight off the attack.
- When people need to trust a company, which can be for a variety of reasons in different industries. However, some industries are opaque in the sense that most people do not really understand how they work. Much of the banking and finance sector is like this. The global financial crisis has illustrated that many insiders, outsiders, and regulators did not really understand how risky some common business practices were. Other industries with opaque design, technology, or production processes, of course, do produce many of the products used in a modern economy. When people lose confidence in these "technologies," the reputations of companies that produce them can help alleviate any fears associated with them. However, if the fear of a technology is too great, then the reputations of the companies producing it will suffer. For example, the reputations of the companies involved in the production of genetically modified foods and nuclear power have suffered over recent years.
- When industries require trust based on faith, such as superannuation (where we give people our money to look after), and religion; or proffer advice such as professional service firms; or issue warnings such as the *Intergovernmental Panel on Climate Change*; or provide information such as universities and the media; or pose risks to the environment such as mining; or have significant influence over our lives such as government regulators; or when matchmakers such as real estate agents, dating agencies, and auction houses seek to entice strangers to transact with each other. A primary role of a good corporate reputation in these situations is to reduce perceived risk.
- When people pay now and get the service later. Insurance and superannuation are two industries where people need to trust that the company they deal with will be around when it is needed and it will pay what is expected.
- When there is an established market for reputation. The reputation of the company is an integral part of the product or service being bought

and consumed. For example, the various annual rankings of business schools have helped consolidate a reputation market for MBA degrees. In turn the good reputation of the business school helps students secure a job and enhance the payback from the degree. There is also a reputation market for investment banks and high-quality luxury goods such as high-valued art sold through the best auction houses.

- When ambiguity exists about what kinds of discretionary behavior are honest and appropriate. For example, as the evolution of the Internet outpaces legal regulations i-companies are often challenged to convince their customers and the regulators that their new initiative is safe, ethical, and does not require costly outside monitoring. Indeed the notion of industry self-regulation is based on the good reputation of the industry-appointed regulators.[9]

At the heart of most of these situations is the issue of stakeholder involvement. When a person is concerned about a purchase, a job, an investment, or forming a relationship with a company, that person will need to rely to some extent on the reputation of the company as a signal of its probity. The company's reputation can lessen stakeholders' concerns about their vulnerabilities being exploited because the agencies of government do not provide the protection needed. It doesn't matter, of course, nearly as much in situations where people are well informed, relationships are superficial, behavior is low risk, and institutions effectively punish organizations that transgress expected behavior.

While there are many situations where a good corporate reputation is invaluable, sometimes companies don't seem to care about their reputation. Some examples are as follows:

- Sellers in a market will never see the buyer again, so there is little risk of either positive or negative word-of-mouth infecting future transactions—such as when tourists buy a gift from a shop in an overseas location.
- People do not need to trust the organization. For example, when people in a transaction are well informed through their own experience or reliable information, or they are confident about their ability to make a good choice. Many low-involvement transactions or low-price purchases from retail establishments fill these conditions.

Another example is when people are already protected by institutions and regulations that govern trade, as by government-offered deposit insurance, which allows people to be largely indifferent about the solvency reputation of the banks that hold their money.

- The company knows that it too big to fail. Often these companies proffer an external illusion of good citizenship, but in their DNA resides a "don't care" approach to corporate reputation management. This character was demonstrated during the global financial crisis when some of the heads of the US auto companies came to meet politicians to ask for financial assistance in their corporate airplanes.
- People must deal with an organization that is too powerful to ignore—such as the social security and tax authorities.
- The financial rewards from some activity are so big that key officers of the company will happily trade its reputation for the dollars on offer. Such a trade-off was at the heart of one of the biggest corporate bankruptcies in Europe, namely that of the giant Italian conglomerate *Parmalat* in 2003. Private equity firms and investment banks have been accused of such behavior.
- When a person's reputation matters more to his or her peers than it does to consumers of the company's products. For example, the legal profession is often accused of promoting behavior that is respected by other members of the profession but is detested by its clients. Then again, many university lecturers have been accused of designing tough courses to impress their colleagues rather than to inform their students.

In summary, a baseline condition for assessing whether to invest in creating a better corporate reputation is to consider whether the people dealing with the company need more trust than is delivered by the institutionally prescribed terms and conditions of their relationship with it. This may be motivated by stakeholders who feel they are vulnerable to the company's activities. No doubt, the additional trustworthiness delivered by a good reputation is economically valuable and can provide a competitive advantage if other companies do not do the same.

A competitive advantage presupposes that there is a market, or many markets for a reputation. But what are these markets and what type of corporate reputation will confer such an advantage? In the next section I briefly address these questions and in the next few chapters elaborate on them.

Markets for Corporate Reputation

If a company's success depends on the quality of its relationships with its stakeholders, of primary importance are company employees, business partners, and customers. Of secondary importance are shareholders, and of tertiary importance are the media, regulators, members of the general public, and the government. The logic of this rank ordering is simply that the contractual relationships of the first three groups are the ones that underpin the company's business model, operations, and sales. The primary role of shareholders is to vote with their shareholding about whether or not they approve of the way managers operate the company. The role of the media is to act as a devil's advocate—check and challenge the company's proclamations and behavior. The role of regulators is to protect the public interest as mandated by the laws of the land. The role of the general public is to benefit from the economic wealth created by the corporate sector. The role of the government is to distribute this wealth for the benefit of the country.

So in the three primary markets for corporate reputation the role of corporate reputation is to attract the best employees, business partners, and customers. And the best people will be those who help the company meet the objectives stated in its strategy. There are two fundamental questions about these markets. One focuses on the size of each market. The other focuses on the type of corporate reputation that will be effective in each market. Answers to both questions are, as yet, not well understood. For example, as I will elaborate later in the book, the companies that base their reputation primarily on their corporate citizenship tend to be less commercially successful, and less broadly respected, than those that focus their reputation-building efforts on creating superior products and services. Research of David Vogel, Deborah Doane, and Timothy Devinney has found that most people are reluctant to sacrifice the functionality or low price of the products and services they want in return for the privilege of buying these products at a higher price from a socially conscious company.[10] Yes, there are some people who will reward the company with their custom and/or praise for being a good corporate citizen, but there are many more of these who will reward it for offering better value than competitors. This observation suggests an interesting precondition for the success of CSR-led corporate reputations. It has been called the "other CSR."[11] Here CSR stands for consumer social responsibility. Unless consumers are prepared to respond in greater numbers to the overtures of CSR-guided companies, the market for virtue will remain small.

Notwithstanding that the consumer market for a good social reputation may be smaller than is often claimed, the market for providing superior functional value to customers is large. A small reputation advantage here can translate into a significant commercial advantage if consumers are prepared to pay for this reputation. In this situation the company generates an overall corporate reputation of being best at something and/or best for somebody. *Apple* is a company that is currently enjoying the fruits of this reputation position. In 2015 it had the highest market capitalization of any US company.[12] *Apple* is a company that has two conflicting reputations. Its reputation for social responsibility is generally poor, but its reputation for producing great products is generally very good. I will return to the *Apple* corporate reputation strategy throughout the book.

The market of corporate reputation in the secondary and tertiary markets is less well developed and, I would argue, less well understood. For example, for shareholders the price/earnings ratio and the total yield (dividends plus change in share price) of the company often represent good, easily available metrics of reputation strength. The P/E ratio combines the evaluation of past performance and expectations into a single forecast while the yield measures the total return potentially due to the shareholder. Both are used by many investors to help judge the value of their investment. Good numbers seem to provide confidence that management is operating in their best interests. In contrast, poor numbers often signal that it is time to question or challenge management decisions. Poor numbers may even trigger disinvestment.

The market for corporate reputation among the media is large and well developed as evidenced by the amount of attention paid to companies. However, it is still unclear when and how this media coverage might have a meaningful impact on a company's commercial prospects. The market for corporate reputation among regulators is to highlight which companies are more likely to attract the attention of a regulator that wants to pursue its mandate by signaling out a company for investigation. Keeping out of trouble is a measure of a good reputation here. The market for corporate reputation among the general public is to reflect the sentiment of a generally under informed group of people. There are hundreds of opinion polls that record such sentiment. However, as the global financial crisis (GFC) demonstrated, even vicious public criticism of corporate behavior that was boosted by wide media coverage had little direct effect on government actions. Most of the big companies in trouble were rescued regardless of their reputation and the opinions of the general public. This response also illustrates the current role of corporate reputation in the market for government assistance. It seems to be almost irrelevant. If a company follows the laws of the land, it is treated like everybody else. And if it is economically or politically important, it is favored. The behavior of the government during GFC now seriously questioned the contention of many academics and social commentators that a good corporate reputation helps secure a company's social license to operate.[13]

2

Corporate Reputation as a Strategic Game

This chapter describes why corporate reputation management is a strategic game. The metaphor highlights that any investment in creating a better corporate reputation than one's rivals is subject to setting goals, understanding the rules of the reputation marketplace, adopting the language of corporate reputation inside and outside the company, and being prepared to measure the value of the investment. These issues provide the basic terms and conditions for the investment in and active management of a company's reputation. The first issue to explore is what are the goals of a good corporate reputation.

Corporate Reputation Goals

The fundamental goal in this game is to develop a better corporate reputation than competitors and thus to secure a competitive advantage. The strategy recommended in this book is to base the company's reputation on the delivery of superior value to the stakeholders who really matter to its commercial success. Hence, to win this game, a company needs to achieve two outcomes. First, it must create and hold a reputation that is better than its rivals. Second, competitors with worse reputations, or those that try to mimic the company's good reputation, must pay a significantly higher cost to do this or receive a much lower return from their efforts. Both conditions are necessary before the better reputation company will obtain the long-term competitive advantage from its investment in creating exceptional stakeholder value.

As with many games, winning involves both defense and offense. In the corporate reputation game we can see these strategies in the goals companies set for their reputations.

Defensive

One goal for a good corporate reputation is to help mitigate the risk that the company will be held fully accountable for its failure to be seen as a good corporate citizen. To achieve this goal, many companies design a reputation risk audit framework and a crisis management response system.[1] The audit aims to identify each major corporate function where a misstep may cause significant reputation damage, and the crisis response system is designed to mitigate the damage. The overall task is to assess the chances of reputation loss and the magnitude of these losses. Each potential reputation loss will then be assessed against the company's appetite for taking the risk that generates the loss. In industries that involve high technology, innovation, exploration of the natural environment, and large-scale production, the participants accept these risks as a natural part of business. Another type of reputation risk occurs from a company's day-to-day activities. According to *The Economist,* many senior corporate managers consider that the major sources of such reputation risk are (1) failure to deal with regulatory and legal obligations (aka compliance failures), (2) failure to deliver minimum standards of service and product quality, (3) unethical practices, and (4) employee fraud.[2]

While most people would argue that a good corporate reputation is needed to insure against risk, paradoxically a "bad" reputation can also achieve this goal. To illustrate this case, consider how *Exxon*'s bad corporate reputation played a role in determining how much money it ultimately paid to settle its civil and criminal liabilities after the *Exxon Valdez* oil spill in Prince William Sound Alaska. The spill occurred in 1989 when the *Exxon Valdez* tanker ran aground and disgorged 10 million gallons of oil into the sound. This resulted in widespread loss of wildlife and serious long-term damage to the marine environment, which in turn resulted in significant business hardship for those people who relied on this environment for their living. It also resulted in a frenzy of media attention, nearly all of which was negative. *Exxon* was dragged reluctantly through the media and the courts. The way the company responded to the media, the 14,000 Alaskans directly affected, and the courts where the company's financial liability was determined became the grist of case studies about what not to do.

However, before passing final judgment on *Exxon*'s handling of this crisis, it is instructive to consider what its reputation was at the time of the oil spill. Tom Bower's description of the oil industry at this time is informative.[3] *Exxon* had the following sharply defining reputation characteristics:

- It had a mystique of omnipotence.
- It was combative with governments.
- It was indifferent to all but its shareholders.
- It was known to "beat opponents to death with lawyers and auditors."

At this time *Exxon* was the alpha male in the pack of major oil companies collectively known as the Seven Sisters.[4] Most employees and shareholders held the company in high regard. Competitors thought the company was a dinosaur. Governments thought the company was too big and powerful to control. And Brian O'Neill, one of the Alaskan plaintiffs' lawyers, thought the company was uncaring, indifferent, and arrogant.

Given the nature of this bad corporate reputation Bower reports that it hindered and then helped *Exxon* in its fight against the financial penalties levied by the courts. At first a display of the tough-guy reputation resulted in Judge Russell Holland raising *Exxon*'s fine from $1 billion to $5 billion in punitive damages.[5] The imposition of this fine then stimulated *Exxon* to further act out its corporate reputation. They expressed outrage and challenged the court ruling. And true to form, by June 2008 they had aggressively pleaded their case such that the final fine was reduced to $507.5 million. This is a classic example of a strong corporate reputation playing the role of defense. Interestingly, *BP* was advised to follow *Exxon*'s lead in defending its liability for the damage caused by the Gulf of Mexico oil spill. Rather than take a conciliatory and contrite stand in court, the company considered pushing back hard in its American legal battles.[6] Ultimately it adopted a softer approach than Exxon.

Despite *Exxon*'s past success in fighting the government and citizens of Alaska, today many of the oil companies seek a good corporate reputation. For example, *BP* re-branded itself as "beyond petroleum." *Chevron* has asked "will you join us" in helping produce "human energy." *ExxonMobil* is "taking on the world's toughest energy challenges." *Shell* has invited us to "find out how they are helping." And *Total* has told us that "our energy is your energy." Notwithstanding that most of what these companies still do is about oil—exploration, production, refining, and retailing, it seems that Big Oil is trying to become Big Energy. The reputation problem here is that most crises generally involve oil. As the 2010 *BP* Gulf of Mexico oil spill demonstrated, the television images of these disasters blanket out all the public relations and corporate branding about energy. However, what these campaigns have probably intended to do is in normal times make it harder for critics to single out one of these companies for public abuse. Here their PR reputation is good enough to play the role of defense.

Offensive

The alternative goal I promote here is to invest to create a better reputation than competitors. This corporate reputation should rely primarily on the value delivered to key stakeholders. For many years *FedEx* adopted this stance. Their internal mantra was that reputation travels "from workplace to marketplace." This reflected a philosophy where employees were the key reputation champions, and a good reputation was generated by delivering outstanding peer to peer service—employee to employee, employees to customers, and employees to business partners. These exchanges were supported by internal and external corporate communication that was aligned around the key drivers of reputation, namely the products and services the company offered to its customers. *FedEx* was seeking a reputation advantage in the marketplace based on its stakeholder satisfaction. Interestingly, at the time of writing this chapter the corporate website did not mention reputation. It stated that "safety will be the first consideration in all operations." Also reputation was not listed in the company's corporate values.[7] My conjecture is that you don't maintain a reputation for excellence among customers and shareholders by being best at safety. Maybe the HR department and operational employees are impressed?

The thesis of this book is that the best corporate reputations accrue to those companies that are seen as significantly better than their rivals. If it is not possible to be significantly better, then there are two other winning reputation strategies. One is to be marginally better. The logic here is that even small differences in a reputation for quality or service can have large long-term payoffs. Over time a marked segregation of companies can occur because of the mild preferences of people for marginally better companies. This is known as a Schelling effect.[8] International economy class air travel demonstrates this effect. Over recent years the Asian and Gulf State based carriers have gradually developed slightly better reputations than many of their competitors for this class of service—and passenger preference has followed.

The second strategy is to offer a very good "local" product or service. This was the idea put forward by the *New York Times* journalist Thomas Friedman in his book *The Lexus and the Olive Tree*. If you can't make a simply better product (like the Lexus) then offer "local" products (olive trees) that give people comfort in their immediate environment.[9] *Starbucks* followed this strategy with its "third-place" approach to selling coffee. Here the *Starbucks* outlet, like the local library, American bar, and the English pub became a safe sanctuary where a person could unwind, relax, work, and talk to other people—while having their daily fix of *Starbucks* coffee. These local establishments gain a good reputation among the local community.

Winning & Then Being Robbed

There is, however, a danger to having the best corporate reputation. Companies with these reputations are more vulnerable to what economists call "hold up." This occurs because when most of the value of a company like *Apple, Starbucks, Google, Microsoft,* and *Nike* is intangible, then angry customers and special interest groups may seek to damage the reputation of the company in order to further their cause. All these companies have been attacked for their supposedly unfair, or uncompetitive, or unethical, or uncaring business practices. The attacks come in the form of interviews with the talking heads of NGOs and special interest groups, and more recently by street demonstrations and Internet campaigns. How a company responds to these "hold ups" illustrates their grasp of the importance of its reputation and its robustness in the face of a direct attack.

Consider the case of *Apple*. In 2012, when do-good protestors demanded that the company treat its workers (or more accurately those Chinese production employees of its subcontractor *Foxconn Technologies*) more fairly, *Apple* effectively ignored their demands. Yes, *Apple* said it was concerned and it would work with *Foxconn* to make improvements, but it committed to nothing that would significantly reduce its profits or increase the price of its products to customers. And it was profitability that was at the heart of this protest. *Foxconn* employees were working long hours because the profit margins offered by *Apple* to *Foxconn* were so slim.[10] So even though there were some street protests and a petition of over 250,000 e-signatures on the *Change.org* website, the company's response was subdued to these groups. Why, because they represented a tiny fraction of their customer base. Also, I would suggest, many of the people who did not agree with the outsourcing of jobs to Asia would not have been too concerned that some Chinese workers were working too hard. Where the protest did matter - was with the Chinese government. Here *Apple* needed to gauge its response so that it would not annoy the government at a time when it is trying to protect its brand image in China.[11]

Winning &Then Becoming the Robber

There is also a dark side to winning a reputation game. The rise and fall of *Enron* is an interesting example of creating a winning reputation, falsely validating its quality, and then using this reputation to defraud the company's employees, customers and investors. In the first era of its life (1986–96) *Enron* helped to reshape the energy markets and other commodity markets in which it owned facilities and traded products. What it did was innovative, noticed, and commented on favorably—by investment analysts, management consultants, the business press, business schools, and many managers. From 1996 to 2001 *Enron* was named America's most innovative company by *Fortune* magazine. The company's share price rose spectacularly on the back of its profitability and positive media coverage.

To help validate its good reputation, *Enron* relied on the reputations of a variety of people and organizations, notably some high-profile members of its board of directors, and their audit firm *Arthur Andersen*. Many people believed that if *Arthur Andersen* certified *Enron*'s accounting practices and its profits, then this financial anchor point of the company's reputation could be trusted. They also used the reputations of the business press. If respected business magazines like *Business Week*, *Forbes*, *Fortune*, *The Economist*, and the *Wall Street Journal* were all praising the company, then it must be good. *Enron* used the reputation of the world's best management consulting firm, *McKinsey & Company*.

McKinsey conducted twenty separate projects for *Enron*, and a *McKinsey* director regularly attended *Enron* board meetings. *Enron* used the reputations of the top US business schools. The company recruited hundreds of their best graduates and was the subject of various flattering case studies.[12] Borrowing the reputations of others is the age-old tactic of gaining respect by association.

During its rise to fame and fortune *Enron* used three other corporate reputation tactics, two that most textbooks said should enhance a company's reputation and the other that should damage its reputation. On the positive side, the company instigated an internal code of ethics that was praised by business commentators; it published a social and environmental report, and supported a variety of good causes. At the 1997 Kyoto climate meetings the company was presented with an award. The second positive tactic was that Kenneth Lay, the company's founder, chairman and CEO told a great story about the company's rise to riches. This story garnered support for *Enron* not because people knew much about the company but because they were seduced by the story. On the negative side, the company violated the principle of transparency. As Bethany McLean, the reporter who finally exposed *Enron,* explained "for all the attention that's lavished on *Enron*, the company remains largely impenetrable to outsiders." She went on to state that "*Enron* keeps many of the specifics confidential for what it terms 'competitive reasons.' And the numbers *Enron* does present are often extremely complicated. Even quantitatively minded Wall Streeters who scrutinize the company for a living think so."[13]

Why did *Enron* fall?[14] A big part of the company operated in the mysterious world of commodities trading. Much of *Enron*'s business involved smart people selling complicated products to not-so-smart customers. Added to this were helpings of greed, hubris, clever accounting practices, and poor corporate governance. All this created a recipe for disaster. It also made understanding how the company produced its substantial profits difficult—even for many of its employees. Only after *Enron* filed for bankruptcy on December 2, 2001, did the full extent of its accounting irregularities come to light. And from this point on the company was savaged in the press.

The *Enron* saga illustrates the best and the worst of playing the reputation game. When *Enron*'s innovation was clearly superior to its competitors, it was rewarded with being regarded by *Fortune* magazine as the most innovative company in America. This provided the company with opportunities to expand, an appreciative workforce, a flow of customers willing to buy its services, and enthusiastic investors. However, when senior management realized that further market-based innovation would not support the same rate of growth, they turned to controversial accounting methods and fraudulent behavior to secure their financial performance. At this point it was *Enron*'s good reputation that provided the opportunity to deceive so many people for so long. The most notable groups who were deceived were employees and the business press. Employees invested their careers and often their savings in the company. The press focused on the share price of the company and failed to ask and answer the basic question of "how did Enron make its money?" Episodes like this and the failure to warn people about the dot.com bubble and the global financial crisis have tarnished the reputations of many business journalists and their media outlets.[15]

Rules of the Game

Every game has its rules. And the reputation game is no exception. But what are these rules? And who sets them?

There are three sets of rules. One set is specified by the macro level aspects of the business environment in which all companies operate. These formal and informal rules emanate from the political system, the judicial system, cultural norms, and kinship patterns. They are slow to change. For example, most advanced economies have a Corporations Act and a set of regulations for companies listed on the stock exchange. These specify rules for incorporation, accounting, auditing, reporting, and so forth. Any violation of these laws and regulations immediately renders a bad reputation onto the company that violated them. For example, in 2000 the US *Securities and Exchange Commission* (SEC) changed the guidelines to oil companies about how they were to report the assessment and value of their oil reserves. These changes caused few problems for *ExxonMobil* who employed eight full-time reservoir engineers and a former *SEC* lawyer to manage its booking of reserves. They did, however, cause serious problems for *Shell* who employed one part-time employee to audit estimates of its reserves. Internal division about how to calculate oil reserves, and the lengthy time it took for the company to downgrade its overstated reserves, were finally revealed in the media. *Shell*'s share price tumbled. The media response was highly critical of the company. The *SEC* fined *Shell* $150 million. This led a senior *Shell* executive to describe the fallout from the company's tardy response to the SEC as "a watershed reputation disaster."[16]

Another example of these rules is the belief in many Anglo-American countries that the courts should avoid second-guessing business decisions that are honestly made but wrong. Hence incompetence will not be punished by a criminal sanction. However, in Germany, Switzerland, and Austria the courts have a concept called *untreue*, which is defined as a derogation of duty that causes real damage to the institution. In Brazil executives and directors can be held personally responsible for corporate failures. In China and the Middle East many companies have been caught out by not understanding the personal responsibilities that attach to management decisions. So for international companies these rules change across jurisdictions. And a miss-step in one country can damage a company's reputation in other countries.

The second set of rules is specified by the individual parties in a business relationship. Their aim is to induce cooperation. They have contractual, ownership, and social characteristics. They are more like arrangements than hard and fast rules. For example, in many Asian cultures the company is an extension of the extended family. Hence, while the private and personal networks of many Asian business societies are social in nature, they also speak to corporate contractual and ownership issues. Sometimes these arrangements contribute to major economic problems. For example, one part of the 1997 Asian financial crisis was characterized as 'good friends and bad loans.' Where macro level rules are weak, these less formal arrangements often act as effective substitutes. Again, breaking these rules results in a deterioration of reputation.

The third set of rules is specified by the company's stakeholders and sometimes the communities in which it operates. The rules imposed by these groups are set by their expectations about how a company will behave. For example, customers expect that the products they buy will be advertised truthfully and 'fit for purpose.' Employees expect to be treated fairly and rewarded for their efforts. Investors expect a return on their investment. Business partners expect to deal with honest and reliable partners. Local communities and their representatives expect that companies provide employment opportunities and do not damage the local environment.

The first two sets of rules are generally understood and adhered to by most companies operating in a particular business environment. However, sometimes we see their power to create a bad corporate reputation when a company from one system seeks to enter a different business system. It is easy for these companies not to fully appreciate the reputation power of the new (to them) sets of rules. Consider the case of the *Huawei*, one of the world's largest manufacturers of telecommunications equipment.

By many accounts *Huawei*'s products are world class and competitively priced. But the company has been effectively banned by the governments of a number of countries from bidding for basic infrastructure projects. These governments fear that the company's networking gear and software could be used by China's security services to listen into sensitive communications. Some people even suggest that the equipment might contain "kill switches" that would allow China to disable the systems in which *Huawei*'s equipment is embedded. The primary reason for this suspicion is that the company and its founder are thought to have formal links with the Chinese government. Other reasons include the company's dealings with Iran, accusations that it does not play by the rules on intellectual property, and the secret way that the company's principal owner runs the company. And because many cyber-attacks on Western companies and government organizations originate in China, *Huawei* is tainted by its country's reputation as a potential threat to other countries.

Huawei has sought to enhance its tarnished reputation by opening up its products to inspection by foreign government agencies and private firms, and embarking on a charm offensive. For example, in Australia they established their first local board of directors, made donations to charities, and sponsored a major sporting team. The first problem here is that the local board is dominated by Chinese directors and contains two Australian ex politicians. At this time a survey of the ethics of Australian professions suggested that only 14 percent of Australians respected their politicians.[17] Thus some people might readily assume that the role of these politicians was not to provide legitimacy to the company but rather to engage in lobbing the Australian government for access to the national network infrastructure. The second problem is that the company's CSR efforts do not focus on its reputation issues. They are unrelated to anything the company does. So far tactics such as these have been unsuccessful in countries like United States, Australia, Canada, and India that are worried about the company's equipment and intensions.

One fundamental reason for *Huawei*'s poor corporate as opposed to product reputation is that the company is in violation of some macrolevel rules of business in these countries, namely those of ownership, governance, and motive. *Huawei* is a privately owned company by its employees and its CEO. While it publishes the same types of reports as a company listed on the share market, these have a level of opaqueness about them that does not instill confidence about the company's motives and governance. Publicly owned companies that abide by a respected Corporations Act and that trade on a share market are easy for governments and skeptics to understand.[18] They provide avenues like audited financial statements and reports from the board of directors that allow inspection of the company's motives and operations. Widespread share ownership also signals a degree of social legitimacy that is not available to a large Chinese private company. Another reason for doubt about the company is that it will not, or cannot prove that the allegations made against it are baseless.

Language of the Game

Games have their own language. For example, the game of politics is played largely as a word game. For example, in the US abortion debate the *Republicans* talk about the evocative notion of "life" while the *Democrats* talk about the abstract notion of "choice." Political linguists suggest that short phrases using concrete words are better than longer abstract phrases.[19] It is better to talk about "air," "water," and "soil" than "the environment." And something like a "Clean Air Act" is easier to understand than an "Environment Protection Act." The test for concreteness is that you can see it or draw a picture of it.

The field of corporate reputations has developed its own language. Some of this has evolved from business strategy such as corporate reputations being called "strategic assets" and companies compete in a "reputation economy." This is all very abstract stuff. Some language is metaphoric such as a company being surrounded by a "reputation halo" or a good reputation acts like a "magnet." This is easier for many people to understand. Some language is peculiar to scholarly discourse about reputations. For example, the people who form reputations of companies are called "stakeholders." Outside the academy however, the words "customers," "employees," and "shareholders" would be better when communicating to lay people. The choice of language matters when the company is trying to communicate about itself.

Because most people have an intuitive understanding of what a reputation is, then using the broad language of reputation throughout a company will signal to insiders that reputation is important. It can do this by using a reputation vocabulary in its everyday discourse. Using this language outside the company will signal that reputation is doubly important. This occurs because, when companies use specific language with outsiders, these people then start to look for instances of such good or bad performance. They are also more likely to use the notion of reputation as an attribute of the organization that affects their decision to engage with it. Thus companies that want to play in the corporate reputation game should use the language of reputation.

There are a number of words that signal that reputation is important. These are based around the word reputation, its synonyms, and words that convey being held in high repute—such as standing, status, admiration, esteem, respect, integrity, honesty, probity, trust, fairness, legitimacy, dignity, and confidence. My experience suggests that these reputation words are not regularly used inside most companies. For example, many annual reports are thousands of words in length but do not contain any of these reputation words. Modern word processing software makes it easy to check this claim.

Games Keep Score against Opponents

In the game of business, growth, profit, and share price are three key metrics for keeping score. However, when the focus shifts to corporate reputations, how to tell who has won and who has not is not so straightforward. In recent years an industry of scorekeepers has emerged. These are the researchers, consultants, and publishers who conduct opinion polls to produce reputation rankings of companies. They argue that these rankings are important because they bestow legitimacy on the winners and stimulate the losers to do better. In some cases this happens, but in many cases nothing happens. When direct competitors are ranked, as happens with business schools, then deans, faculty, students, and alumni have been known to pay attention.[20] And the deans are likely to instigate change to improve their ranking. However, when disparate companies are ranked, the winners are pleased, the losers are a bit disappointed, but neither group is motivated to do anything to change next year's ranking.

As noted in chapter 1, CEOs suggest that it does not matter to them whether their company has a better reputation than some of its peers. For example, when an ad hoc sample of Internet users rates a mixed group of companies, it may help sell newspapers and raise the topic of reputation in the community, but it does not define competition. In chapter 8 I discuss three broad types of reputation measures, namely what a content analysis of the media suggests, what a customized measure of reputation might tell a company, and a new type of measure that tells whether a company's reputation is actually used by its stakeholders to help them choose one competitor over another.

Opponents Take up Positions on the Field

One of the fundamental tenets of marketing is that of positioning. This is mostly communicated through the branding of the company and its products and services. In the corporate reputation context, companies adopt positions to differentiate themselves from competitors and to reflect what they are best at or who they are best for. These desired reputation positions are generally signaled by the company name and/or its corporate slogan. Corporate identity consulting firms like *Landor Associates* and *Wolff Olins* help companies choose names, logos, and slogans to signal their desired reputation position. Some of these combinations are better than others. For example, if you do not know the company *Bupa,* its name does not suggest what it does and thus who it is for. And to make matters worse, the company does not use a slogan to suggest what it does and how it differs from competitors. It is an international healthcare group serving 22 million customers in 190 countries. This new name comes from its original name—*BritishUnitedProvidentAssociation.*

Corporate identity and branding can be used to suggest what a company desires to be admired and respected for and to differentiate it from its direct competitors. In this way the corporate identity symbols combine as a signature of the desired reputation of the company. For example, for many years the German auto manufacturers *BMW* and *Mercedes Benz* positioned their cars and companies against each other on their engineering excellence. In the luxury car market this was an attribute that was highly valued by customers. It was also a capability that many people thought that German automobile companies were best at. Hence, rather than say "we make the best cars," each company adopted a slightly differ position:

- *BMW*—the ultimate driving machine.
- *Mercedes Benz*—engineered like no other car.

Both of these slogans told employees what to build and they told customers what to expect. In a similar way the old *Compaq* personal computer name, which suggests small, and the slogan, which was "inspiration technology," spoke to employees and customers.

Corporate identity and branding is like designing the front door of a house. It is one of the first things a person notices. And it signals to come in or stay away. It often provides the first impression of the company, and later it signals and signifies what to expect. In these ways good corporate identity and branding can help a company with a good reputation trigger emotions like trustworthiness that are inspired by this reputation. Because this is so important, I will return to this topic throughout the book.

In contrast, a company with a bad reputation will use its corporate identity to hide from public view. For example, many of the so-called sin companies that make alcohol and tobacco products use holding companies with obscure names to like *Altria* to remain below the radar of the general public. While the regulators and shareholders know who they are, most members of the general public are blissfully unaware of who owns and controls the companies that make these products.

In the reputation game it is important for corporate branding and identity to signal the type of reputation that is being used to create a competitive advantage. The *BMW* and *Mercedes* positions noted above are signaling a capabilities-based reputation. *Compaq* is signaling a customer experience or value-based reputation position. The new generation of so-called benefit corporations is signaling a character-based reputation position. Through the use of their statements of vision, mission, ethics, and codes of conduct, and their various corporate social responsibility activities they are promoting the narrative of "doing good." The *Bupa* set of identity symbols (its name accompanied by a wriggly line) is signaling nothing. It is certainly not the only company to get no free reputation points from its identity and branding.

3

How Corporate Reputations Are Formed and Work

If a company wants its key stakeholders to admire and respect it, then it needs to know what is the basis for these evaluations. It needs to understand how corporate reputations are formed in the heads of its stakeholders and how they might use them to engage with the company. This understanding will help a company change the reputation-enhancing factors over which it has control and monitor the factors that it can't control. There is a lot of consulting advice available to draw on. There is even now a modern reputation consulting industry. Because these practitioners tend to have their own specialty, they look at reputation management through their own prism. Thus corporate reputation management is a "branding problem," or an "identity problem," or an "advertising problem," or a "PR problem," or a "stakeholder management problem," or a "corporate social responsibility problem," and more recently an "Internet problem." The essential idea here is that better branding, identity, advertising, social media, citizenship behavior, and/or PR will result in a better reputation. A good example of this approach is that of the UK PR firm *Bell Pottinger Private*. Their corporate slogan is "Better Reputations. Better Results," but it really should be "Better PR. Better Reputation. Better Results." However, this communications-based approach to reputation management has resulted in a lot of confusion about the true nature of corporate reputations.

Another source of advice is the *The Oxford Handbook of Corporate Reputations*, a major scholarly treatise on corporate reputations.[1] This is a collection of independently authored essays rather than an integrated treatment of the two fundamental questions of interest to managers, namely how are corporate reputations formed and how do they work? So this chapter will pull together some of this material into a simple model of how stakeholders form their reputation of a company and then how they might use this reputation to help them decide whether to engage with or avoid the company. A good place to start is by briefly examining the current landscape of corporate reputations. How reputations were formed and used in the past conditions how they will be formed and used today.

The Corporate Reputation Landscape

The notion of reputation has existed for centuries. My Webster's dictionary says that the first known use of the old Anglo-French and Latin words for reputation was in the 1300s. In traditional Chinese society reputation is one of the principles of Feng Shui where people are recognized for their contribution (fame) and given credit for this (reputation). Also the notion of 'reputation' is like the notion of 'face'.[2]But there are two senses of 'face'. The word *lian* stands for society's confidence in the integrity of a person's character. A person who has lost this face cannot operate successfully in society. *Mian-zi* denotes distinction, as earned from having achieved success in life. This affords a person status, dignity, and respect. All these notions of reputation are intuitive for most people. Hence it is easy and meaningful for them to perceive that someone or some company has a good or bad reputation. As you will see throughout this chapter, many scholarly notions of corporate reputation align with these ancient ideas, ideas that have stood the test of time tend to be important and useful.

My other Heritage dictionary defines reputation as "the general estimation in which a person or thing is held by the public." Many scholarly definitions reflect this meaning. However, over the history of business the concept of reputation has evolved under terms such as honesty, discretion, integrity, judgment, and character.[3] These were the perceived characteristics of the probity of an individual or an entity such as a company or government. This is the concept of reputation used throughout this book. Because the focus is on business entities, I use the term "corporate reputation" as the catch-all term for all these evaluations.

In the late nineteenth century, as business became more geographically dispersed and the face-to-face contact of business people diminished, less personal means of assessing business partners evolved. Institutional agencies emerged to complement and sometimes supplant the primary role of personal reputation in business dealings. Credit reporting agencies were formed, banks assumed more of the risk in financial transactions, limited liability companies shared the risks of ownership, accounting and later auditing firms helped companies understand and report their financial performance, and governments introduced laws and regulations protecting the parties to trade. Now the reputations of these entities mattered as much as the people involved.

Business enterprises soon discovered that one of the primary roles of a good corporate reputation was that it reduced the risks of the counterparties involved in business transactions. And this in turn reduced the various costs involved in doing business. For example, because a party with a good reputation could be trusted to honor its promises, the other parties it dealt with did not need to invest as much in gathering information about their probity or writing detailed contracts or designing and implementing various mechanisms to monitor their behavior. In this way the good corporate reputations of business partners, ratings agencies, and government greased the wheels of commerce. This scenario ensured that it was in everybody's best interest to create and maintain a good corporate reputation.

During the last 100 years, however, a new scenario evolved that reshaped the role of corporate reputation in many aspects of contemporary business. The scenario was highlighted by two sets of factors. One was the government and quasi-government regulations that proclaimed how the parties to standard types of business transactions should behave. For example, Corporations Acts defined the rights of shareholders. Accounting bodies and stock exchanges designed generally accepted financial reporting procedures. Various consumer protection regulations stipulated many terms and conditions for commonplace transactions. Workplace regulations shaped many of the terms and conditions that can be offered to employees. As more of these regulations were implemented, the role of corporate reputation to mitigate many types of transaction risk diminished. For example, many people do not think much about the reputation of the companies from which they buy their utilitarian goods such as groceries, clothing, and household appliances.[4] If these types of products are not fit for purpose the manufacturer or the retailer is required to replace them. The tendency for governments to mandate rules and regulations for commerce is not necessarily a bad reputation outcome. Government-backed rules and regulations establish a set of minimum standards by which companies are judged. These make it easy for people to gauge good and bad corporate behavior.

Even in a highly regulated environment corporate reputations still serve to help mitigate two types of risk. One is related to the asymmetric nature of the information that the parties to trade have about each other. When one party knows little about the other, a good corporate reputation can help lower search costs and reduce the risk that the party will act in an opportunistic fashion. Another type of risk relates to the reassurance that a good corporate reputation provides that aspects of a product or service that are difficult to evaluate will be of the quality expected. The good corporate reputation provides a source of trust and sometimes product differentiation. For example, the strong reputation of *Harvard Business School* helps to attract MBA students and executives attending its programs by signaling that the pedagogy will be of a high standard. It also helps to establish credibility for its case studies and the articles in the *Harvard Business Review* magazine that are used by its students and competitors. *Harvard*'s reputation has also helped the school charge premium prices, attract high-quality faculty, students, and corporate recruiters, and secure a vast financial endowment.

The second set of factors that reshaped the landscape of corporate reputations was a number of economic crises, stock and housing market bubbles, and episodes of corporate malpractice. These focused a spotlight on the broad commercial and social responsibilities of companies and the other entities that support a market economy. Two insights emerged from the discussion surrounding these "tests" of corporate responsibility. One was that during this time the master image of the modern corporation in many developed countries evolved from the factory to the bank. Whereas the prior dominant image of the company was an entity that manufactured and sold products and services, it slowly became one that focused on making money, in an ever growing stream of profits. Because these were sometimes designed by the accounting and treasury functions of the company, this area became a new source of business and reputation risk. For example, in his book *Oil: Money, Politics and Power in the 21st Century* Tom Bower describes how the big oil companies moved away from their mission of helping supply civilization's lifeblood to a new mission of trying to maximize their profits by means such as oil trading (hedging and speculation), political lobbying, and avoiding regulations and taxation.

Within this context many companies and professional business advisory firms proclaimed that they were amoral. They were merely intermediaries between buyers and sellers. However, they embraced the profit motive to such an extent that they began to be characterized as creating "fast money." Books like *Masters of the Universe* by Tom Wolfe, *Extreme Money: The Masters of the Universe and the Cult of Risk* by Satyajit Das, *Wall Street Versus America: A Muckraking Look at the Thieves, Fakes and Charlatans Who Are Ripping You Off* by Gary Weiss, and *Infectious Greed* by Frank Partnoy paint a very unflattering picture of the new financial alchemy and its destructive consequences. From a reputation perspective, it became obvious that many of the people and some of the companies in the financial services sector were happy to invest in creating a very good reputation in order to later use it for their direct financial advantage. Here a good corporate reputation was not something to be passed on to the next generation of the firm but rather something to be cashed out for a massive financial gain. Authors of the above-mentioned books often characterized the senior managers of modern financial corporations as entering into a Faustian contract—they sell their souls to the Devil in exchange for wealth.

The second observation from this era of business was that the dominant companies in the economy became the banks and financial institutions. Traditionally the role of these financial intermediaries and the accounting and law firms that supported their deals was to fill the gap in trust and expertise between entities that sought and provided capital. In this environment the reputations of the professional firms were very important. They were "rented" to the entities who issued capital in order to give confidence to the parties seeking capital. As Jonathan Macey explains, in countries like the United States much of the value of a good corporate reputation as a signal of the probity in these and other business situations has now been supplanted by a vast profusion of laws and regulations.[5] And as this legal swamp grew in size and became more toxic in nature, its inadequacies were exposed as a substitute for the natural tendency of firms to invest in maintaining a good corporate reputation. More and more firms began focusing on black letter law compliance and maneuvering around the regulations. This in turn prompted some US regulators to threaten to prosecute companies for supposed noncompliance in order to be seen as upholding the law. (In the United States, this mode of operation has the added bonus of raising money via fines and out-of-court settlements to fund the regulators.) Incrementally, the old-fashioned role of a good corporate reputation as a signal of probity was replaced by regulatory compliance motivated by litigation.

Many aspects of this new master image of the modern corporation were reaffirmed during the global financial crisis (GFC) of 2007–2008 when governments were forced to rescue financial and nonfinancial enterprises from their financial misadventures. It has become the background story that now defines many people's idea of the nature of the modern corporation. The reputation problem this poses for companies today is that many are tainted by the sins of the companies involved in the GFC. No company can be implicitly trusted to do the right thing. Their attempts at genuine corporate social responsibility (CSR) are often belittled. Their attempts to get governments to reduce the ever-expanding morass of rules and regulations are rebuffed. Regulators are now regarded as protectors of human rights. And they are being encouraged to crack down on some long-standing corporate practices like tax avoidance. The mantra is that companies have become more socially irresponsible.[6] This situation has been characterized as "the high cost of low trust."

While this low-trust environment is a concern, it does present an opportunity for some companies.[7] The concern arises because trust is a source of competitive advantage. The condition can occur whereby one party to an exchange is vulnerable to the actions of the other party when it is difficult or costly to accurately determine the quality of what is offered—or when one party makes a much bigger transaction-specific investment than the other party. If protective institutional, or legal, or social governance mechanisms do not exist, then one party can take an unfair advantage of the other. Companies that do this gain a reputation for being untrustworthy, or opportunistic, or a swindler. However, a low-trust environment also presents an opportunity for companies to establish a reputation for not exploiting the other party's vulnerabilities. These companies will gain a reputation for being trustworthy. And in a low-trust environment there is plenty of scope for companies to establish this reputation position.

Given the recent history of the modern corporation and the low esteem in which business people are held, it seems reasonable to suggest that the overall reputation of corporate America, Australia, Canada, and other developed countries, is now less than exemplary. The grand challenge is how to rebuild this overall reputation. The micro challenge is to do this one company at a time. To do this requires knowledge of how reputations are formed.

A Working Definition of Corporate Reputation

While some of the academic literature builds on the common dictionary notion of reputation, many scholars use their own nuanced definition of the concept. Thus a tour through the literature often results in a good deal of confusion about precisely what is a corporate reputation?[8] Thankfully, most of these definitions are derived from one of three complementary theoretical perspectives.[9] One is a social-constructionist view, according to which corporate reputation is the broad public recognition of the quality of the firm, its probity, and behavior. Most of the specialized academic literature endorses this view.[10] Another is a game-theoretic view whereby a firm's reputation signals its hidden characteristics and likely future behavior. For example, the *BMW* and *Mercedes Benz* corporate slogans noted in the previous chapter reflect this view. A third is an institutional view where the reputation position of the firm relative to its peers defines its status. The commonality across these three perspectives is that each is based on the beliefs and expectations of people about a company.

A problem with this field of scholarship is that the concept of corporate reputation is often conflated or confused with other similar concepts. Hence what we need are some working definitions of corporate reputation and these other constructs. These definitions will help use navigate through the literature. And if they are linked to a major concern of the company, they will help to indicate where it should focus its attention in order to improve how its key stakeholders evaluate it. Table 3.1 provides a set of these working definitions.[11]

Table 3.1
Corporate reputations and related constructs

Construct	Definition	Concern
Organizational identity	Central, enduring, and distinctive characteristics of the organization	Who we are
Corporate identity	Nomenclature and symbols used to identify the organization	How to recognize us
Corporate brand	Promise made by the company about the value it offers or a statement about what underpins this value	What we offer, our capabilities, our point of difference
Corporate image	Salient beliefs held about the organization	What people think about us?
Corporate reputation	Estimation in which the organization is held	Are we good or bad, admired, respected, and held in esteem?
Corporate status	Organization's reputation standing relative to others	Are we better or worse than our peers or rivals?
Reputation equity	Stock of trust, perceived risk, and support afforded by the organization's reputation	Is our corporate reputation valuable?

All the descriptions of corporate reputation so far provided and the dictionary definition fit within the social-constructionist perspective. Within this tradition a recent review of the literature suggests that there are three dominant conceptualizations of corporate reputation: namely being known and prominent, being known for something, and generalized favorability which ranges across a spectrum of good to bad.[12] The first two conceptualizations are cognitive and based on the beliefs a person has about a company. The third conceptualization is evaluative. And all three conceptualizations directly support the idea that a company's reputation can be judged on the basis of it being known as "best for something" and/or "best for somebody."

The Formation of Corporate Reputations

Some years ago Charles Fombrun wrote a seminal treatise on corporate reputations. It was called *Reputation: Realizing Value from the Corporate Image*.[13] Fombrun's thesis was that images are the perceptions and impressions people hold about a company while a reputation is the general estimation in which it is held. He then proposed that the primary mechanism by which perceptions are turned into evaluations is by meeting the expectations of stakeholders. A few years after Fombrun's book, I suggested that an additional mechanism would also convert a corporate image into a corporate reputation. This mechanism was the values the person held against which they compared the behavior of the company.[14] The example of this mechanism I noted earlier dealt with the legal tax avoidance practices of companies. Some people think this is moral, others think that it is amoral, and others think it is immoral. The first group may enhance their reputation of a company if they found out that it practiced tax avoidance. Why shouldn't a company use a legal means to reduce this cost? The second group would think that this behavior was irrelevant. The third group may degrade their reputation of the company because they think that all companies should make this financial contribution to the government so that it can pay for defense, welfare, and other social services.

Combining both Fombrun's and my ideas suggests that what people believe about a company gets turned into a corporate reputation when the person compares what a company does with their expectations and judges this behavior against their personal values. Expectations will be determined by the rules of the corporate reputation game outlined in chapter 2 and the things the company says about itself through its corporate branding, advertising and public relations. They will also be created by the company's past behavior, especially the quality of the products and services it offers relative to competitors and its behavior during a crisis. Additional factors that help set expectations are what the media says about the company, its corporate governance practices, and the industry with which it is associated.

Yet a person's values will be formed by their family, culture, education, and religion. None of this can be influenced by the company. The best it can do is to understand what these values are and how they might impact on the evaluations of corporate behavior. For example, for centuries there has been a religious inspired hatred of banks and money lending.[15] In Australia this hatred has been immortalized in the common saying that "the banks are bastards."[16] So presented with such a problem, a bank could track how its profit-making activities are viewed through the prism of the values of its stakeholders and if any of its extracurricular behavior helps to compensate for the way it makes its profits. For example, do people regard extra-curricular CSR activities as the payment of a social tax, or do they think that it is simply a diversionary activity to deflect attention from the bank's profitability?

The diagram shown in figure 3.1 (read from left to right) combines these ideas to explain how corporate reputations are formed. It also suggests how corporate reputations "work" to produce a set of effects that is commercially valuable to a company.

Figure 3.1 tells the following story:

- People believe many things about a company (their Corporate image) that depend primarily on who it is (Organizational identity), what it makes (Capabilities) and sells (Products and services), how it

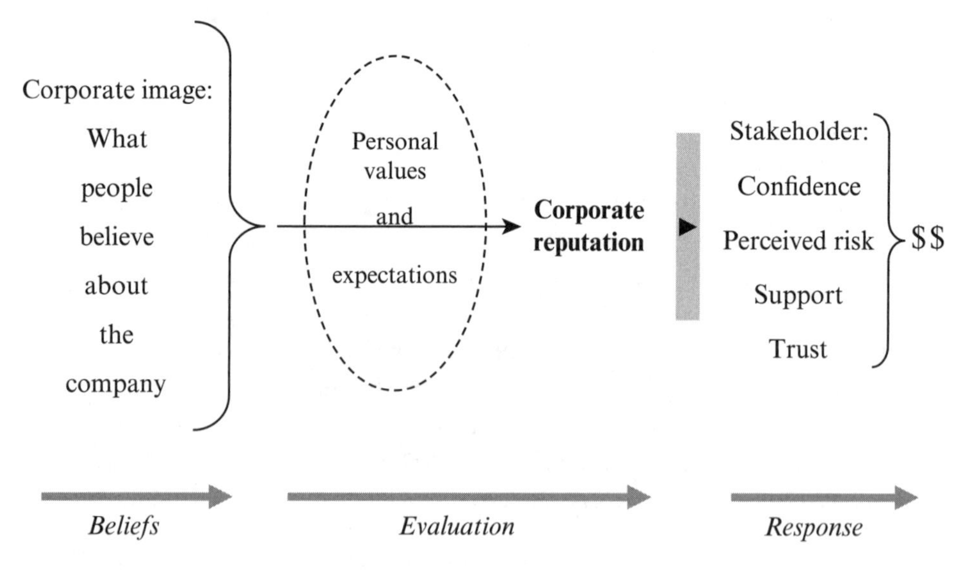

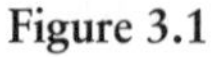

Figure 3.1

How corporate reputations form and work

behaves (Behavior), what it says about itself (Corporate brand and Corporate communications), what is said about it (Media profile), and the industry with which it is associated (Industry image). The beliefs about an industry will often set the baseline for the image of all the associated companies.

The beliefs that are important are the ones that are salient, that is, those that are top-of-mind. In cognitive psychology, the structure of these beliefs is called a schema or a script. In business, they are often referred to as the perceived attributes of the company. Once formed, these knowledge structures profile the company and lead the person to expect certain things from it. And the strength with which these beliefs are held will act to influence how new information about the company is interpreted. For example, if a person's beliefs are strongly held, then new information that clashes with them is less likely to be influential. This is why many corporate communication campaigns are impotent. They are not persuasive enough to change the knowledge structure of the person to whom they are directed.

The final characteristic about beliefs is that their salience often depends on the context in which the person wants to engage with the company. For example, many MBA students believe that working for a major financial institution or a management consulting company as their first job after graduation provides the best platform to launch their career. However, the reputations of many of these firms are less than exemplary. They are known to exploit their junior employees. Then again, they are known to teach them a set of skills that MBA programs do not. Hence it is not unusual to find that a person holds a mixture of good and bad beliefs about a particular company. These do not compete with each other for supremacy, but rather they are invoked to characterize the reputation of the company in a particular situation. Thus a company may have a good reputation as an initial employer but a bad reputation as a long-term career choice.

- A corporate reputation is formed when a person's image of the company is compared with his or her values and expectations. It is often expressed as the admiration, respect, and esteem a person holds of an organization at a point in time. A simple expression of the reputation a person holds of a company would be saying that Company X has a "good" or "bad" reputation. A more nuanced expression is when a person says that Company X has "a good reputation for its product quality (or whatever)" and "a poor reputation for its philanthropy (or whatever)." How such positive and negative evaluations are combined to form the company's overall reputation is still somewhat of a mystery.[17] This is a current hot research topic.

- The basic role of corporate reputation is to help people gauge the risk of dealing with or relying on an organization. Another way of expressing this is to say that corporate reputation is a surrogate for trustworthiness. Well-reputed organizations are less risky to deal with or rely on because a good reputation acts like a performance bond offered by the company to the other party. If the company does not deliver what its reputation suggests it should, then it will suffer some reputation loss and thus not be as trustworthy for following encounters. A bad reputation is also valuable to people because it helps them avoid engaging with these organizations.
- Last, as chapter 1 argues, a corporate reputation that is better than one's competitors should result in financial gain.

One of the fundamental ideas inherent in this description of reputation formation is that because different groups of people have different relationships with an organization, we should expect each stakeholder group to have a (slightly) different reputation of the same company. Their relationship with the organization focuses their attention on different attributes of it and makes these more salient and more important. Hence their mixture of beliefs will be different. Thus a company does not have a reputation, it has many reputations. And this means that different measures of reputation might be needed for different groups.

A second idea embedded in the description is that for a company to be defined by its industry limits how it will be perceived by its stakeholders. The company is always described as one of those—airlines, banks, credit card companies, hotels, etc. Its reputation will inevitably be described as a good or bad airline or better or worse than another airline. And if people don't like airlines, then the reputations of all the members of the industry are so constrained. Hence, if the industry image is predominantly negative, the challenge is to reposition the company into an adjoining industry with a better image. Thus we see gambling companies saying they are gaming companies. Fast food outlets become family restaurants. Garbage collection becomes a sanitation service. And so the list goes on. However, rather than encouraging people to link a company to an industry, the proposal developed in chapter 5 is that the company be defined by the value it offers to its stakeholders. This is a marketing approach to reputation development. The central idea is to focus stakeholders' attention on the benefits and solutions to problems delivered to them rather than the character or competence of the company in a particular industry.

There are two management messages embedded in the diagram. One is that changing a person's beliefs is the most likely route to reputation change. Traditionally this has been done from a corporate communications perspective, using the levers of advertising, public relations, sponsorships, social media campaigns, corporate identity and branding, and corporate social responsibility activities. As noted later in chapter 6, corporate storytelling is missing from this list. The second message is that a person's values and expectations will moderate the effectiveness of any initiatives a company may implement to improve its desired reputation. Because companies tend to spend less time trying to understand these factors than designing their corporate communications, it is worth exploring the nature of these two moderators.

Values and Expectations

Values

Understanding people's values is not a straightforward exercise because they are made up of enduring beliefs about appropriate modes of conduct and preferred end-states of existence.[18]Values are important because they motivate choice behavior, justify past behavior, and set standards by which people and companies are evaluated. Thus companies face three challenges in this area. One is to know what values stakeholders hold. The second is to determine what they mean for corporate behavior. The third is to work out how to communicate the company's values orientation to stakeholders so that it aligns with their values.

The first two issues involve understanding how values moderate perceptions of corporate behavior. For example, a basic value in many societies is the Golden Rule—we treat others as we would want them to treat us. However, as we move across cultures, many other values come into play. Australians are thought to hold five other mainstream values that define their outlook on life—equality, fairness, tolerance, aspiration, and respect.[19] What is interesting about these values is that two of them are couched in the language of reputations, namely fairness and respect. This should be a strong signal to Australian companies that their reputations are important. Indeed the first three values lead to a general belief that no one is superior, nor should they think they are. Thus a company that is seen to put itself above its stakeholders is likely to suffer a reputation backlash. So, if an Australian company decides to fight a regulator, it should do this in a way that preserves the respect of the legal system. How different sets of business-related values influence corporate reputations is one of the fundamental questions that needs a lot more research.

The third issue for companies is how to present their values orientation to stakeholders so that this aligns with the business oriented values of key stakeholders. For example, most people believe that companies are in business to make a profit. But the way they are perceived to make their profit can violate certain values. A study by Don Porritt found that a company's reputation was damaged when it was perceived to make its profit by working employees harder and/or implementing a strong user-pays approach to customer service.[20] The off-shoring of jobs as a cost-cutting strategy would probably result in a similar derogation of reputation. Thus there are "good" and "bad" profits, both of which signal the character of the company.[21] Internally many companies try to compensate for any perception of bad profit making by developing a narrative about their good character. Statements of values and ethics and social or environmental reports are published to illustrate desirable character traits. However, because most people seldom see these documents, the narrative is lost. Hence highly visible corporate socially responsible activities like the sponsorship of a good cause are now being used to communicate good corporate character.

There is an industry of social research organizations, market research firms, and public opinion pollsters to help companies understand the values of various stakeholder groups. While some of their reports focus directly on values, others survey the beliefs and evaluations of people about the professional integrity of the people who run and are employed by companies. One such a longstanding study in Australia by the *Roy Morgan* pollsters indicates that most Australians don't have a high opinion of many business people.[22] For example, in 2014 only 52 percent of the general public believed that accountants were highly ethical and honest. Some of the other scores were—bank managers 43 percent, lawyers 38 percent, company directors 24 percent, business executives 18 percent, stock brokers 16 percent, union leaders 12 percent, advertising people 8 percent. So it is not surprising that similar surveys of the ethics of companies often generate low scores. Hence for people who base their reputation of a company on its character, these beliefs trigger a significant discount in its reputation.

Expectations

To help understand people's expectations, most companies employ the services of a specialist market research firm. From a reputation standpoint the crucial issue is what should a company expect to happen to its reputation when it meets thc expectations of people? What should it expect when it exceeds or falls short of these expectations? Research in psychology and customer satisfaction has found that many people react quite differently to having their expectations surpassed or not met. The basic psychological principle here is that "bad is stronger than good."[23] Hence the rewards and penalties for these two effects are not symmetric. If I re-interpret this research from a stakeholder corporate reputation point of view, it suggests that when a company exceeds its stakeholders' expectations by a small or moderate amount, it should expect only a very modest improvement to its reputation. To get a big improvement, it must surprise and delight them. In contrast, when a company falls short of the expectations of a group of stakeholders, even by a small amount, the fall in reputation can be quite large relative to the disappointment experienced. These two response functions are shown in figure 3.2. The managerial implications of these are profound. First, companies must be careful not to fall short of what is expected of them, by even a small amount. Second, to get a reputation boost from exceeding expectations will require significant "overperformance."

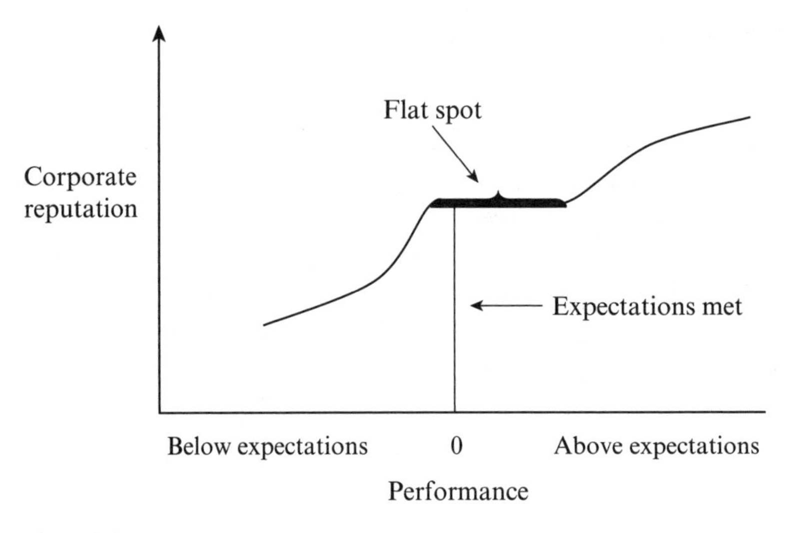

Figure 3.2

Reputation gains and losses from exceeding or falling short of stakeholder expectations

Third, because people update their expectations after they encounter a company or view its performance, then corporate reputation is a dynamic construct.

Character & Competence versus Value Delivered

A look across the academic and consulting literatures suggests that many companies are being advised to ground their desired reputations in their character and competence (aka capabilities). These two factors are key parts of the DNA of the company. Corporate behavior and communications reveal and promote these foundations of reputation. And hopefully stakeholders form their salient beliefs based on this information rather than the information they are exposed to in the media. In this context activities like CSR would suggest character, while winning a customer excellence award from the *J.D. Power* would suggest competence. Some behavior like tax avoidance would suggest both competence in cost minimization and a character trait of being prepared to game the legal system.

There is some merit in basing a corporate reputation on these two attributes. Competence signals that the company is good at what it does and probably makes quality products and services. Competence is also a key part of the company's strategy. In the next chapter it becomes part of the economic logic of the company. Character signals that the company is less likely to engage in opportunistic behavior that is detrimental to its stakeholders. In the next chapter it is a key part of the normative logic of the company.

Looking at the character and competence of a company may also help explain some of the outcomes on a company's reputation when it is involved in a crisis. For example, if the crisis involves the competence of the company, it may be perceived as far more damaging than if it involves its character. Many crises that involve price fixing between competitors seem to have a transitory effect on the reputations of the guilty parties, whereas crises that involve operational competence seem to have a longer lasting effect. For example, the fine art auction and real estate house of *Sotheby's* was involved in the sale of illegal antiquities in 1997 and a price-fixing scandal in 2000. The sale of illegal antiquities involved the basic competence of the company to establish the provenance of the items sold, and it has resulted in a continuing stream of reputation damaging accusations about the company being a part of the illegal art market. In contrast, the price-fixing agreement it struck with its competitor *Christie's* illustrated the character of both rivals. While it resulted in much negative publicity for both houses, the jailing of one of the co-conspirators, and the imposition of fines, its effects have now passed into the history of these two houses.

However, the problem with trying to establish a good reputation on the basis of corporate character is that it is easy to fake. And sooner or later this will be exposed. Shakespeare even had a term for this type of behavior—"seeking the bubble reputation."[24] The case of *Enron* noted earlier is a standout example. Also there is research that indicates that some companies are using CSR activities like philanthropy as a smokescreen to cover up their misbehavior.[25]This uncharitable view of extracurricular CSR is that it is being used to launder a bad reputation.

The alternative reputation foundation developed in the remainder of the book is that of a strategy-led, stakeholder-focused approach to reputation formation. Here the primary focus is the stakeholder rather than the company. The idea is to create and deliver superior value to stakeholders. The roles of the character and the competence of the company are to be points of proof of why and how the company can genuinely satisfy stakeholders' needs and solve their problems. This is a classic marketing approach to reputation formation. Its basic premise is that if a company is simply better at satisfying its stakeholders than its competitors, then it will develop a better reputation for this endeavor. And as the next chapter explains if this reputation is strategy led then it has a better chance of delivering a competitive advantage.

4

Strategy-Led Corporate Reputations

How can a company demonstrate to its key stakeholders that it is strategically committed to being of good character or delivering better value to them? There are the usual prescriptions:

- Suggest that the board of directors take direct responsibility for oversight of the company's desired reputation.
- Make corporate reputation one of the key performance metrics of the CEO.
- Routinely measure corporate reputation and share these "numbers" throughout the company.
- Ask line managers to play a more active role in making sure that their departments do nothing that might damage the company's desired reputation.
- Use corporate communication to tell the world that you care about the issues that they care about.

There is nothing wrong with any of these suggestions except that they are secondary to how to really address this issue.

My suggestion is that reputations need to emerge naturally from the company's DNA, strategy and corporate governance before any of the previous tactics will work. It is these in-built mechanisms that help create either a positional or status-based competitive advantage for the company. Here a positional advantage occurs when the company is perceived to be either best at something and/or best for somebody. For example, *Apple* has become known as the preeminent lifestyle brand in the technology industry. This position is based on the innovative consumer interfaces of its products. The late Steve Jobs had a fetish for such design. His philosophy was "design should be simple, yet have an expressive spirit, aka simplicity is the ultimate sophistication." He knew that great design produced an emotional reaction that attracted and retained *Apple*'s customers. Establishing a reputation for this was the positional advantage that obsessed Jobs while he ran *Apple*. In contrast, a status-based advantage occurs when the company's reputation is based on a similar platform as its competitors but it is seen to be better than these rivals. For example, for many years *Singapore Airlines* was voted to have the best in-flight service of any international airline.[1] Both types of better reputation generally engender more confidence and trust, and attract more customers.

For a number of reasons strategy-based corporate reputations are strong and enduring, and therefore they build reputations that are more trustworthy:

- Reflect the viability and effectiveness of the company's strategy. For example, *Apple*'s good reputation signals that its focus on design is a sound strategy.
- Focus and forge other parts of the organization that are crucial to the success of the strategy. For example, *Apple*'s reputation for creating the best personal lifestyle technology products fosters and reinforces the company's internal culture to develop even better and bolder designs.
- Make the company's future behavior more predictable to stakeholders. For example, each new iWhatever from *Apple* is expected to be better than anything else on the market.

In this way strategy-based reputations provide reassurance to all parties about the long-term strategy and expected behavior of the company.

In contrast to the reputations that are built into the DNA of the company are those that are designed around corporate communication campaigns or the provision of CSR activities that are unrelated to its core activities. A grand example of a communication approach was the one adopted by the oil company *BP*. Under the zealous leadership of Lord John Browne the company promoted a vision designed to seize the high moral ground from other members of the often criticized Big Oil cartel. Through extensive public relations and marketing campaigns, and some token environmental projects, *BP* tried to convince itself, its customers, and the general public that it was a new breed of energy company. *BP* now stood for "beyond petroleum." There were three problems with this campaign. The first was that some members of the board of directors did not buy into the idea.[2] The second was that surveys of the American public and investors showed that many people were puzzled by the claim. The third problem was that oil exploration, extraction, refining, and distribution clearly drove (then and now) its business model. And a number of accidents demonstrated that these operations were risky to workers and the environment. That the "beyond petroleum" reputation campaign was always really a bolt-on exercise was further confirmed by an advertising agency executive who worked on the campaign. He described it as "mere marketing" rather than a genuine attempt to "change the paradigm."[3] Because BP did not really commit to becoming an energy company rather than an oil company with a new green and yellow corporate livery, it could not really be trusted to put the interests of the broader community before those of its shareholders. This came to be demonstrated during the 2005 Texas City oil refinery explosion, the 2006 Prudhoe Bay oil spill in Alaska, and then again in the 2010 Gulf of Mexico oil spill.

Strategic Corporate Reputations

To illustrate strategy-based reputations, I'll describe three broad types of company whose reputation is created by their corporate governance, mission, DNA (i.e., their normative and economic logics) and strategy.[4] I call these social enterprises, owner capitalists, and sustainable enterprises. Social enterprises are driven primarily by their normative logic, owner capitalists by their economic logic, and sustainable enterprises are driven by both logics. As one of my colleagues noted, what differentiates these companies from each other is how they reconcile the tension between making profits and adhering to a set of social principles:

- Owner capitalists put profits before any vague social principles.
- Sustainable enterprises make profits that are aligned with sustainability principles.
- Social enterprises put profits after their chosen social principles.

At the present time because sustainable enterprise style companies are seen as a publicly acceptable compromise, many companies are experimenting with the idea of becoming more like this. Hence this is as much an inspirational idea as it is the source of a good corporate reputation. Time will tell if companies can overcome the challenges and compromises presented by this business model to effectively enhance their corporate reputations.

Social Enterprises

The poster child of the social enterprise company used to be the old *Body Shop*. Under the direction of its late founder Anita Roddick, the *Body Shop* was a good example of a company that practiced a "who we are is what we sell" approach to business. The normative logic of the company was to "do well by doing good." Principles such as the use of environmentally friendly materials and no animal testing were used to guide product development. Target customers were cosmetic buyers who were environmentally conscious. Anita Roddick personified the corporate brand and told a great story about how the company was formed and came to be a respected player in the worldwide cosmetics market. Not everybody believed the character-based claims made by the company.[5] And, alas, in 2006 the *Body Shop* was acquired by the French cosmetics company *L'Oréal* and has become one of the many brands in its portfolio. A key reason for the *Body Shop*'s takeover was shareholder discontent. This is the bane of many social enterprise style companies that are listed on a stock exchange. Sooner or later they must satisfy their shareholders' desire for ever-increasing financial returns.

Many companies that implement the corporate citizenship model of reputation formation use their character to position themselves as a social enterprise. For example, *Seventh Generation* is a company that makes natural household cleaning, health and beauty, and baby products. Their corporate slogan "caring today for seven generations of tomorrows" explains their name. The company mission is to reduce the environmental impact of their products while at the same time increasing their performance and safety.[6] Here CSR is embedded directly in their products as opposed to being an add-on attribute. At the time of writing, this company has a small share of the markets in which it competes. Neither the plea to consumers to act responsibly nor the reduced environmental impact of the products has been strong enough to create a sizable competitive advantage.

Today one of the new generation social enterprise companies is *Patagonia*. It was formed by a group of mountain climbers and surfers who promoted a minimal impact style of recreation activity. The love of the wild and beautiful places they visited inspired them to set up a company where some of the economic rewards are used to participate in the fight to save these environments. The company makes clothing for "silent" sports—climbing, skiing, snowboarding, surfing, fly fishing, paddling, and trail running. Its mission is to "build the best product, cause no unnecessary harm, use business to inspire and implement solutions to the environmental crisis."[7] One of the founders has described *Patagonia* as "the slow company" because it has adopted a philosophy of sustainability and long-term profitability.[8] However, scanning their corporate website reveals that being simply better, namely "building the best product," is a major part of their strategy.

Patagonia is a benefit corporation. To qualify, a company must have an explicit social or environmental mission, and a legally binding fiduciary responsibility to this mission. It must publish a Benefit Report in accordance with recognized third-party standards (e.g., *B corporation*) about its social and environmental performance. The idea of becoming a B corp is to position the business as one committed to a social or environmental purpose. Chartering as such a company also means that the company must formally answer to a range of stakeholders, not just shareholders. Had the *Body Shop* been a B corp, Anita Roddick might have been able to resist the demands of her shareholders to sell out to *L'Oréal*, a company that stood for many of the things she opposed.

The current reputation problem with positioning a company as a social enterprise is that the idea of "doing well by doing good" has become a tired management cliché. It can be interpreted in a wide variety of ways, most of which can be found on the websites of large public companies. Also many of these companies seem to be reacting to incremental social change rather than trying to create a new future. Together, these circumstances seem to be reducing the potency of this reputation strategy.[9]

Owner Capitalists

Under the direction of Jack Welch, *General Electric* was an owner capitalist style of company. When he took control Welch wanted *GE* to become "the most profitable, highly diversified company on the Earth." During his twenty-year tenure as CEO, *GE*'s sales grew from approximately $28 billion to $130 billion, and its market value grew from approximately $14 billion to $410 billion. Toward the end of his era, both *Fortune* and the *Financial Times* voted *GE* as the most respected company in America and the world. When Welch retired, he received a severance package worth approximately $417 million.

Jack Welch was a hard-driving, self-opinionated CEO. Under his leadership *GE*'s mission was "We Bring Good Things to Life"—the corporate slogan. His management philosophy revolved around empowering employees and making all the parts of the company profitable. His corporate philosophy was to keep *GE* growing. During his tenure Welch grew the financial services division of the company (*GE Capital*) by so much that it generated more than half the company's revenue. In effect he transformed *GE* from a manufacturing company to a financial services company with a number of unrelated manufacturing divisions. His record at *GE* established him as one of the prominent business leaders of his generation. The business press acted as his cheerleader. He glorified his success in three books—*Jack: Straight from the Gut*, *Winning*, *Jack Welch Speaks*. *GE*'s record of growth and financial success made the company a poster child for the owner capitalist style of company. Here shareholders are the stakeholder group who really matter, and profitability and growth is the economic logic that guides these companies.

In 2000 Jeffrey Immelt took control of *GE*. Like many new CEOs he made a change to the company mission slogan to signal his ascendancy. *GE* now signed all its corporate advertising with the slogan "Imagination at Work" to signal the company's focus on innovation. In 2005 the company launched its "Ecomagination" business program—described as "a commitment to imagine and build innovative solutions to today's environmental challenges while driving economic growth."[10] Ecomagination can be regarded either as a clever way to signal a central pillar of the company's strategy (green innovation) or as an attempt to put a "green" spin on many of its other manufacturing activities (e.g., locomotives and jet engines). A look at the company's annual Ecomagination reports indicates that revenues from these projects are a small but growing part of the overall business. Two of the highlighted quotes in the chairman's letter to shareholders in the 2012 Annual Report, however, leave no doubt that *GE* is still a true owner capitalist: "We want investors to see *GE* as a safe, long-term investment. One with a great dividend that is delivering long-term growth." Also, "At $100 billion of revenue with 15% margins, we are the largest and most profitable infrastructure company in the world."

The current reputation problem with positioning a company as an owner capitalist is that "community moralities" often sit uncomfortably beside the financial return morality of shareholders. This becomes a concern when a company with an owner capitalist reputation decides to operate in a public space. For example, the Australian based so-called millionaires' factory *Macquarie Bank* has been positioned as an owner capitalist by the media. One of its principle lines of business is to take control of major roads, airports, and utilities. From a community perspective, these are all part of the public infrastructure. Hence *Macquarie* needs to be careful how it presents itself to the public to manage the perception that a profit-oriented public company can do a better job of running these projects than the welfare-oriented government from which they were acquired. As the journalist Gideon Haigh noted, "an unelected elite making big money from handling what the public used to own: it's a target-rich environment, if ever there was."[11]

After the global financial crisis there has been more focused attention on the ethics and social fairness of some owner capitalist style companies. Here the somewhat romantic notion of the social enterprise is often used as a benchmark against which these companies are judged. And when the old Milton Friedman truncated quote of "the business of business is business" is trotted out, the contrast is stark.[12] Thus in the current socioeconomic climate there is hesitancy for many people to publicly proclaim their support for this style of company.

Sustainable Enterprises

If *GE*'s Ecomagination program was a separate enterprise then it might be considered a good example of a sustainable enterprise. Here the normative logic of the company is to address environmental challenges while its economic logic is to do this profitably. Michael Porter of the *Harvard Business School* advocates a similar, but slightly different approach. His clarion call is for companies to create "shared value."[13] Porter argues that companies should recognize that social needs, not just economic needs define markets.

GE's Ecomagination and Porter's shared value are wonderful ideas—in theory. And many companies are trying to improve their desired reputations by moving in the direction suggested by these principles. However, both of these ideas run into trouble when a company is faced with having to make a trade-off between capturing and sharing the economic and social value they have created, and whether this should involve a short term or a longer term time horizon. There are many cases where there is conflict between these decisions. And the way the conflict is resolved will substantiate the company's desired reputation, or put it at risk. For example, if pharmaceutical companies significantly reduced the price of many of their drugs, they would create massive short-term social value for health systems and patients. However, they use practices such as "evergreening" to prolong their patents and keep prices high.[14] They say it is to fund the next generation of drugs, but their critics argue that it is to support their share prices and dividends. Because of this they receive much negative publicity.

Nestlé ("Good Food. Good Life") faces an interesting social dilemma. As the world's biggest food company, the rising obesity rates of people in the countries where it sells most of its products put it at the center of attention regarding how it is helping or hindering the fight against this growing health problem.[15] While it says that it is examining its product portfolio to make many of its products healthier, the company still sells a wide range of unhealthy products, sometimes to unsuspecting customers in emerging markets.[16] Notwithstanding this situation, *Nestlé* became the first company in 2006 to implement a shared value approach to some of its business. The company website says that it focuses its efforts on nutrition, water, and rural development. The program is built on compliance with the law and various codes of conduct, environmental sustainability, and creating shared value. However, there are a number of reputation problems that stem from the credibility of their claims. One is that the company provides no cost–benefit accounting of the value it creates and how this is shared between itself and society. Another is that there is no attempt to link the program back to the overall strategy of the company. Finally, *Nestlé* makes no attempt to compare its performance with its rivals or its peers. Hence the leverage that this program could provide to the company's desired reputation is muted by its poor reporting. *Nestlé* is not alone here.

Johnson&Johnson is also a company that prides itself on its social contribution. In its 2010 Responsibility Report they provide an "economic value" accounting summary of these activities. The strength of this quasi cash-flow statement is that it provides a snapshot of how much money was paid to various stakeholder groups. However, its weakness is that it does not relate most of these payments to the various stakeholder groups nominated in the company's Credo as being of primary importance. Thus we see a disconnection between who the Credo says really matters to the company's performance and who the shared value initiatives focus on.

Another example of a company that is yet to receive the full reputation advantage due from its sustainability initiatives is *Walmart* ("Save money. Live better"). Over recent years this giant company has embraced a program of gaining significant improvements in efficiency and waste reduction. Its scale has allowed it to push its suppliers to also focus on these issues. The company has seen much of this effort flow directly to its financial bottom line. And environmentalists have applauded the commonsense waste reduction that has flowed from many of these efforts. However, the *Walmart* business model, like that of many growth-inspired companies, is unsustainable. It is based on an ever-increasing stream of discretionary consumer spending on products that are delivered by international supply chains. And this is fueled by a share market expectation that the company should grow faster than the economy. Thus what companies like *Walmart* are really doing is being a bit less unsustainable. They may be buying time until they can transition to a more environmentally sustainable economic model, but then again, they may not. If they do become sustainable, then their reputations will really change.

The current reputation problems for many large companies that want to position themselves as sustainable capitalists are twofold. One is that they are perceived to be fostering pet projects in a sea of corporate irresponsibility. The other is captured in the old proverb that "you can't be a part of the solution if you are a cause of the problem." On close inspection, the sustainable activities of many of these large companies look more like a cost reduction initiative, or the discovery of a new market opportunity, or the payment of a social tax rather than a fundamental change of business model. Thus, while many of these initiatives deliver desirable social and environmental outcomes, they seem somewhat superficial. They would seem less so if companies committed to significantly increasing the proportion of company revenue they raised from these activities.

Components of a Strategic Corporate Reputation

Figure 4.1 outlines the key elements of a reputation grounded in the DNA and strategy of the company. The top part of the diagram asks the question about the size and development of a market for reputation. Do stakeholders demand that the companies that they engage with are of high repute? The next part focuses on the DNA of the company. This is made up of its normative and economic logics, and how these combine to deliver the company's stated objectives. Different combinations of these produce social enterprises, sustainable enterprises, and owner capitalists. The bottom part of the diagram focuses on how the communications and actions of the company shape its desired reputation.

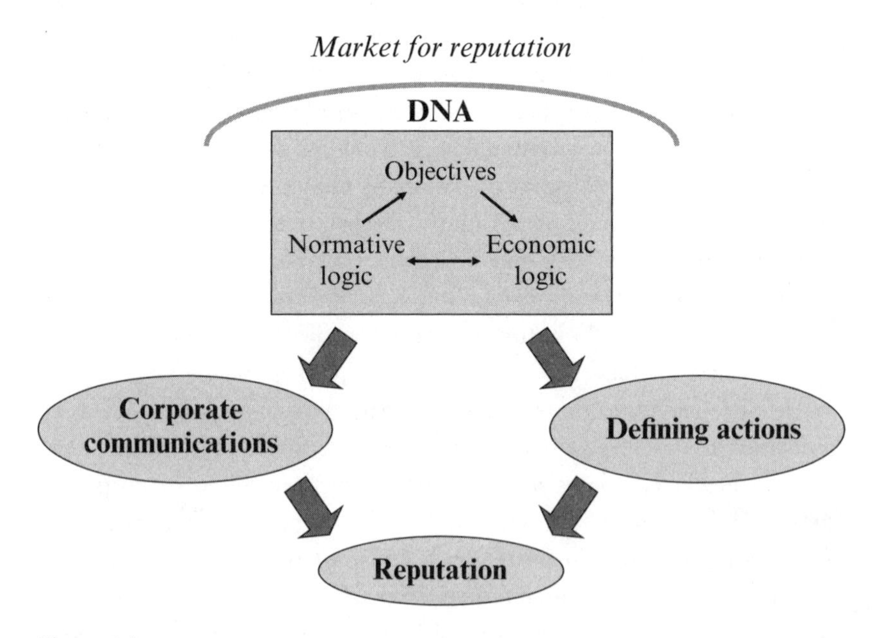

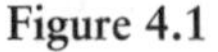
Figure 4.1

Components of a strategy-based corporate reputation

The Market for Reputation

As noted in chapter 2, there are multiple markets for corporate reputation. Some are more developed than others in the sense that the attributes of what constitutes a good reputation are well known and agreed upon. An example of one set of well-developed markets is that of university business schools. Each year schools from around the world are ranked in a number of different so-called reputation polls. These annual league tables are scrutinized by the staff and faculty of the school, current students, alumni, and the senior managers of the parent university.[17] A school's ranking can add prestige and status to its parent university, and it is often used in its promotional material. All this suggests there is a big and well-developed reputation market for business schools. In contrast, the lack of such tables for television stations suggests that the reputation of a television station is not nearly as important as it is for business schools.

The key issue for companies wishing to use their reputation for the offensive or defensive purposes outlined in chapter 2 is to understand the strength and nature of the demand for a good corporate reputation. The discussion in chapter 1 and the first part of chapter 3 is instructive here. While the claim made by the *Reputation Institute* that all companies operate in a reputation economy is overstated, it is reasonable to assume that most companies would benefit from having a better reputation than they currently possess.[18]

Reputation DNA

At the heart of any corporate reputation is the DNA of the company. In figure 4.1 this is characterized by the objectives of the company and its normative and economic logics. The objectives of a company guide the relative emphasis given to the normative and economic logics of the company. When they are stated in financial terms and specific targets are promised to the share market, they are seen to favor the economic logic of the company. These targets play a profound role in driving the actions that employees take and thus the corporate behavior that shapes the company's reputation. And the more difficult these financial objectives are to achieve, the more they hold the company's existing reputation hostage to their attainment. In recent years over ambitious financial objectives have been at the heart of many corporate scandals. In contrast, when objectives are stated in nonfinancial terms they provide more scope for other aspects of corporate behavior to shape reputation.

In the language of chapter 3, normative logic includes the character of the company. This can often be found written down in statements of vision, mission, ethics, and values. It is also found in the corporate governance principles and the organizational culture of a company. As noted in chapter 3, some companies paraphrase their normative logic in their corporate slogan. The economic logic of a company includes its competence and its generic approach to business. Three types of generic business strategy made famous by Michael Porter are differentiation, overall cost leadership, and focus.[19]

From a reputation standpoint, the most difficult decision managers make about the objectives and normative logic of their company is which stakeholders *really* matter. At the heart of this decision are two related issues. One is the legal form of incorporation and the other is the model of corporate governance used in the boardroom. As noted earlier, there are now some specific corporate forms that are designed to highlight nonshareholder priority such as the benefit corporation. Then there are public companies where directors can adopt either a narrow shareholder or broader stakeholder view of their responsibilities. However, there are other forms that make it difficult to discover the objectives of the organization and its prioritization of stakeholders. For example, private companies, trusts, partnerships, and private equity groups are deliberately opaque about who really matters.

Within this mix of corporate forms there is no single global model of governance. For example, for many Anglo-American companies the orthodoxy is to proclaim that shareholders are "first among equals." This is wonderfully vague. In contrast, many European companies are designed to support a more sociodemocratic model of the firm. This has historically been called the Rhinelandish model where shareholder interests are balanced, and sometimes even outweighed by the needs of employees and local citizens. Unlike the Anglo-American boards that have an essentially rules-based approach to corporate governance, many European boards have a more principles-based approach to corporate governance.

In Asia countries like China, Hong Kong, India, Indonesia, Japan, Malaysia, Philippines, Singapore, Thailand, South Korea, and Vietnam have some quite different company structures (e.g., state-owned enterprises and family-controlled conglomerates) and approaches to corporate governance. While there are some overarching characteristics such as a major shareholder (state, family, individual, armed forces, or major company) that foster related party transactions, these countries have different cultures of governance and formal regimes. Many of these are opaque to non-Asian managers. No wonder it is hard to fathom out who is really important.

In contrast to the vagueness of the Anglo-American and Rhinelandish approaches and the opaque nature of corporate governance in Asia, the *Ritz-Carlton* chain of hotels has been clear about putting the customer first.[20] A similar priority was proclaimed by Howard Schultz when he ran *Starbucks*. His mantra was "people first and profits last."[21] However, the company's recent exposure as a serial exponent of tax avoidance illustrates how priorities can change. Herb Kelleher, the founder of *Southwest Airlines,* also had a simple philosophy for setting stakeholder priority. He said:

> You put your employees first. If you truly treat your employees that way, they will treat your customers well, your customers will come back, and that's what makes your shareholders happy.[22]

This statement is clear about both the priority of stakeholders and the logic that underpins it. It speaks to the intent and thus trustworthiness of the company.[23]

The reputation problem with all these approaches to corporate governance and the setting of stakeholder priority is that the company's normative statements are often violated during a crisis. Consider the case of Australia's biggest airline *Qantas*. In October 2011 *Qantas* suddenly grounded its entire fleet of aircraft and locked out its workforce as a way of precipitating federal government action to help expedite the settlement of a long-running industrial dispute. As a result 98,000 passengers were stranded around the world, politicians were angry because they were surprised and embarrassed by the company's actions, employees went ballistic, and some anti-union CEOs from other companies applauded. Many people in the general community were horrified that an Australian company would inconvenience so many unsuspecting Australian travelers. The media had a great time berating the company's senior management and interviewing stranded passengers. *Qantas,* however, claimed that stakeholder anger was the price it had to pay in order for management to gain more control over the strategy of the airline. It later spent an estimated $200 million dollars trying to restore the trust it lost during the crisis.

At the heart of the *Qantas* dispute was what really mattered to three key groups of stakeholders—senior management, operational workers (pilots, ground crew and maintenance workers), and shareholders. Senior management wanted a new strategy that required more employee flexibility and cost cutting to increase the profitability of the airline;[24] employees wanted job security, higher pay, and less off-shoring of work to lower cost countries, and shareholders wanted a better share price and more dividends. In effect the three groups were arguing about how to share the financial value created by the company. Using the language of reputation, the issues here were stakeholder legitimacy, the fairness of profit sharing, and honesty with affected parties. It is at times like these that an answer to the question of who really matters becomes painfully apparent.

From a stakeholder perspective management's decision to damage the company's reputation can be viewed as either normatively stupid or economically rational. Most of the media commentary tended to support the former explanation. However, another way of interpreting what the managers of the airline did was to trade away part of the company's good reputation for the chance of helping secure its financial future. This is an economically rational decision. If a good corporate reputation is a rent-producing asset, then it should be used. If it is damaged in the process, then it can be restored, in this case at a cost of $200 million.

A look at the annual report of most big companies and the corporate governance principles buried therein is a good place to discover the overarching objectives of the company and the normative and economic logics that are intended to deliver these. For example, the reputational DNA of *Macquarie Bank* is to "drive superior and sustainable shareholder value over the long term through the alignment of the interests of shareholders and staff."[25] There is nothing squeamish or opaque about this statement.

The generic approaches to making profits of differentiation, overall cost leadership, and focus also provide a powerful anchor point for reputation building and promotion. For example, the world's largest furniture retailer *IKEA* employs a cost leadership strategy. Its UK website says that the *IKEA* business idea is "to offer a wide range of well designed, functional home furnishing products at prices so low that as many people as possible will be able to afford them." Their operations "use inexpensive materials in a novel way to minimize production, distribution, and retail costs." Their customer value proposition is sometimes referred to as Scandinavian design at Asian prices. To deliver this, they are clear about who they target (the thrifty producer-consumers), what they offer (ready-to-assemble furniture, soft furnishings and accessories at affordable prices), and how they do this (through an integrated approach to design, manufacturing and transport, products that pack flat, and a serve yourself retail format). Among their employees and loyal customers, they are highly regarded for their success.

The law firm *Wachtell, Lipton, Rosen & Katz* (referred to as *Wachtell Lipton* on the company website) is a good example of a focused, differentiation approach. In the field of US law firms *Wachtell Lipton* stands apart from and above its rivals. The firm was founded in 1965 in New York where it still resides—it has only one office. It commenced operations with a narrow suite of practices which it still has. It started with a transaction as opposed to a relationship client focus and a lower leverage ratio (partners to associates) than the other major US law firms, and still has both these attributes. It quickly became extremely profitable and prestigious and it still is. It is known for its innovative thinking (e.g., it came up with the "poison pill defense" that prevented hostile takeovers), transaction-based fees (as opposed to hourly billing), and dealing with nonroutine legal matters. What gives *Wachtell Lipton* its powerful reputation is the differentiated who, what, and how choices it has made and persisted with, that provide higher margins on its work than its rivals. A leverage point for its corporate reputation is the recognition it receives in the US legal reputation polls.[26] This helps confer legitimacy on the firm's strategy and position in the legal firm status hierarchy that is highly prized by US law firms. It is also an important way to manage the expectations of potential clients and competitors.

Four things help reinforce the strong economic logic based reputations of firms like *IKEA* and *Wachtell Lipton*. One is a strong organizational culture. The second is a better customer value proposition that leads to commercial success. The third is a good corporate story about the organization and its leaders, which is often amplified by favorable media commentary. The fourth is the irrevocable commitment of resources made by the organization. These commitments shape the risk profile of the organization. And it is this risk that gives an organization's reputation much of its credibility as a signal of future behavior. Thus the risk of being held hostage to its reputation is an indirect measure of the trustworthiness of the company.

Before moving on, I will flag a warning about building a corporate reputation around the DNA of an organization. It is well illustrated by the phone-hacking tale involving Rupert Murdoch and *News Corporation*.

The Reputation Dark Side of Companies with a Strong DNA

They caught us with dirty hands.

Rupert Murdoch, July 19, 2011

The story of phone hacking in Britain first came to light in 2005 when the *News of the World* newspaper was accused of illegally accessing the phone messages of Princes William and Harry. It escalated dramatically in 2011 when the paper was accused of raiding the messages of a murdered schoolgirl. Media scrutiny by Murdoch's rival newspapers and government enquiries revealed that journalists at the paper, under the direction of their editors, paid private investigators to hack into the phone messages of more than 4,000 UK citizens, including some politicians and senior police. The journalists also paid some police to give them private information about people and stories. Murdoch and his editors frequently entertained senior British politicians. A key strategy of his newspapers was to aggressively support one or the other of the major political parties.

Wikipedia provides a clinical account of this sorry tale of the British press, politicians, and police succumbing to the influence of Rupert Murdoch and his newspapers. However, various books about Murdoch and *News Corporation* suggest that at the heart of the scandal was a strategy to beat competitor newspapers that was underpinned by a strong culture of get the news at any cost. This culture was directed by Murdoch and enforced by his editors. Even though the phone hacking, police bribes, and use of private investigators were routinely referred to by employees as the "dark arts," the strong culture that delivered circulation success legitimized this behavior. When it was exposed Murdoch and his senior managers first directed a campaign of denial, then obfuscation, then they blamed others, then they professed hurt feelings, contrition, acceptance of limited responsibility, and finally regret that was signified by the closing of the *News of the World* paper.

When companies have a very dominant, or in *News Corporation*'s case a tyrannical CEO, the culture of the organization comes to reflect the ethics of the leader. For example, the *News Corporation* board includes Murdoch's siblings, and for eight consecutive years between 2003 and 2010 the business ratings company *The Corporate Library* (now part of *Governance Metrics International*) gave the company's corporate governance an F grade—the lowest possible.[27] If this type of company also has market power, then some business philosophers suggest that it is easy for these companies to become rogues. The following quote captures this sentiment.

> Power tends to corrupt, and absolute power corrupts absolutely. Great men are almost always bad men.
>
> Lord Acton, 1887

Actions Speak Louder Than Words

Finally, the lower part of the figure 4.1 focuses on the actions and communications of the company. Communications are designed to promote the company's desired reputation, and as noted earlier, they are often designed around its character and competence. For example, for *Qantas* this desired reputation is outlined on its corporate website. It wants to "build a reputation for excellence in safety, operational reliability, engineering and maintenance, and customer service."[28] To back up the customer service element of this statement, the airline also has a customer charter on the website. However, this is cheap talk. The most recent clearly reputation-defining actions of the company were illustrated by its dispute with its employees.[29] And, as is often the case, the actions of a company that have a significant impact on its reputation are a direct consequence of the financial objectives and strategy of the company and thus its prioritization of stakeholders.

As I will argue in chapter 6, rather than making some vacuous statements about the character and competence of the company, a better basis for reputation communications is a coherent story about its past, present, and prospects. Stories are a powerful vehicle to communicate why someone should be prepared to trust the actions of a company. Thus a corporate story should be the grounding narrative for all reputation-enhancing communications.

In the next chapter I will outline another key element of this story, namely how the company creates and delivers value to its key stakeholders. These products, services, and employment opportunities should be the key reputation-defining actions of every company. And if they are simply better than those offered by competitors, there is a good story to be told about them and the company that offers them. This is a very self-interested view of corporate reputation formation. If a person thinks that a company wants to serve their needs better than its competitors they will admire and respect it for these efforts.

5

Simply Better

My thesis is that the best organizations tend to acquire better reputations than their competitors, and they tell good stories about themselves. But what does "best" mean? Once an organization has established legitimacy in a market, it then has to become known as the best at something or the best for somebody. For example, the UK grocer *Tesco* used to be best for customers who wanted good value—delivered by its "good, better & best" policy, and to be recognized for their loyalty—delivered through its *Clubcard* loyalty scheme. And *Apple* is still best at designing personal electronic products. Its employees work hard at this and customers recognize their achievements and value the iProducts highly. When an organization is significantly better than its rivals, its corporate reputation is reflected in its recognized and trusted name.

When an organization is worse than its rivals, often the feral media vent their frustration by ascribing new meaning to the company name. For example, many years ago these companies were re-branded: *DHL* = documents hopelessly lost; *Ford* = fix or repair daily; *British Airways* = bloody awful, *UBS* (the bank) after its financial crisis in 2007 = used to be smart, *LOTUS* (the UK cars) = lots of trouble, usually serious; IBM = I've been misled. Since the obvious hubris of its "beyond petroleum" re-branding campaign, *BP* has been particularly vulnerable to this type of anti-corporate sentiment. For example, it has been labeled: burning the planet, big problems, broken pipelines, and bloated profits.[1] Sometimes even a profession gets re-branded—public relations people are commonly referred to as "spin doctors" or "flacks." These signatures say not to trust what these people and companies say or what they offer.

In the second Steve Jobs era, *Apple* became a standout example of the 'making the best offer to customers' approach to reputation building.

The company's star product brands— the iPod, iPad, iPhone, iTunes, Mac PCs—were loved by their users and respected for their innovative design. Their advertising was engaging. Their retail stores were designed to be temples for the faithful. The sales people were the disciples of the brand and created a good buying experience. Numerous books, articles, and social media stories about *Apple* and Steve Jobs created a mystique about the company. At the time of Job's death *Apple*'s stock price placed the company at the top of the stock market ladder.[2] This position of excellence was also affirmed by the *Fortune* business magazine reputation polls in which *Apple* was voted as the world's most admired company each year from 2008 to 2015.[3] The *Financial Times* newspaper also reports that *Apple* is now one of the world's most valuable consumer brands.[4]

Yes, *Apple* had some warts on its corporate reputation, but most people were not interested to find out what these were. And if by chance they did become aware of a blemish, they didn't let it significantly devalue their reputation of the company or its products.[5] Thus the good parts of *Apple*'s reputation overshadowed the bad aspects of its behavior, and these gave it a competitive advantage that was difficult for its direct competitors like *Samsung* to match.

The *Apple* example highlights the three basic parts of my preferred reputation-building strategy:

1. Become a company that is perceived to offer significantly better value to the stakeholders who matter to the company's success than competitors.
2. Make this the strategic priority of the company.
3. Create a compelling corporate story to remind people of who you are, what you stand for, and how this creates excellence.

These three elements are shown in figure 5.1.

The key factor in this model is that an organization should offer a value proposition that is much better than the ones offered by competitors. But what does this goal actually mean? In the case of *Apple* its iProducts are generally regarded as much better by their customers and even occasionally by their competitors. For example, Bill Gates is on the record as saying that some of *Apple*'s products set the benchmark for competitors to emulate. Steve Jobs has said that "for most things in

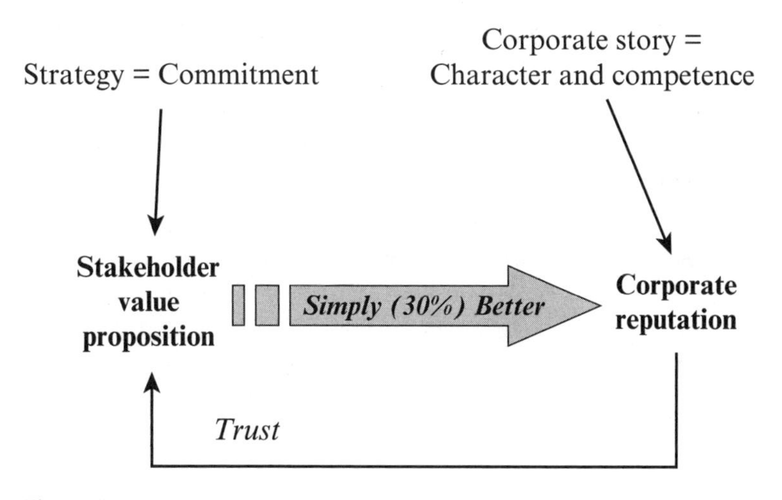

Figure 5.1

Stakeholder value + Corporate commitment + A good story

life the range between best and average is 30% or so."[6] This 30 percent margin is a good rule of thumb to strive for—hence its inclusion in the figure above.

In a stakeholder-driven world a company that is simply better than its rivals is seen to be acting in the best interests of its stakeholders. And when the provision of this benefit is fairly shared between the company and its stakeholders it fosters being seen as fair and trustworthy. This chapter outlines how to design the best offer to each stakeholder group in order to achieve these outcomes. To illustrate being simply better, I'll start by retelling three old stories. They are about *IBM*, the *Sydney Olympic Games,* and *Rolls Royce*. The *IBM* story is summarized in a saying common at the time in the corporate world:

Nobody ever got fired for buying *IBM*.

When *IBM* was the King of the mainframe computer market, they understood a wonderful paradox that helped make them successful—*IBM* sold their mainframe computers, operating systems, and service, but many of the buyers were not really interested in the hardware, software, or for that matter the support. Consider the situation faced by an organization buying a big mainframe computer. The buyer was typically a big organization acquiring the mainframe to run its mission-critical operations, payroll, and accounting. This was a complex situation, and the buying group who were assigned responsibility for making the choice of computer consisted of a variety of managers, only a few of whom knew much about hardware or software. Also the purchase was risky—in terms of the amount of money involved, the lock-in to the vendor's equipment, and the chance that the system would not deliver what a variety of different users wanted. As tenders were called and the evaluation process unfolded, it became clear that *IBM* was one of the better and more expensive options, but they were reluctant to offer any form of discount. There was often a technically better option on the shortlist of prospective vendors. But, more often than not, *IBM* got the sale. Big Blue, as they were called, was the clear market leader.

As a member of the buying group who did not have extensive knowledge about computers, software, or computer vendors, consider how you would have felt. You are about to make a buying recommendation that will have a major impact on the organization's operations, competitiveness, and future viability—and regardless of how much homework you do during the buying process, you are still not completely confident that you are on top of every aspect of this complex decision. If the purchase turns out to be a good one, some people may remember that you played a part in the correct decision. If the purchase turns out to be a poor one, as many such purchases did, then many more people will remember your participation, and some will blame you for it. If highly respected *IBM*, the market leader, puts up a reasonably competitive proposal, it is quite an easy decision to award them the contract—even though the IT people on the buying group might say that Vendor X had a better cost-performance package. Why? Because, by awarding the contract to *IBM*, you are buying the new IT system and an insurance policy for your personal reputation. In the event of poor performance your refrain will likely be: "If the highly respected, market leader's system would not deliver, then no other system would either! Hence don't blame me—we bought the best on offer at the time." IBM sales people were adept at selling the corporate and personal benefits of their IT packages.

Another example of "making an offer that can't be refused" occurred for the purchase of the main stadium for the 2000 Olympic Games in Sydney. The organizing committee wanted a world-class facility for the opening and closing ceremonies and for the athletics. The stadium would be used after the games by the citizens of Sydney for various sporting events. A stadium to seat 100,000 patrons is a very expensive piece of infrastructure. Tenders were called and proposals submitted. All the short-listed proposals could provide a world-class facility. However, one proposal stood out from the rest. Not only would it build the stadium and do its fit-out, it would also arrange for the financing of the venture. As a member of the buying group for this project the choice is easy—you get a world-class stadium and you don't have to worry about financing the deal. This package won the contract.

The third story was told by the late and legendary Peter Drucker.[7] He discovered an old prospectus for *Rolls Royce* that stated that the cars would have "the cachet of royalty." The company originally restricted sales to customers of whom they approved—preferably titled ones. They also priced their cars as high as a small yacht—about 40 times the annual income of a skilled mechanic or prosperous tradesman. What this sales strategy achieved was to signal that a *Rolls Royce* car was simply better than anything else one could buy. And at the time they probably were. For many years the name *Rolls Royce* was synonymous with high quality.

These are three examples of designing a simply better offer to a specific group of customers. Behind their success was insight about the latent and expressed needs of the customer. These needs were functional, economic and psychological. Some were expressed, such as we need a world-class Olympic Stadium, while some were latent, such as we are worried about how to pay for it. Good salespeople master the art of understanding all these types of need before making their offer.

Now here is a more contemporary and contrived example of gaining a corporate reputation for producing the best products in the category. It is also an example of how a good corporate story is crucial to building and maintaining this reputation.

Wine Glasses

When drinking beer or wine it is nice to drink from an elegant glass. They look and feel good in the hand. An elegant glass, especially in a restaurant can enhance the overall experience of consumption. In large part it does this by changing what you expect from the wine and the resulting experience tends to live up to these expectations—especially when the wine costs a lot of money. And some people who drink wine have been convinced that the nature of the glass from which they drink actually affects the taste of the wine. The idea here is that the shape of the glass collects the aroma of the wine and it also directs it to different parts of the mouth to emphasize the wine's best characteristics. Hence champagne, fortified wine, and different varieties of red and white wine should all be drunk from different shaped glasses. But where did this idea come from? Answer—the makers of wine glasses. However, in properly designed blind taste tests involving untrained wine drinkers, this effect is hard to find.[8]

Notwithstanding this the family-owned Austrian glass company *Riedel* has crafted a reputation of excellence for its leadership in the field of designing wine glasses. *Riedel* call themselves "The wine glass company."[9] I have underlined the word "The" in their corporate slogan to reflect the central position they have claimed in the market for wine glasses. If *Riedel* is the wine glass company, then everybody else is forced to adopt a different position—such as being the cheapest, or most durable, or most fancy, or having the biggest range, or being the most popular, or whatever. Now a look at the *Riedel* corporate website is an exercise in being educated about wine glasses—bowls (shape, size, and rim diameter), stems and bases. What is noteworthy is that the education is wrapped around the story of appreciating wine. For example, "A person interested in wine is led by color, bouquet, and taste, but often the glass is not considered as an instrument to convey the wine's message. Over the years *Riedel* has acquired some interesting scientific explanations as to why the shape of the glass influences the bouquet and taste of alcoholic beverages." And so it goes on. *Riedel* has a great corporate story targeted to "people interested in wine" that is often endorsed by sommeliers, fine dining restaurants, and wine critics. So here we have a company that creates elegant wine glasses and supports this quality by referring to their features and using the testimonials of others as points of proof. *Riedel* is "best at wine glasses."

The principles that apply to creating desirable products and services migrate easily to building relationships with all a company's key stakeholders and thus enhancing its desired reputation. In the discipline of marketing this approach is called creating a customer value proposition. Here I will call it creating a stakeholder value proposition (SVP).

As noted earlier, because each group of stakeholders has a different relationship with a company, each will need to be offered a different SVP. In the *Riedel* case there are three broad groups of stakeholders. One is the untrained wine drinkers. The second is the professional wine merchants—sommeliers, wine tasters and critics, the wine media, fine-dining restaurants, and business partners such as wine shops and companies like *Celebrity Cruises* that promote *Riedel* glassware. The third is the 940 employees at the company's five factories in Europe where the glasses are made. The first two groups will require only slightly different SVPs. Employees, however, will require a very different offer. It is interesting to note that there is no mention on the *Riedel* corporate website of shareholders (because they are a family-owned company) or the communities in which the company operates (presumably because they are not thought to be crucial to the company's desired reputation as being best at wine glasses).

The overall corporate reputation of *Riedel* will be based on three SVPs as shown in figure 5.2. The proximity of the two top SVPs is used to indicate their similarity. As the description above suggests the overlap of each SVP with the company name represents its contribution to the company's

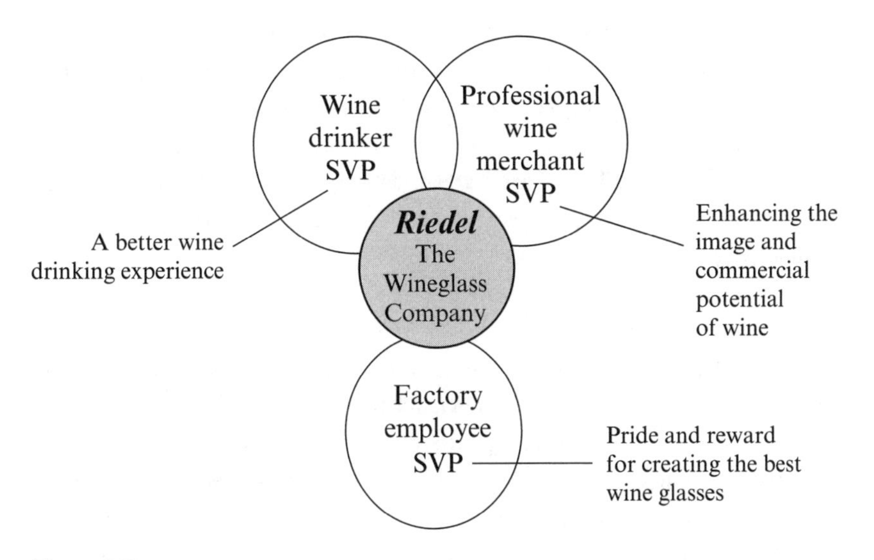

Figure 5.2

Structure of Riedel's overall corporate reputation

overall reputation. While *Riedel* has only three key SVPs, large public companies will typically have more groups of stakeholders to placate—employees, customers, business partners, shareholders, and sometimes the media and the communities in which they operate. Hence a diagram like the one in figure 5.2 will need to accommodate the stakeholders who really matter.

Stakeholder Value Propositions

Formally defined, a SVP is the person's set of resulting experiences from dealing with a company. In the case of the buyers of *IBM* computers, their resulting experiences were as much about buying a personal insurance policy for their career as it was with the service provided by *IBM*'s equipment. For retired shareholders who are interested in the dividends a company pays, a big part of the resulting experience is the lifestyle that these payments secure. Hence the reliability of the dividend is of paramount importance. For a new employee, the resulting experience will include being paid a good salary and the prestige that accompanies this sum of money. The point here is that resulting experiences can be many and varied.

What resulting experiences are not is a list of attributes of the product or service received. Nor are they platitudes about how the organization values its employees, respects its shareholders, provides the best quality to customers, or contributes to the local community. All companies issue these proclamations. Many are paternalistic and often patronizing statements rather than an expression of the set of experiences the group really wants.

The Components of a SVP

At the heart of a compelling SVP is usually a single core benefit offered or a significant problem solved. For *Riedel* these were noted in the preceding figure. Either will provide a positive resulting experience from dealing with the company. For example, when *Apple* introduced the iPod portable music device, the advertising for the product included the tagline "1,000 songs in your pocket." For people who love their music, this was a fantastic experience and one they were prepared to pay a premium price for. *Apple* also understood that the "i" that preceded this and its other products stood for "individual" not "information."

Uncovering this core benefit/solution requires becoming the stakeholder—a task that goes way beyond listening to them in focus groups or reading research about them. To illustrate this point, consider the senior automotive executive who could not understand why so many car buyers disliked the experience of buying a car. When asked about his car-buying experience, he confessed to not having bought a car, or for that matter having his car serviced for the last twenty years. In his case a new car was part of his salary package. When he had driven it for 1,500 kilometers, someone automatically replaced it with a new one, so that his old car could be sold as a "demonstrator." It was impossible for this senior manager to empathize with most car buyers about the frustrations involved during the car-buying experience. To help overcome this type of myopia in some companies, managers are asked to practice the mantra of "buy your own dog food"—or better still, "buy and eat your own, and your competitors' dog food." The idea here is that all managers should experience their own, and competitors' products and services as their customers do.

Another difficulty with developing a strong SVP is called "the engineer's lament" (sorry engineers) or the "academic's lament" (sorry colleagues). It is stated as: "It is hard to give someone what they want, when you know what they need." This lament often leads to designing an SVP as a set of features. For example, in the early part of my academic career I designed my courses for students on the basis of I knew what they needed to know. If I could present this material in an interesting way, then my teaching ratings were OK. Later in my career when I started to work with executives, I had to change my approach. Now I started my course design by finding out what problems were troubling the managers and then designing a program around exploring these problems. The set of resulting experiences for both of us improved.

There are always some notable exceptions to this customer research-led approach. One was practiced by Steve Jobs at *Apple*. He never did any customer research. His approach was to look at existing products, uncover their limitations, loudly denigrate them to his employees and others in the industry (in terms such as "these things really stink"), and then relentlessly push his hardware and software engineers to significantly improve what was offered. He was a perfectionist who did not tolerate being told something could not be done. While the outcomes of this approach were many product successes, Walter Isaacson's biography of Steve Jobs details the personal cost to him and many of his associates of following this bullying approach.[10] Because most companies do not have such a visionary CEO/product developer and they are not prepared to drive their employees to the extreme, a program of ethnographic research is often a better approach to providing the feedstock for developing value propositions.

The other key component of a SVP is the price paid to achieve the experience received. Setting the right price is one of the most difficult decisions managers face. For example, in consumer markets the three basic options are to (1) skim the market by setting an initial high price and reducing it over time, (2) set a low initial price and keep it there, or (3) set a price to capture the value represented by the benefits delivered. In July 2007 when *Apple* introduced the iPhone in the United States, it was priced at $599. Many people considered this to be a value-based price. The design and image value of the phone supported the high price. The price was a signal of quality rather than a measure of sacrifice. And then *Apple* did something that tarnished its reputation and the trust of its customers.

Two months after launching the iPhone *Apple* dropped its price to $399. People who had bought the phone for $599 felt ripped off. And they let *Apple* know of their displeasure. Steve Jobs' initial response was to publish an open letter to customers defending the company's actions. He said that such price reductions were standard practice in technology markets. In effect he said that *Apple* had used a skim price rather than a value price. The problem was that iPhone buyers didn't expect such a price reduction so quickly. Had the price come down just before the release of the next version of the iPhone, these buyers may well have accepted the logic of *Apple*'s pricing strategy. But this was not the case. In order to try to appease the early buyers *Apple* then offered a $100 of store credit to these people for products in its stores.

The key to being stakeholder focused is to concentrate on the benefits and/or solutions to problems that the person wants from their relationship with the company. As noted above, these can be:

- Functional—the company does what is expected.
- Psychological—the resulting experiences are gratifying.
- Economic—the "price" of this relationship is acceptable.

At the heart of designing a set of benefits and solutions is to find out what type of relationship each stakeholder group wants with the company. In the next section I'll describe this. Then I'll illustrate a technique for designing a SVP.

Stakeholder Relationships

As a marketing academic and consultant I observed some of the best commercial relationships to be between companies selling to their key account customers. For example, during one assignment I observed how the senior partners of a major law firm really understood what a relationship was with their biggest client. It was like a new marriage. In contrast, some of the worst relationships I observed were based around the customer loyalty programs of large airlines. These programs illustrate how difficult it is for a company to have a "relationship" with hundreds of thousands of people.

At the heart of both good and bad relationships was the understanding that relationships are emotional, and that they involve shared responses and responsibilities. For example, in the case of the law firm the engagement partner described his client relationship in terms of:

- Who gives what.
- Who gets what.
- When things are due.
- How disputes will be resolved.

In the case of the airlines and many consumer goods companies, the nature of the commercial relationship is often not understood by the customer. Companies know they are having a "commercial relationship" with their customers where the terms and conditions are laid out on the website. However, many customers think that the relationship is supposed to be more like a "personal relationship" where their loyalty actually entitles them to special consideration. And here lies the problem. If both parties don't agree about, and abide by the terms and conditions of "their relationship," then it is difficult for a company to create and deliver a strong SVP.

A good way to help understand this problem is to segment each group of stakeholders into "relationship groups." For example, a company's customers might be partitioned as follows:

- *Sleepers*—people who are yet to be convinced that entering into a "relationship" with the company is worth their effort, such as infrequent customers.
- *Transacters*—people who know that they don't want a relationship with the company, such as people who buy low involvement products merely out of habit.
- *Brand loyals*—people who like your brand and want it to stay the same, such as people who buy the same brand even though others are readily available.
- *Opportunists*—people who will exploit any offers made by the company, such as infrequent travelers who link their credit cards to an airline frequent-flyer program so that they can use the points to buy products on the airline's website.
- *Partners*—people who believe they will benefit from a closer association with the company, and who are willing to contribute to the relationship, such as people who are prepared to be involved in market research studies and new product development projects in return for privileged access to corporate events.

In order to manage the expectations of these groups, the "relationship" needs to be designed and communicated differently. Also this type of research can help the company identify which of its customers will be susceptible to more psychological aspects of their offer. For example, most wine glass buyers start off as sleepers or transacters because they are indifferent to or skeptical about claims that a wine glass can enhance the wine-drinking experience. However, *Riedel* likes to target those who like to appreciate wine and share the experience with friends. These people are the ones invited to attend a *Riedel*-sponsored wine-tasting event. The company has found that it can convert many of these wine lovers to its point of view about the impact of their glasses on the wine-drinking experience. And from then on, drinking from a *Riedel* glass provides an emotional connection to the company. These people are also more likely to softly promote *Riedel*'s glasses to their friends. In effect they have been converted from sleepers to partners or brand loyals. The key to designing a strong SVP is to understand the type of relationship desired by each stakeholder subgroup.

In the case of shareholders, their motivation for investing in a company is the key to designing a strong shareholder value proposition. Many day traders are like transacters. They can be usefully ignored. Institutional investors and active investors are like partners. They like to be thoroughly informed. Speculators are like opportunists. Their behavior and recommendations need to be monitored. Passive investors are like brand loyals. They need periodic reminding about how well their shares are performing.

There are three simple ways to segment employees. One is by whether they "work to live" or "live to work." People in the second category may do this because they want to create something of lasting value, or they may use work as a way to improve their life, or provide an enjoyable social experience, or it might throw up challenges not available elsewhere. Many of the employees in *Riedel*'s factories would likely fit into this category. People in the first category may view work as a source of livelihood or because it provides an immediate economic gain. Each type of employee will seek a different type of employment relationship with the company. And those who live to work may be better reputation champions for the companies they work for.

A second segmentation scheme is to assess whether the employee is more loyal to his or her craft or profession than to the company they work for. Many professionally trained people have this characteristic. These people will become reputation champions when the company's values align with their professional values. A third way to segment employees is to note whether they are in or outside the core group of the company. The core group is those people who are entrenched in the organization and who see it as their role to keep the spirit of the enterprise alive. These are the real internal reputation champions. Sometimes a CEO will not be invited to join this group. When this happens the CEO's reputation-enhancing initiatives may be ignored. This was one of the problems experienced in *BP* when John Browne introduced the "beyond petroleum" corporate communications campaign. Because the core of most oil companies revolves around its engineering expertise, anything that runs counter to this core value is likely to be regarded as rubbish, especially by the entrenched insiders.

Designing a Stakeholder Value Proposition

The key to designing a strong stakeholder value proposition is to emphasize what is being received rather than what is offered. I'll call what is offered the features of the SVP. The role of a feature is to "prove" that what is received, namely the benefits, solutions to problems, and resulting experience can be delivered. A useful way of thinking about this is that a:

- Feature does something.
- Benefit gives something.

Marketing managers use this style of thinking to understand the core benefit or unique selling proposition of the products and services they sell. For example, a cordless electric drill has four main features—it is cordless, has a rechargeable battery, can drill through wood and other materials, and uses a number of different size drill bits. However, what is bought is quite different. What is bought is the ease and safety of making holes of various sizes almost anywhere. And the resulting experience is usually "a job well done." The *National Geographic* magazine became iconic because what people were really buying was not a well-produced, interesting magazine about various parts of the world, but rather cheap educational travel. A modern equivalent is those travel programs on television. The resulting experience for some people is more confidence about how and where to travel, and for others it is a good reason not to travel. Banks, which many of us love to hate, sell a variety of financial products and services, but most of us buy wealth creation, management and protection, and transaction management and security. The resulting experience is often as simple as peace of mind. Charles Revson, the founder of the *Revlon* cosmetics company really understood this idea. He once commented that "In the factory we make cosmetics; in the drugstore we sell hope." As cosmetic prices will testify, people will pay a lot of money for hope.

Insight about what is bought, like those in the previous examples, typically comes from research, intuition, and testing a variety of value propositions. A good advertising agency can be helpful here. The way I start thinking about what is offered and what is bought is to create a value proposition "onion" diagram like the stylized one in figure 5.3. I use the metaphor of an onion because you have to peel away the outer layers

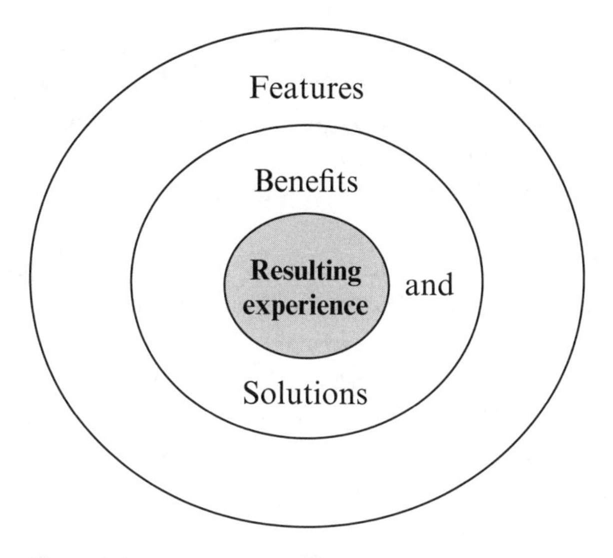

Figure 5.3

Stakeholder value proposition onion

of the onion (the features) to get to the best part (the benefits). Also the process often produces some tears of frustration.

These onion diagrams are essentially creative doodles. I start by writing down a description of the stakeholder group I am designing the offer for. I give them a descriptive name. For example, *Riedel*'s factory workers might be called craftsmen and craftswomen and their customers wine lovers and wine merchants (to reflect their commercial interest in the company's glass wares). The names should reflect the essence of the group's identity and how their relationship with the company might help them achieve some desired outcome. For example, in the mobile phone market the business customer segments might be called—hermits (they do not move from their desk very often), corridor cruisers (who frequently wander around the office), road warriors (who travel domestically), globe trotters (who travel internationally), and networkers (who talk and text wherever they go).

The next task is to list all the features that might be offered to the stakeholder group. Then I link each feature with a benefit or solution to a problem that research, experience, and intuition has uncovered. For some features there will be no obvious link. At this point I have a messy list of feature-benefit pairs. To create some order from this chaos, I shift as many of the feature-benefit pairs as I can into an onion diagram. I do this as a paper and pencil task. Yes, it is old fashioned, but what typically happens is that a lot of shuffling around of these features is necessary before a clear picture emerges. During this process the center of the onion is left blank.

Figures 5.4 and 5.5 show hypothetical onions for *Riedel*'s factory employees and wine lover customers. They try to capture the things that provide value for the people who take pride in making and using the most elegant wine glasses and decanters. In essence, the SVP for employees focuses on *Riedel* being regarded as a great place to work. Thus it will be composed of a mixture of elements that describe—the company such as its history, performance, and management; the workplace environment such as physical working conditions, promotion opportunities, and job demands; utilitarian factors such as remuneration and leave entitlements; and how the excellence of what is being made is recognized. The SVP for

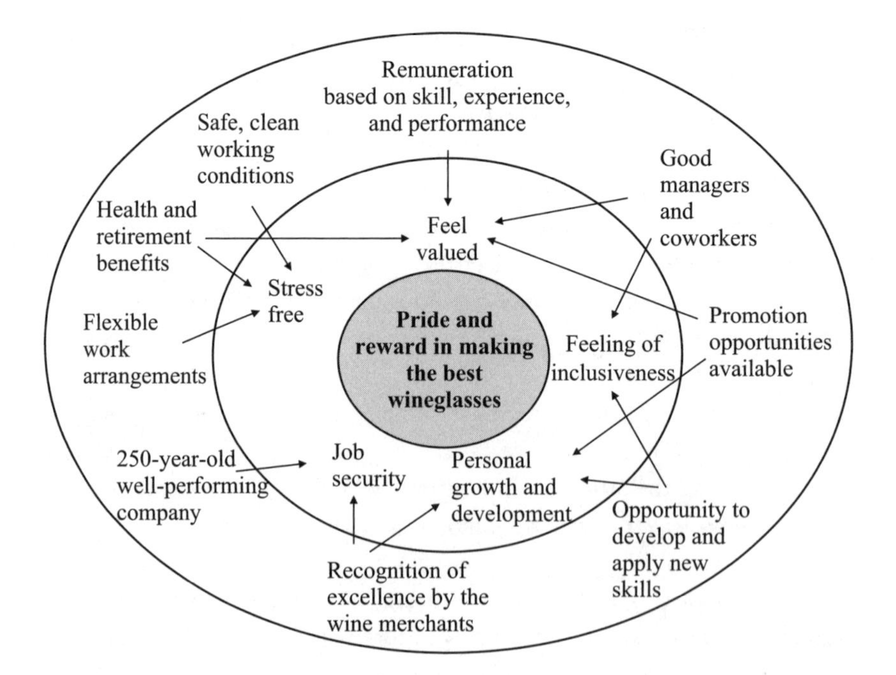

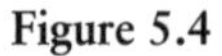
Figure 5.4

Riedel factory employee value proposition onion

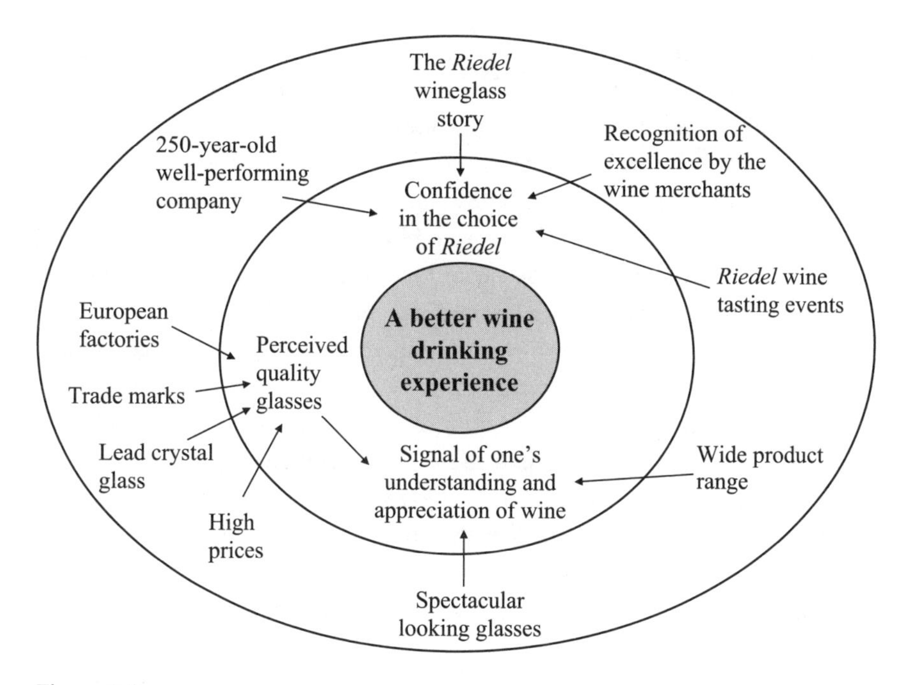

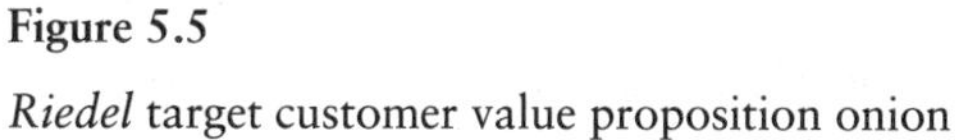
Figure 5.5

Riedel target customer value proposition onion

the customers focuses on enhancing the wine-drinking experience. Here the idea is to link the features of the company and its range of glasses to allowing the customer to enjoy their wine and to signal this to their fellow wine lovers.

The final thing to do with these onions is to recognize that each is a hypothesis, meaning a conjecture that needs to be tested. In fact two tests are needed. One is to check that the elements in the onion reflect what the stakeholder group really wants and whether they think that the company can deliver this better than competitors. Focus groups and surveys can be employed to answer these questions. Market research firms specialize in this type of research.

The other test is to check that the core of the SVP aligns with the reputation strategy of the company. For example, in the 1990s the Netherlands-based global electronics company *Philips* had a reputation as "a reliable consumer electronics company." This was the essence of their desired corporate reputation position. The problem here was that the company saw itself as much more than this, and its strategy demanded that it be more than this. Like its competitors *Philips* had big growth targets that being "reliable" would not achieve. The company had been investing a lot of money and effort in becoming more innovative. To reflect this strategic initiative, the company re-branded itself as "Let's make things better," which was really a rallying cry for employees. A decade later the corporate brand slogan became "sense and simplicity," as would describe the resulting experience of using its products. In 2013 the *Philips* brand slogan became "innovation and you." At this time the story on the corporate website said that *Philips* "demonstrates our innovation capacity by translating customer insights into meaningful technology and applications that improve the quality of people's lives."[11] The company's aspiration is to become "best at innovation" by being guided by the needs of their customers. As the patchy record of the success of many of the company's past new products suggests, this is not an easy path to implement. Also being the most innovative company is a contested position in the field of electronics.

To guide the creation of SVPs and to ensure that they contribute to enhancing the reputation of the company requires a framework to listen to the expectations and values of key stakeholders. I call this listening to the voice of the stakeholder.

Voice of the Stakeholder

Researching what stakeholders want a company to do for them is both an art and a science. The art is to know what questions to ask, and the science is to gather this information in a valid and reliable manner. Here I will focus on what to ask. The previous discussion suggests that four types of information are needed to understand the concerns of a group of stakeholders. This is their values, expectations, relationship with the company, and their resulting experience. These four types of information are shown in figure 5.6.

Figure 5.6 suggests that these four types of information provide answers to four reputation-related questions. What does the person want from the company, here defined as aligning with the person's values and meeting their expectations? Was the person's engagement with the company meaningful, in that each shared similar values and wanted a similar

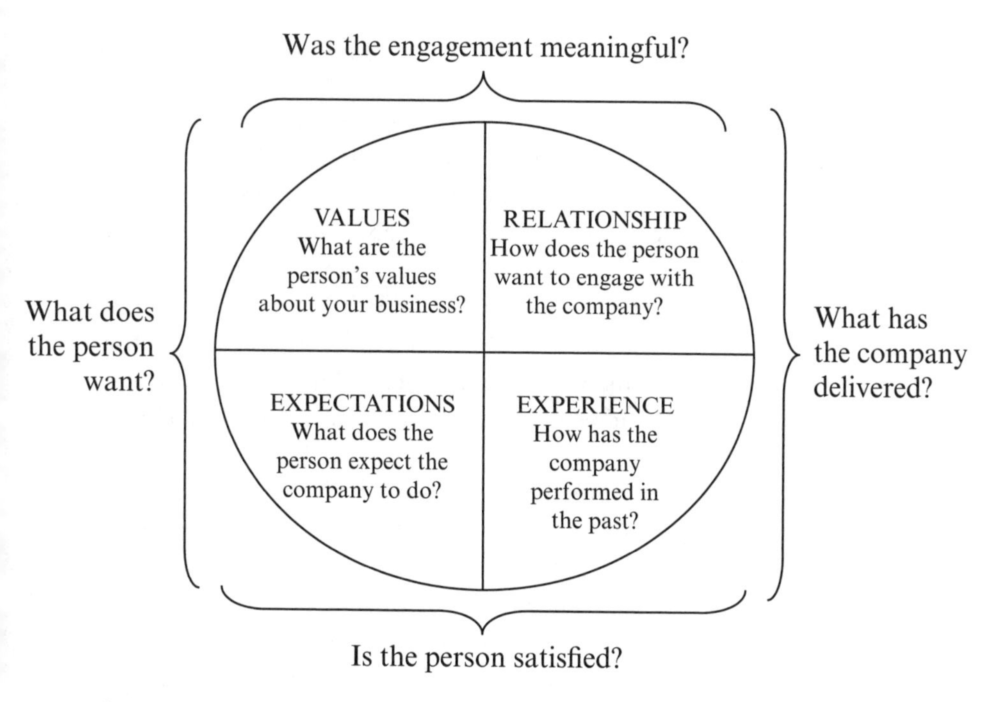

Figure 5.6

Voice of the stakeholder

type of relationship? What has the company delivered? Is it perceived to be best at something or best for somebody? This is the stakeholder value proposition the person has experienced. Is the person satisfied, here defined as did the experience delivered by the company meet the person's expectations? Answers to these questions speak to the quality of the company's SVP. The consequence of poor answers to any question suggests a less than optimal SVP.

The next aspect of a corporate stakeholder value proposition to consider is whether it can be branded in order to help communicate the central part of the SVP onion diagram to stakeholders. Here the discipline of marketing has much to contribute.

Branding Corporate Stakeholder Value Propositions

One lesson from the world of marketing is that branding a customer value proposition can help communicate its core benefit to the target stakeholder group. This is often done with a corporate slogan or tagline. This idea of signing off the company name probably came from the mottos that schools and universities often use.[12] Many of these were written in Latin and now sound somewhat quaint. Some of my old favorite product slogans are *Coca Cola* "it's the real thing"—this immediately relegated *Pepsi* to a lesser status; *AT&T* "the right choice"—the confirmation of a good choice: *Nike* "just do it"—was a call to action by buying *Nike*'s shoes; *CNN* "be the first to know"—for those people who need to know first; *Apple* "the power to be your best"—another call to action; *De Beers* "a diamond is forever"—something to treasure and please don't sell it and flood the market with excess diamonds; *American Express* "Don't leave home without it"—a reminder to use the product; *L'Oréal* "Because I'm worth it"—pure flattery; *US Army* "be all you can be"—a call to personal development; *BMW* "the ultimate driving machine"—a claim to be simply better; *SAS* "the business airline of Europe" —for people like you, and *Federal Express* (*FedEx*) "when it absolutely, positively has to be there overnight"—when speed matters; *LG* "life's good"—describes the customer experience delivered by their appliances. Each provides a good reason to buy the product.

In the corporate world the problem is how to brand the company in a way that speaks meaningfully to its key stakeholder groups without offending other people. Because this is a difficult task many companies avoid the challenge. It is simply too hard to come up with a corporate slogan to please everybody. There is some justification in this decision because sometimes these slogans actually work against the thoughts automatically elicited by the company name. For example, seeing the name *Walmart* might prime thoughts of value, economy-priced merchandise, and a sterile store environment for people who know the retailer, while seeing the name *Nordstrom* primes luxury, high-priced merchandise, and a nice store environment. However, when a company adds a slogan to its name such as *Walmart*'s "Save money. Live better," people may consider this to be a persuasive marketing tactic that is designed to influence their behavior. They then are inclined to correct for the influence of this tactic. Correction here entails counter arguing with the claim and introducing negative evaluations of the company.[13]

An alternative is to try to create a broad corporate brand slogan that speaks to everybody. The problem with most of these is that they often wind up talking to nobody because what they say is meaningless. For example, who owns these corporate slogans—"go further" (*Ford*); "sponsors of tomorrow" (*Intel*); "hello tomorrow" (*Emirates* Airlines); "make.believe" (*Sony*); "inspired by purpose" (*Procter & Gamble*). These are clichéd words without meaning. They do not speak to either what makes the company special or what it might provide to its key stakeholders. Thus they do nothing to enhance the company's desired reputation. Maybe they would be better written in Latin. Now if the company has a poor reputation and wants to hide from the public, then using a meaningless corporate name often works. Earlier I noted the example of the tobacco company *Altria*.

Another corporate branding tactic is to create a coined brand name that has some deep meaning. Two such names are *Accenture* and *Verizon*. The problem with these is that someone has to explain who the company is (a management consulting and technology services firm and an American broadband and telecommunications company) and what the name means (accent on the future; truth and horizon). And then most people, even many employees instantly forget what the name means. To try to overcome this problem sometimes the company adds a slogan. For *Accenture* this is "High performance. Delivered." Despite what the company says on its website, if you do not know who *Accenture* is, then the name and the corporate slogan wouldn't help much.[14] You have to see *Accenture*'s corporate advertisements to understand the slogan and the company's brand position. These showcase client success stories and the company's capabilities.

Sometimes a company creates a slogan that captures the essence of both its employee and customer value propositions. The old *Harley-Davidson* slogan "live to ride, ride to live" is a good example. It captures both the motivation for owning a *Harley* and the resulting experience of using it. And because many of the people who make these bikes also ride them, the slogan has meaning for the company's employees. Two of their other slogans were "turn on your own thunder" and "the legend rolls on." Again, both of these speak about the resulting experience of being a *Harley* employee and owner. And they will resonate with the people who see the company's products and its customers. The strong, distinctive culture of the company, its employees, and its customers makes it easier for

Harley-Davidson to create a stronger corporate brand than companies that try to be all things to all people.

Many corporate brand slogans and corporate advertising make a promise or they state a leadership position. Some notable examples are *GE*'s "we bring good things to life," "imagination at work" and "ecomagination"; *Cathy Pacific*—"arrive in better shape"; *Airbus*—"setting the standards" (which makes sense only when they were bigger than *Boeing*); *Avis*—"we try harder"; *Bose*—"better sound through research"; the old *Compaq* (*HP*) personal computer company—"inspiration technology"; *DuPont*—"the miracles of science"; *Bayer*—"science for a better life"; *Holiday Inn*—"the world's first choice"; *Mitsubishi*—"better built, better backed"; *Mont Blanc*—"The art of writing"; *Nestlé*—"Good food. Good life"; *RollsRoyce*—"trusted to deliver excellence." Granted, many of these are not highly creative, but the point is to remind internal and external stakeholders about the raison d'être of the company or what it offers.

Good corporate branding should reflect the central theme of the company's SVPs offered to key stakeholders. For example, *BMW*'s old slogan "The ultimate driving machine" told employees what to design and build, and it told customers what to expect. *Riedel*'s "the wine glass company" attempts to do a similar thing. In contrast, *3M*'s old slogan "innovation" said what the company was good at and reminded employees what to do, but it failed to link this corporate capability to its better products. You have to go to the corporate website to find out how good this company really is. Most customers don't do this, and so the old corporate slogan was somewhat muted. Recently the corporate slogan was upgraded to "Innovative Technology for a changing world," and currently it is "Science. Applied to Life." These are better, but they could equally apply to many technology or life science companies.

As we will see in the next chapter, corporate stories provide the context for corporate brands. When stakeholders know this story and buy into its message a good corporate slogan acts to trigger these memories. Why many of the corporate slogans above were fairly meaningless was that nobody can recall the company story from which they are derived.

Signals of a Weak Stakeholder Value Proposition

To finish this chapter, I'll briefly note how to assess when a SVP is likely to be weak. If the following signals are weak, it should trigger some formal investigation. Recall the traditional measures of SVP strength for the following stakeholders:

- Customers—satisfaction, loyalty, and positive word-of-mouth.
- Employees—engagement, identification with the company, retention, confidence in senior management, a lack of industrial disputation, and respect for customers.
- Business partners—commitment, satisfaction, and respect for the organization.
- Shareholders—amount invested, trading pattern, and confidence in the future of the company and its management.
- Local community—proud to have the organization as a member of the community.

When stakeholders respond to the company in such positive ways, it must be doing something right.

Over the years I have noticed the following early warning signals of trouble:

- When a company makes considerable profit in areas outside its core operational sphere. Here the business model of the company is not aligned with the SVPs of its target customers. For example, the co-branded credit card loyalty programs of some airlines are their high-performing profit centers. People earn frequent-flyer points using their credit cards to buy things like furniture, wine, and travel goods. So, if the most profitable part of an airline has little to do with being an airline, then what is it? And should a person base his or her reputation of the company on its airline activities or its rewards program?
- When customers or media commentators negatively rename or describe the company. For example, discount airlines became known as "peanut airlines," and bankers have become "banksters." These terms should be a warning signal.
- Very mixed media coverage signals confusion. Very negative media coverage signals problems.

- When an industry is forced to appoint an ombudsperson to mediate disputes. The Australian banking industry has one of these.
- When the company has to bribe its customers to buy its products or services. Many radio stations run "give-away" promotions where they offer money for the lucky listener who phones in. Car companies offer money back rebates from the manufacturer. Hotels offer free nights. If your product is any good, people will pay the asking price.

Because the idea of SVPs originated in marketing, it is appropriate to go back to this discipline for guidance about how to more formally evaluate the strength of a value proposition. The industry of firms that measure the brand images of products and companies do this type of research. In addition to the above, their studies also focus on the three basic perceptions of whether a brand is perceived by people to be relevant to them, distinctive from competitors, and is what they promise deliverable by the organization. These three perceptions will provide additional insight into the strength of a SVP. Any competent market research firm can do this type of analysis.

To summarize this chapter, the key to being seen as simply better by important stakeholders is the strength of the SVP offered—relative to the strength of the SVPs offered by rivals. The more precisely that a SVP can be described:

- The less chance there is for confusion inside the company about what needs to be done to create and deliver this value.
- The more focused the communication about the SVP can be, and thus
- The less chance for uncertainty in the minds' of key stakeholders about what is offered and what their relationship with the company entails.

Thus a good SVP helps manage the expectations of both the key stakeholders and the employees responsible for creating and delivering stakeholder value. As I will emphasize in chapter 9, these line employees are the ambassadors for a company's reputations.

6

Corporate Storytelling

Every company could tell many stories about itself, and some like *Enron* did. The various *Enron* stories focused on its corporate character and Kenneth Lay, the principal character who ran the company. As noted in chapter 2, they helped to create a very powerful reputation for the company. So powerful in fact that many people were duped by these stories into being a customer, or investing their money or their labor in the company. The various *Enron* stories illustrate many of the key aspects of a corporate story and the impact that it can have on creating an image for the company and transforming this into a reputation of distinction, or not as the case may be.

To elaborate the role of corporate storytelling for reputation formation I'll start by telling a short tale of the thirty-year life of the *Australian Graduate School of Management*— the *AGSM*. I will tell this tale as most people would, namely as a descriptive chronology. To turn it into a more engaging corporate story requires some development, which I will describe after I recount this version of the story. To turn it into a good reputation story requires more focus.

I joined the *AGSM* in its second year as a PhD student and stayed until the end when I was an associate dean. This is my story of an organization that I grew up with and later helped run. For most of its life it was rated by the *Financial Times* as offering the best MBA degrees in Australia. As you will see, it was an interesting and sometimes challenging place to work. And we were a group of people who were not universally liked by some of our other Australian colleagues.

The Australian Graduate School of Management Story

As a brand name the *AGSM* still exists. Some people even think that it is still a proper business school. For the first thirty years of its life it was an autonomous graduate business school. But in 2006 it was gelded. Over the next few years most of its faculty left, and its programs were submerged into those of a much bigger faculty. In essence, the *AGSM* became a Post-it note brand name.

The Beginning

It all stated well enough. After a report about the poor quality of graduate business education in Australia, the federal government committed to funding a national graduate school of management. Thus the *AGSM* was established in 1976 as a separate postgraduate school in the University of New South Wales.

The first dean was a well-respected Australian academic. He sourced his founding faculty from overseas. They were an eclectic group of 12 young and aged scholars who were dedicated to building a center of excellence. Initial funding was $2.33 million from the federal government. The first programs were for full-time MBA, PhD students and fee-paying executives. They proved difficult to fill and the first class of MBAs totaled just 31 students who were willing to bet the next part of their careers on a new venture. Initially the *AGSM* looked more like a small medical school than a traditional university faculty. It quickly developed a tangible esprit de corps. The size, structure, and source of funding of the new school signaled that the *AGSM* was very different to the then and now large university faculties of economics and commerce. Over its first decade the *AGSM* quickly gained a reputation as a small, privileged clique of high achievers.

The Middle Years

During the next twenty years the *AGSM* prospered. It grew to become about a $40 million operation that could survive at this scale but could not grow without making some fundamental changes to its programs and institutional arrangements. This problem, and our independent relationship with our parent university, ultimately came back to kill us.

During this period the *AGSM* became more like a professional practice than a university department. The school developed a strong internal culture among the student body and the faculty. We were much more collegiate in our decision making than a traditional faculty. We were also housed in our own self-contained building, which had a great library, reliable computing facilities, accountants, good restaurant, executive accommodation, and a well-stocked wine cellar. We attracted some important donations that were quarantined from the university. We paid salary supplementation based on a formal performance appraisal system. We had three ex-management consultants as deans. And we did not pay any "tax" or "dividend" back to the university. For many years "we ate what we killed."

The school also developed some defining character traits that set it apart from most other Australian university faculties. For example, all faculty were expected to participate in decision making, and each person's opinion was appreciated; the MBA programs were priced at what the market would bear rather than being pegged to other university courses; student teaching evaluations were put in the library for all to see; some faculty were allowed to specialize as teachers or researchers; people were paid well above the standard salary scale for excellent performance; teaching executives and executive MBA students often required travel away from the university and working on nights and weekends; a large proportion of the faculty were professors as opposed to the few professors in most faculties; consulting was done through one's private account or through an *AGSM* company rather than through the university's consulting company; we were happy to be ranked annually by the *Financial Times* against our global rivals; a board of directors participated in the governance of the school, and sometimes the directors were called on to pressure our parent university to modify its claims on *AGSM* resources.

During this period the *AGSM* attracted and developed some outstanding students, teachers, and researchers. A few of the faculty were headstrong and at times a bit difficult to manage. They would act like sole traders in a market rather than members of a college. One source of tension was the business model of the school—teaching made the money but research was held internally in high esteem. At one point, a faculty revolt resulted in one of the deans being terminated. Some people found the *AGSM* environment uncomfortable and left. Some spent the greater part of their working life there.

The End

In 2006 the university appointed one of our previous deans as vice chancellor. His primary mandate was to put the university on a more secure financial footing. To do this, which he ultimately did, required some tough decisions. To signal to the university community that such decisions were forthcoming, he then proceeded to "shoot his own dog"! Immediately after his appointment he called a joint meeting of the *AGSM* (about 40 faculty) and the university's Faculty of Commerce and Economics (about 240 faculty). Here he announced that the two entities would merge under the leadership of the dean of the faculty. The die was cast. A short, unsuccessful attempt was made to reverse the situation, or at least wrest control of the leadership. All attempts failed.

A number of reasons motivated this decision, none of which were satisfactory to most of the members of the *AGSM*. Hence, within a couple of years approximately a third of the faculty left, a third was happy to join a much less demanding environment, and a third decided to stay until their generous superannuation became due.[1]

Postscript

The *AGSM* brand name settled down to be a Post-it note that is attached to a small number of postgraduate degrees and executive courses. The brand name has a couple of dedicated administrative staff but no separate group of faculty. Without these it cannot be regarded as a real business school.

Notable Omissions

This corporate story has some notable omissions. All would need to be addressed before it would "work" to consolidate the *AGSM*'s old reputation or create a new one.

One is that my rendition of the *AGSM* story deliberately lacked the development of a dominant organizational character trait that would appeal to your business-related values or expectations. By emphasizing a deep inner desire to do something (aka mission) and some signature behaviors, I could have positioned us as a pioneer—we were established to re-energize Australian management education and became the first school to implement many modern management practices. I could have positioned us as a rebel or a challenger—we would routinely challenge many university orthodoxies. For example, most of the faculty did not join the academic union, and most were prepared to drive through the occasional picket line on a day of strike action to come to work. Another position could have been that of excellence—our research productivity and teaching excellence routinely outperformed that of our commerce and economics colleagues at the *University of New South Wales* and in other Australian university business schools. The positioning of an organization is what shapes its reputation position by showing that we were best at something or best for somebody.

My narrative also lacked a face. I gave some hints that individual academics could have been used to humanize the organization. And the dean who became vice chancellor and gelded the school to which he devoted nine years of his working life could have been made into a pivotal personality. Powerful corporate stories generally have some strong people as principal actors. These help other people identify with the organization.

A third omission is that there are no disasters, obstacles, turning points, or competitors. Many corporate stories chronicle how the organization overcomes some type of adversary. This is often a point of proof of a strong character or some special competence. For the *AGSM* the major issue was funding. Despite the best efforts of our various deans, we only every raised a very small endowment. Our program fees were our principal source of revenue. So our "profit story" was that we were an "eat what you kill" operation. At a small size, operational funding was not a serious concern, but we did not have enough in reserve to fund significant growth.

A fourth omission is that there is no moral to the story. Two could have been easily developed. One along the lines of it was a mistake to geld a viable, strongly branded, internationally reputed institution. The reputation story here is that often the reputations of a university's professional schools (business, engineering, law, medicine, etc.) boost that of the parent university. Now the *AGSM* story becomes one of poor brand management and poor strategic decision making. An alternative story line is that of growth and/or re-invention. Here the *AGSM* was merged into a larger institution that could serve the needs of a broader Australian business community. This is a good outcome, and if the integrity of the *AGSM* brand had been retained, it would have allowed the school's reputation to spread to a wider community. What is interesting is that for the first few years after its demise, when people talked about the old *AGSM,* both of these storylines competed for supremacy.

The final omission was that there was little direct discussion of the value we created for our various stakeholders. Many students went on to successful careers. Many of the faculty built successful careers. The reputation of our parent university was enhanced by our success. And our executive programs helped some companies to become more successful in their endeavors.

The choice of facts to highlight, organizational character, outstanding people, turning points, and value created, all offer ample scope to write a variety of stories about the old *AGSM*. The storyline chosen may seek to create a desired reputation based on character, competence, citizenship, and sometimes profitability. These are "who we are" stories. Alternatively, the storyline may focus on the people who really matter and what the company does best for these stakeholders. These are "best for somebody and/or best at something" stories.[2] To be believable, the new *AGSM* story will have to be true enough to fit with the memories of the people who knew the organization when it existed. When these memories fade, the story can be rewritten by its current owners.

To recap, there are some key aspects to good corporate reputation stories:

- Stories are personal—the facts, defining moments, key people, and situations faced are all introduced and framed by the storyteller.
- Language matters—if the corporate story is to help build and maintain a good reputation, then it must use the language of reputation in its telling.
- History matters—what has happened in the past conditions how new information about the organization is presented by the storyteller and interpreted by his or her audience.
- Key people and the defining characteristics and experiences of the organization highlight its overall character.
- A strong story will contain similar elements and convey a similar reputation position when told by different people.

- You don't need to spell out every detail of the story. The well-organized absence of information will draw people into a story. In this way they become co-producers of the story. They are then likely to believe it more.
- The primary audience for a corporate story is employees. If they don't believe it, then nobody will. And outside the company employees are its primary storytellers.

With hindsight one of our biggest mistakes with our *AGSM* story was that many more people knew our name than knew any of our stories. We had some interesting stories to tell that fitted with the worldview of a modern business school, and that many people in the local business community and business academics in Europe and America shared—but we didn't tell them. We lived our story as students, administrators, and faculty, and we allowed our deans to periodically change our corporate identity symbols instead of all of us telling and retelling our story. As marketing consultants say, "just because people know your name doesn't mean they know who you are."

There is one facet in the AGSM story that bedevils many very profitable companies. It is how to tell the corporate profit story in such a way that it is not seen as greed by members of the general public. In chapter 3 this problem was called the bottom-line backlash effect. A common strategy to avoid such an effect is to try to deflect attention from super profits by telling a corporate citizenship story. Most big companies implement this by writing some type of social or environmental report and posting it on the corporate website. Some of these win awards and the praise of NGOs. However, apart from some curious academics and journalists, I wonder who else reads these reports. For example, let me ask you the reader, how many vision statements, codes of conduct, ethics statements, and sustainability reports have you read of the companies that you regularly deal with? In fact, have you even read your own company's current statements?

Another strategy is to use corporate advertising to focus the attention of stakeholders and members of the general public on something other than profits. For example, the "Designed by Apple in California" advertisement is 1 minute and 30 seconds long. It echoes the message in William Isaacson's biography of the late Steve Jobs that product development at *Apple* is conducted by "engineers and artists, craftsmen, and inventors" and it is a long process—"for every yes there are a thousand nos." It also notes the product development strategy of the company—"We spend a lot of time on a few great things."

Interestingly, one of the best places to find a rendition of a company story is in *Wikipedia*. For example, there is much more informative detail about the European electronics company *Philips* here than on its corporate website! Also these entries seldom focus on the profit side of a company.

So here is the dilemma. A well-established company has far too much history to tell and far too many aspirations to convey, but it still needs to tell a story about itself. So how could it fashion such as story? My suggestion is that it takes a leaf out of the leadership book of the *Royal Navy*.[3] This highly respected institution uses two types of story. One is of the long-wave variety and chronicles the formal memory of the navy. On entering a naval institution, one can generally find a book that notes past naval activities on that date. The role of these episodes is to show what individuals did in situations large and small and thereby inspire others to tackle the challenges of the day. The other type of story is short-wave in nature. Here navy personnel are encouraged to tell stories called "dits" about what is happening on a day-to-day basis. These serve to assimilate knowledge and insights and to reinforce the Navy's collective consciousness. The aim is to get both types of story to focus on reputation-enhancing issues.

In a corporate reputation context the long-wave story focuses on the values, purpose, character, competence, and past deeds of the company. These factors can be illustrated by linking them to defining moments, critical challenges overcome, and key employees. In essence this is the story about how the company achieved the reputation that it currently enjoys or endures. A version of this type of story can usually be found on the corporate website. In contrast, the various short-wave stories need to focus on the value the company is creating for its different groups of stakeholders. These stories encourage employees to talk to each other, and if they can focus on stakeholder value creation, then they are speaking about how the company is creating a better corporate reputation. These stories are generally shared "around the water cooler" and at other informal gatherings. For many years *FedEx* told a number of these stories about its heroic attempts to deliver its parcels.

To further make my case for the efficacy of corporate storytelling, let me proceed by selling the power of corporate stories.

The Power of Stories

Parents and grandparents know the power of a good story. So do moviemakers and the writers of fiction, documentaries, television dramas, biblical texts, the armed services, and so the list goes on. Comedy and jokes often involve a short story with an unexpected ending. Anecdotes are mini-stories. So are most news reports. Thus, at an intuitive level, we all know the power of a good story.

On the scientific side the case for developing a corporate story is supported by two sources of evidence. One is Howard Gardner's scientific work in the field of cognitive psychology.[4] His research supports the efficacy of using stories to convey ethical and moral principles and to change people's minds. Here the story of a company gives people a reason to believe something about it that aligns with their values and expectations. Anita Roddick, the late founder of the *Body Shop,* was a master storyteller about her company and what it stood for. Likewise is Richard Branson and his various *Virgin* stories. Stories also provide the context in which new information about the company will be evaluated. The second type of evidence comes from the work of Stephen Denning and Annette Simmons on inspiration, influence and persuasion through the art of business storytelling. Their work provides much of the compelling anecdotal evidence about why stories are a powerful communication tactic to activate emotions and to engender trust and confidence in leaders and their companies.[5]

Howard Gardner regards stories as one of the four "contents of the mind."[6] They have a powerful influence on what we learn because of their pervasiveness and intuitive appeal. Also, because they often speak about values and morality, which sits at the heart of the reputation of individuals and companies, they are a natural medium to convey a company's character, good deeds, and aspirations. In a corporate context they are more believable, more memorable, and they generate more enthusiasm than the various sanitized statements of mission, vision, ethics, and codes of conduct that companies routinely produce and that often remain invisible inside the organization. Hence, while these statements of intent are useful as inputs into a corporate story, they are no substitute for it.

The task facing a corporate communicator is to craft a corporate story in the language of corporate reputation with content appropriate to foster a desirable reputation position. To illustrate how this task may be achieved, I'll outline what I suggest should be the raw material for such a story.

Who We Are Style Reputation Stories

One type of long-wave reputation story is based on the identity of the company. It is a "who we are and what we do" type of story. The content of this type of story is scattered throughout many a company's website. This information is often organized as a chronicle. The timeline is usually some version of what we did yesterday, our record today, and what we will do tomorrow. The past history of a company is relevant when it guides the values of the present, shapes the current identity of the organization, and/or helps sustain the faithful and bring in new recruits. Information about today acts as a bridge between yesterday and tomorrow. Information about tomorrow is meant to be inspirational. Balance across these three time periods is a key aspect of this type of corporate story. When there is a heavy emphasis on yesterday, it may suggest that the company is past its prime. A too heavy emphasis on the current situation may resemble a report card. And a too heavy emphasis on the future may sound too prophetic.

To illustrate this challenge, consider the task faced by Carly Fiorina when she became the CEO of *Hewlett Packard* in 1999. As an *Economist* reporter noted, *HP* had become a hardware has-been, unable to keep up with the Internet age.[7] What Fiorina was confronted with was that *HP* had a proud history as a founding member of Silicon Valley that was supported by a very strong culture called the "HP Way" that she thought was now stifling innovation. Her options were to create a new corporate story based on a new future or one that acknowledged the past. The first option would be perceived as either ignoring or challenging *HP*'s history, and it probably would have created resentment among longstanding employees.

The risk with the second option was that the past could easily distract people's attention from engaging a new future.

Fiorina chose the second option, but she cleverly reframed the past as a prelude to the future. *HP* was to again function according to the old "rules of the garage" that William Hewlett and David Packard had used to drive innovation in the company's early years. However, current 'star' employees were used in the company's communications to suggest that this generation of employees were the spiritual descendants of the founders. Not only did this approach show respect for the past, it empowered all of *HP*'s employees to take key roles in the future. The corporate slogan at the time was "invent," which was a reminder of the past and a plea to employees to keep their focus on innovation. It was also designed to position *HP* as "best at innovation." The problem here was that many of the company's innovations were not successful in the marketplace. Thus one of Fiorina's key tasks was to get more of *HP*'s products into homes and offices. As noted when discussing *Philips*, having a reputation for being innovative is only worthwhile if customers think that this provides something valuable to them.

Another source of content for "who we are" reputation stories comes from the measures of corporate reputation reviewed in chapter 8. These measures typically ask people to rate a company on a number of factors, such as the quality of its products and services, the engagement of employees, corporate profitability, leadership, and community responsibility. Sometimes the list can be 20 or more such factors. When companies take these measures seriously, there is tendency to manage to the measure. That is, they focus on the factors that they can control that produce the highest reputation score. It is just like managing to one's key performance indicators. In these situations it makes sense to craft the company story to speak directly about these factors. However, the problem with this approach to storytelling is that while each factor is important, it is difficult to wrap them all around a central theme or timeline.

Figure 6.1 identifies the feedstock for the "who we are" style of corporate story. Here various aspects of the company's mission, character, competence, moral purpose, and modes of behavior form the basis of the reputation story. If the corporate story resonates with the values, expectations, and self-interest of key stakeholders, they are likely to believe it.

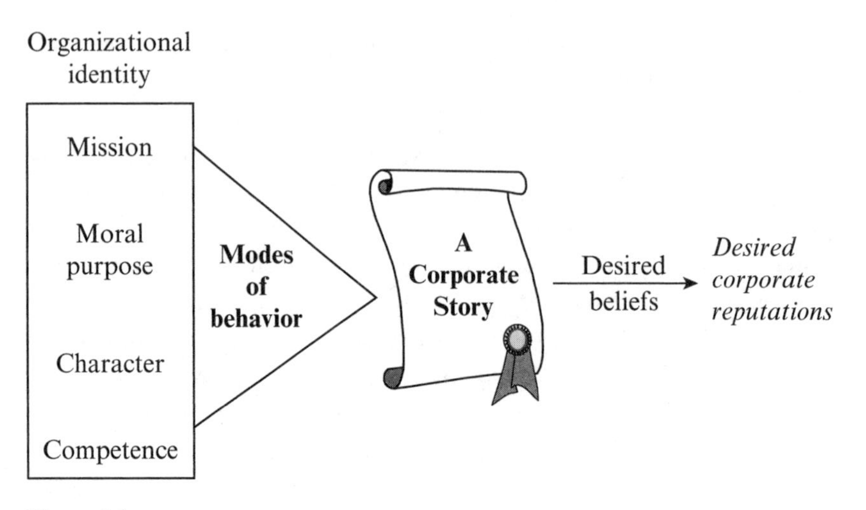

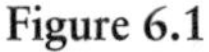
Figure 6.1

Components of reputation stories

Looking across the corporate landscape suggests that some companies decide to anchor their story around a mission that appeals to our values and emotions. Eleven archetypal types of company are:

- *Altruistic companies*—exist primarily to serve their stakeholders. Most charities, not-for-profit organizations, government departments, schools, hospitals and churches are designed for this purpose. In the corporate world where a profit imperative exists, altruism gets translated into "doing well by doing good." This comes in a variety of guises such as a giving people a great deal. For example, the low-cost airlines have this purpose. *Disney* was founded to make people happy. The new benefit corporations appeal to this emotion.
- *Excellent companies*—exist primarily to be the best at whatever they set out to do. For example, when *BMW* proudly advertised its cars as "the ultimate driving machine" and they were better than their competitors, the company was pursuing excellence. Excellence is often the aspiration of the big professional service firms, especially the big law firms. To signal and re-affirm excellence, companies must often charge a price premium and/or figure prominently in the league tables that rate industry competitors.

- *Discovery companies*—exist primarily to be creative and build something new. They often have massive research institutes. Many of the old chemical companies and many of the new biotechnology companies have this character. As noted earlier, *3M* and its stream of new products is another example of such a company.
- *Hero companies*—some exist to overcome a major problem. Many pharmaceutical companies are trying to find a cure for major diseases. Others companies exist to lead or challenge an often bigger incumbent on behalf of a specific group of customers. *South West Airlines* started out as a challenger-hero when it first entered the Texas market and challenged the two incumbent airlines. Richard Branson's various *Virgin* companies enter markets to challenge big, lazy incumbents, and if they are successful, they emerge as heroes.
- *Pioneer companies*—exist to explore or create new markets. *Amazon*, *Google,* and *YouTube* are examples of this. Sometimes they create a profound new experience for people. Sometimes they simply make an existing task so much easier or better. Sometimes they redefine an existing market such as *Cirque du Soleil* with circus-style entertainment.
- *Lifestyle companies*—exist to provide people with a better or unique lifestyle. *Apple* has done this via its many iProducts. *Facebook* has done it with its social networking. Cruise lines such as *Carnival, Disney, Holland America, Norwegian, Princess,* and *Royal Caribbean* have done this with their ocean cruising. *Harley-Davidson* has designed itself to appeal to some unique lifestyle groups such as motorcycle gangs and affluent weekend riders.
- *Everyday life companies*—exist to facilitate our daily lives. Big retailers like and *IKEA*, *Walmart,* and *Tesco* have a mission to make everyday living easy and/or less tedious, and sometimes even enjoyable. For example, *Walmart*'s slogan of "save money, live better" now reflects this purpose. *Tesco*'s core purpose is "we make what matters better." *IKEA*'s mission is to make low-priced products that help people live a better life at home. *Starbucks* retail outlets that are positioned as a "third place" that is neither home nor work fosters this position.
- *Infrastructure companies*—exist to provide the backbone infrastructure of the nation. These are the companies that help build or run the airlines, railways, telecommunications networks, electricity grids,

road systems, distribution systems, financial systems, and the like. The big challenge for these companies comes after they are privatized. Now their profit motive is set off against the lingering expectation that they will still deliver on their broad-based community service obligation.

- *Watchdog companies*—exist to monitor the activities of other organizations on behalf of a particular group of people. For example, audit firms play this role for shareholders. Some media firms still do this for the community. Before the global financial crisis the ratings agencies used to be trusted to provide an independent evaluation of the creditworthiness of companies and countries. *Greenpeace* is still actively engaged in monitoring corporate environmental behavior.
- *Protection companies*—offer services that protect the assets, health, or lifestyle of people. These companies trade on the fact that many people perceive that there is risk associated with many of the things that they do. Insurance companies have become profitable serving this need. Some pharmaceutical companies adopt this stance. Police and fire fighters also play this role.
- *Public service organizations*—are agencies that administer government policy. The most liked tend to dole out welfare, and the most disliked tend to collect revenue. For organizations like these that can't change their missions, style matters a lot. People sense indifference, pomposity, and arrogance, and they also sense the opposite.

When a moral purpose draws on the philosophical ideas that shape a society, then anchoring a corporate reputation to such a moral purpose automatically gains the company a certain amount of respect for trying to do what is right and what is worthwhile.[8] An interesting example of a company that does this, but does not fit easily into the categories listed above, is the *Tata Sons* conglomerate of India. The company has more than 100 operating companies whose products and services touch the lives of many people in India on a daily basis. Charitable trusts own 66 percent of *Tata Son*'s shares. Thus the role of the business is to generate profits for its charitable trusts to distribute. And as one divisional head noted, "Return on capital is not at the center of our business. Our purpose is nation-building, employment and acquiring technical skills."[9] The company's corporate slogan is "Leadership with trust" explained on the corporate website as "to improve the quality of life of the communities it serves globally, through long-term stakeholder value creation." Interestingly, one of the key items on the agenda of the *Tata* Group Executive Council is to "preserve and enhance the reputation of the *Tata* name." A *Tata* brand custodian and chief ethics officer is a member of this council.[10]

The risk of grounding a corporate reputation in a moral purpose is that the message can get lost in the implementation. For example, to achieve their aims, *Tata Sons* must deal closely with numerous parts of the Indian government and civil service, and such relationships will always generate accusations of corruption and crony capitalism. Also it is easy for hero and watchdog companies to be regarded as villains. This was the fate of *Monsanto* when it heroically tried to develop genetically modified foods. *Greenpeace* has often been criticized for the way that it goes about trying to hold companies to account for their actions. However, when corporate morality resonates with the values of a stakeholder, the company is establishing deep roots for its reputation.

Whether reputation stories are grounded in corporate attributes or anchored to a moral purpose, a critical component will be the signature modes of behavior of the company. These express the mission, character, morals, and competence of the company. Modes of behavior demonstrate how the company creates value for itself and its customers; deals fairly with employees, customers, and business partners; and fulfills its expressed obligations to other stakeholders. As noted earlier, it is during times of crisis that modes corporate behavior are starkly contrasted with corporate rhetoric. For example, when *Qantas* grounded its fleet of aircraft and stranded its passengers around the world in 2011, it deliberately violated two conditions in the Customer Charter outlined on its website—its commitment to getting its passengers to their destination on time and to notifying them about delays of which it is aware.

Because the mission of some companies leads to behavior that doesn't enhance the long-term interests of society, they spin a counter story about their morality. For example, to handle the growing public concern about the use of the carbon fuels, many of the big oil companies are spinning stories about their active concern for the environment on their corporate websites and through their corporate advertising campaigns. Typically these stories state the company's concern for the environment and then present their initiatives to dampen the harmful effects of their products. For example, *Chevron* has branded itself as a "human energy" company (the current corporate slogan). They invite people to share their views and ideas with the company (see chevron.com/weagree). In this way people are being invited into a part of the corporate story. The problem with this type of "we are aware of the problem and are trying to fix it" story is that many people consider that companies that are responsible for creating an ongoing problem can't also be a part of the solution. They are working against their own self-interest. The big processed food companies encounter this problem. Their advertising campaigns say "consume more" while the PR campaigns say "consume less" or "consume responsibly." Far more money is spent on advertising than public relations.

As noted earlier, corporate advertising, identity symbols, and slogans like "human energy" are branding devices. They are designed to both signal and signify a company's overall mission or morality—to both employees and external stakeholders. These devices were used extensively by Carly Fiorina to communicate to *HP*'s employees, customers, and investors that the company was reinventing itself to be a major player in the information technology market space. An early series of advertisements showed a picture of the garage where William Hewlett and David Packard started their company. Other advertisements featured "star" employees as purveyors of the company's mission. The corporate slogan was stated simply as "invent." And at this time a part of the company website was devoted to using these devices to help tell *HP*'s story.

Best at and/or Best for Style Reputation Stories

The other major type of reputation story is grounded in the narrative of being seen to be best at something and thus being best for somebody. While many of the "who we are" stories hint at being best at something, they seldom take the next step and state who they are best for. They don't tell people why being best at something like innovation is beneficial to them, for example, because it generates new products that solve their problems. From the stakeholder value perspective introduced in chapter 5, these stories don't describe the set of resulting experiences from engaging with the company. And herein lies the major shortcoming of many "who we are" stories—because they don't speak directly to anybody, they tend to speak to nobody. Scanning the *Wikipedia* entries and the corporate websites of *Philips* and *HP* suggests that it is much easier to talk about what these companies try to be best at rather than who they are best for.

In the previous chapter I mentioned the *3M* company as one of the world's best corporate innovators. It is a good example of a leading company that is now trying to tell people why its considerable expertise in innovation is useful to them. This company probably has the best record of commercial innovation among modern corporations. It has a wonderful history and tradition of innovation.[11] It has given us everything from the Post-it note to a range of life saving medical products. For many years these Post-it notes were used to express the company's competence in innovation to its customers. This novel product captured the imagination of people in all walks of life.

The front page of *3M*'s current US corporate website introduces a link to a section about how the company's innovation capability benefits a wide range of different people.[12] The section titled "3M Story" describes many of the company's life changing products. The shortcoming here is that the product is positioned as the hero in these stories rather than the person who uses the product. Seldom are the end-user benefits that are delivered by these products illustrated on the website.

I would suggest that most people who buy or use or benefit from most of *3M*'s products do not know that they are from *3M*. Hence the corporate capability showcased in the *3M* Story section on the website does little to broadcast to the ultimate beneficiaries of its products the company's innovative reputation. And as I noted in the previous section, nor does its corporate branding—"Science. Applied to Life." So what would I advise *3M* to do? Here I would steal an idea from *Intel*. Many years ago when *Intel* (the chip maker) and *Microsoft* (the operating system) were key parts of most of the personal computers that people used, *Intel* ran an advertising campaign with the slogan "*Intel* inside." They were training people to insist that their new PC had the latest *Intel* chip inside. Then, and only then, would they chose a brand that had this chip inside. From all accounts, this was a clever and very successful campaign. Maybe *3M* could enhance its long-standing "innovation" slogan with a reminder to consumers to make sure that this is a product "powered by *3M* innovation" or with "*3M* inside." It would then be easy for corporate advertising to showcase *3M* employees designing better (more innovative) products that delivered benefits to customers. Now employees become heroes, and customers have a reason to seek out *3M* products. This type of corporate branding would help strengthen the company's desired reputation as "best at innovation."

At the *AGSM* we had a similar problem to *3M*. We were more product focused than customer focused. In order to redress this imbalance, we needed to tell our prospective students why they should consider doing their MBA with us rather than a competitor. We selected three pieces of information to include in our recruiting story. One was the average salary increase a student could expect. This information was also a key factor in the *Financial Times* ranking of MBA programs. It speaks about the financial benefit and the payback time of doing an *AGSM* MBA. The other two pieces of information were where students were most likely to be employed after graduation, and some testimonials from successful alumni. This information speaks about the resulting experience of doing an *AGSM* MBA.

The main story line in a "best at therefore best for" reputation story focuses on stakeholders first and the company second. Focusing the corporate narrative on products and services is a halfway compromise. Sometimes stakeholders get the message, but often they don't. The reason for this is that most people like to hear about how they might benefit rather than how good your products are.

Three Roles for Reputation Stories

To be commercially valuable, a reputation story needs to help attain and retain the stakeholders who matter to the company's success. As noted earlier, these people are the company's target customers, and the employees and business partners who create value for these customers. For *3M* the core employees are the scientists and engineers who can innovate to produce beneficial new products and services. Target customers are the people who are prepared to pay *3M*'s premium for these simply better products. Business partners are the firms that will help *3M* apply its innovative capability and market its new products. The role of management is to arrange funding for and facilitate these activities. In essence *3M*'s reputation story is about how the company explores to create new products and then exploits what it creates to be commercially profitable. The exploration and new product development attract employees, business partners, and customers while the commercial viability of these new products retains these groups and satisfies the company's shareholders.

The basic template to understand stakeholder value creation was laid out in chapter 5. These stakeholder value templates can be used to help craft a reputation story. The elements to emphasize are the cores of the onions of each group. For *Riedel* the pride employees have in making the best wine glasses produces a range of products that enhances the wine-drinking experience of discerning consumers. This makes it easy for business partners like wine merchants and sommeliers to promote *Riedel* glassware and profit from their efforts. All this is captured in the core of the *Riedel* onion, namely, "The wine glass company." If *Riedel* can establish a reputation as the wine glass company, everybody else has to find a different reputation position. Told well, this story can help attract the best available employees, customers, and business partners. And practiced well, it will retain these people as loyal and engaged partners. If the company strategy is a good one, then *Riedel* will survive and prosper.

Another role for a reputation story is to help reestablish the company's past reputation. This is sometimes called a "springboard" story.[13] It is often told by a new CEO appointed to restore a company's past glory. The *HP* story mentioned earlier was an example of this. The job of these stories is to inform and motivate employees to embrace a program of change and key stakeholders to accept it. Because a new future is uncertain, these stories are often told without a great deal of embellishment to encourage the listener to participate in inventing his or her version of it. The stories about two of *IBM*'s previous CEOs, Louis Gerstner and Samual Palmisano, are illustrative of this genre.

- *Original story*—In its formative years *IBM* had an interesting story to tell about its spiritual leaders Thomas J. Watson, Sr. and Jr., its origins selling business machines, a radical innovation in the system 360, and market leadership as reflected in its nickname Big Blue. This story combined aspects of discovery and heroism.

- *Story lost*—In the 1990s *IBM* failed to re-invent itself and nearly became a collection of Baby Blues. In 1993 *Fortune* magazine called *IBM* a collection of dinosaurs.
- *Story re-crafted*—Under Louis Gerstner's leadership, the company re-invented itself and became the global leader in e-business consulting and technology. This story was one of a leader-hero.
- *Story changing*—Under CEO Sam Palmisano, *IBM* began to reconfigure itself from the *e*-business company to a provider of "on demand business," which was its then corporate slogan.
- *Story stalled*—Under the next CEO Virginia Rometty, *IBM* sought once again to become an innovation company. This was expressed as "continuous transformation," which was explained on the company website as helping *IBM* transform itself and its clients transform themselves. This slogan was illustrated using the company's "Smarter Planet" initiative, which showcased its principle achievements. I suggest that *IBM*'s story stalled because many IT-based companies were pursuing similar initiatives. Also, after reading the website and an interview with the CFO Mark Loughridge, I still cannot figure out how the company could become the leader in its field and which stakeholders would respond to their overtures.[14]

Some company stories are told around the character and exploits of the founder. Richard Branson is a master of this. His numerous books and blogs about the *Virgin* group of companies with himself and sometimes his employees as key characters have made him a modern-day hero and *Virgin* a challenger brand for many customers. His philanthropy and personal exploits are used to embellish these reputations. The power of these stories is that they are much more personal than most other types of corporate story. Also it is harder to attack a likable rogue like Branson, or obsessive nerd like Steve Jobs, or respected elder statesman like Bill Hewlett than a faceless company. The two big problems with this twinning approach of founder and company is the potential damage done by a personal indiscretion of the founder and what happens when he or she dies. This is one of the problems facing *Apple* in the post Steve Jobs era.

Howard Gardner provides two reasons why stories fail. One is that they are full of hyperbolic narrative, something used by many CEOs when they are sprucing the growth prospects of their company. A second reason is that many stories underestimate the resistance of the various counter-stories that circulate about a company. This has been a major problem for *Monsanto*'s story. As an enthusiast for genetically modified foods, Robert Shapiro used this discovery to trumpet how *Monsanto* could help alleviate worldwide famine and malnutrition. However, the good reputation potential of this story was countered by the stories of many disparate groups about the dangers of "experimenting with nature."

Storytelling

Any corporate reputation story has a big job to do. It must speak to different stakeholders in a way that resonates across their diversity. And it must do so in a credible and engaging manner. Hence help is often needed. For example, to help Jack Welch talk *GE* into becoming one of the world's greatest companies and to convince outsiders that it was, he used the services of speechwriter.[15] Warren Buffett also uses an editor to help write his annual letters to *Berkshire Hathaway* shareholders.[16] Moreover presidents and prime ministers use speechwriters. So here lies a source of expertise that is readily available to most companies.

The brief to a speechwriter will dictate whether the company decides to tailor its story to each group of stakeholders or use one story for all. My suggestion is to create a story that has attributes of both these options. Four parts of a corporate story should remain the same, namely mission, moral purpose, character, and competence. These are the things that underpin the trustworthiness of a company. They also guide employee behavior and provide the moral authority for making tough decisions. The part of a corporate story that should be changed to facilitate communication with a particular audience is the core of their stakeholder value proposition. This will customize the expression of the company's mission, morals, character, and competence in order to help people like it and resolve any doubts about its expected performance.

The *Qantas* dispute noted earlier provides a perverse illustration of this principle. In this case the senior managers of the airline chose a set of actions that contradicted the story they had fostered for the last twenty years. Over this period *Qantas* was positioned, and accepted among many people in the community as an iconic Australian company. Its corporate branding portrayed this through its slogan the "Spirit of

Australia" and its symbol the flying kangaroo. Its story and its branding aligned with the Australian values about what was appropriate behavior toward its employees and customers. To many people it was unthinkable that the airline would unexpectedly and deliberately strand its customers in foreign countries in order to win a dispute with its employees. Had the company warned travelers about this action prior to canceling all their flights, this behavior would have signaled their concern and respect for their passengers. It would have reaffirmed the good character of the airline with this important group of stakeholders. It would also have signaled to the Australian employees that paying customers were equally important. And as noted earlier, it would have honored the pledge in its customer charter.

The Medium and the Message

In November 2005 the giant US retailer *Walmart* found itself at the wrong end of a story titled "Walmart: The High Cost of Low Price."[17] What worried the corporate affairs people was that this unflattering documentary movie might become a cult hit like Michael Moore's 1989 unsympathetic portrait of *General Motors*—in *Roger & Me*. To counter and hopefully disarm the story, *Walmart* released its own movie "Why Walmart Works & Why That Makes Some People Crazy." In effect their idea was to fight "movie with movie," a tactic that illustrates the power of the medium used to convey the message. And one that echoes Marshall McLuhan's enduring observation that "the medium is the message." Advocates of the power of social media make a similar claim.

Now, if the medium becomes a key part of the message, then selecting an appropriate medium to communicate a company's reputation story is a crucial part of its success. The traditional approach has been to use a mix of different media for internal and external stakeholders. For internal stakeholders the often unrelated statements of mission, vision, and values talk about the character, aspirations and morals of the company. Internal newsletters and the company's various annual reports then chronicle behaviors that signify these attributes. However, seldom do these newscasts contain explicit cross references from organizational outcomes back to these guiding statements. And seldom are they prefaced by a précis of the desired corporate story. In effect the corporate story is split up across different media, and more often than not, it fails to be integrated by anybody other than the CEO in his or her occasional addresses to new employees and shareholders. Such fragmentation dilutes the effectiveness of the official corporate story.

Likewise, for external stakeholders, a holistic corporate story often goes untold. They may glimpse parts of it in the annual report, a corporate advertisement, a media article, a corporate video, an Internet blog, or on the company website. And if the company is big, there might be an entry in *Wikipedia*. Often when a company changes its corporate identity symbols, the public relations department will tell a story about how this new expression of identity expresses the soul of the company. However, for most companies there is seldom a continuing effort to explain the character and competence of the company and how this helps deliver an engaging set of stakeholder experiences. As noted at the beginning of this chapter, this was one of our failures at the *AGSM*. Unlike our distant ancestors, we did not sit around the campfire and tell and retell our story so that it became a powerful folktale. However, on the few occasions when we did sit in our dining room next to the wine cellar with our students these became emotional events. Over time our building became a sacred site for these special functions.

The crucial issue for most big companies is how to cost-effectively tell their story to the stakeholders who really matter. And to do this in a way that helps each group understand their role and contribution to the company's success. While face-to-face communication is generally considered to be the most effective medium, it is not cost effective for most large companies. Nowadays corporate websites have a crucial role to play in corporate storytelling. They can be easily updated to reflect current events and to address critical commentary. They can be beautifully illustrated with images and interviews. However, the big problem with most company websites is that parts of the corporate story are scattered all over the place. For example, when I wrote the first draft of this chapter, the *HP* story was told in the About Us, Newsroom, Investor Relations, Global Citizenship, and Former CEOs sections. And none of these sections referred to any other section. It was a complete mess. When I did the latest revision, the US website had changed and these parts of the story had disappeared.

Illustrating and Reinforcing the Story

Many years ago I was told a story about the appointment of a new managing partner of one of the world's premier consulting firms. The first thing he did was to review all the current engagements of the firm. This uncovered one engagement that he did not think lived up to the reputation of the firm. He went to the client and got permission for his firm to redo the assignment at no cost to the client. I call this a "signature act." It demonstrated what the firm stood for, and it signaled the importance of a good reputation. Every company needs some of these signature acts to help it tell the right story of the company.

Whether or not they realize it, most companies have many such signature acts. The *AGSM* had two that I was routinely involved in. One was our faculty meetings. They were conducted in a robust way where rank counted for little relative to the power of one's evidence and persuasion. The other was that we taught some classes on weekends. And if they involved teaching executives or executive MBAs, the course director lived in with the course participants, sometimes for a period of up to four weeks. A colleague and I got into trouble with the participants on one executive course when we started it on Mother's Day (a Sunday). Both these signature acts signaled to outsiders, especially other parts of our parent university, that we were different from a traditional Australian university faculty.

As the example of the *Royal Navy* suggests, stories involving signature acts need to be shared. One that became legendary among MBA students was the *Goldman Sachs* recruiting process. It was an endurance test that involved 10, 20, 30, or more interviews with 10 or 20 members of the firm. Another set of signature acts involving MBA education became a best-selling book titled *Snapshots from Hell.*[18] It was about the first-year experience at the *Stanford Business School.* Signature acts vividly demonstrate the culture of the company. In this way they help to set the expectations of people who deal with it.

Evaluating the Reputation Story

For a reputation story to help establish and enhance the company's reputation, it must get traction inside and outside the company. Media analysis is a common way that companies use to assess how well their story is being repeated to outsiders. The leverage points in the traditional and newer Internet media are the journalists and opinion leader bloggers. Interestingly, few companies periodically measure the reputations of these people to help them understand why they get the media coverage they do.[19]

While having the corporate story accurately reflected in the media is important, what is more important is for employees to accept it. On a personal level it is important to gauge if the corporate story makes them feel inspired about creating something better, or like the company more, and sometimes tell the story to other people. A less reverent measure of acceptance is to ask them where they consider the story falls along the 4B-spectrum of being seen as "bullshit," "blather," "boasting," or "better company." If the story does not resonate inside the company, it will not be portrayed by employees in their encounters with outsiders. And if outsiders do not accept the story, they will ignore it, or worse still, begin to actively counterargue with it. Qualitative research among employees and important stakeholder groups can be used to track acceptance. Monitoring the Internet is also important. This research should seek to detect if opinion leaders are starting counterarguments or rumors, and if gossip is spreading.

Finally, the most powerful corporate stories become legends. Now that Steve Jobs has passed away, the story of *Apple* under his reign is taking on a mythical nature. A good example of this is the movie *Steve Jobs.* Such mythmaking makes it harder for the characters in the new *Apple* story to live up to the legacy of the past. Another example of this phenomenon is the story of the *All Blacks* rugby union team in New Zealand. This team has such a rich and strong heritage that every player caries the responsibility of meeting the expectations of the entire country when they run out onto the playing field. As a final reminder to the team members of their responsibilities to the legend of the *All Blacks,* the team performs a Haka (a traditional Maori challenge) on the field facing their opponents at the beginning of each match. Ceremonies like this add a sprinkle of fairy dust to the occasion, and just as importantly to the story of the team.

7

Managing Corporate Reputations: Top Down

Now that the foundations for creating a better corporate reputation are in place I can direct attention to three key aspects of implementation:

- Managing the things that really matter to creating a winning reputation.
- Keeping score by measuring what stakeholders really think about the company.
- Keeping out of trouble by avoiding some of the common behaviors that undermine an otherwise good reputation.

The link between the first two activities is captured by the old saying: "If you can't measure it, you can't manage it."

In recent years there have been a number of books written for managers about how to manage their company's desired reputation. I have ten of them on my bookshelf, one of which I wrote in 2001.[1] All these books make a number of sensible recommendations, but all make some naive assumptions about the internal workings of companies. In the last decade various corporate scandals, a number of books written by corporate insiders,[2] and the global financial crises have exposed many myths about the difference between corporate proclamations and the behavior of organizations.

There is an old proverb about war that says that a battle plan seldom survives its first contact with the enemy. The same seems to be true inside many companies with respect to the reputation battle plans expressed in the top-down statements of mission, vision, ethics, and codes of conduct. When a crisis occurs that requires accommodating one group of stakeholders at the expense of others, some of the broad-based good intensions in these statements are sacrificed on the altar of necessity. The *Qantas* Customer Charter referred to earlier is a prominent example.

Many companies also have two inbuilt structural problems regarding the management of their desired reputations. One is that what happens in one part of the organization can damage the reputation of the whole organization. And generally the people who run the different parts of the organization do not have the right to sanction the activities of their peers in other parts of the organization. For example, the tax policy of the company is set in an isolated part of the organization with no responsibility to or oversight from other parts of the organization. The other problem is that plans and budgets tend to treat operational divisions as profit and cost centers rather than stakeholder value creation centers. There is a profound difference for a line manager between being asked to increase sales or reduce costs and creating more value for his or her stakeholders. The problem a profit focus creates is that the good reputation that would flow naturally from the value a company creates for stakeholders is easily corroded by the organization's own budgets and bottom-up key performance targets. These principal drivers of an employee's daily behavior crowd out the good intensions embedded in the organization's vision, values, and ethics statements. Here what is formally rewarded dominates what is sometimes informally praised.

Because it is so easy for these daily drivers of individual behavior to corrupt the organization's reputation intensions, I start this chapter by proposing how to solve this issue. There has to be an opposing force strong enough to counteract the natural tendency to manage to one's short-term performance targets. Then I return to the vexing question of how to manage stakeholders. It is their conflicting demands that are often at the heart of reputation damage. Finally I make some observations about how the persona and behavior of the CEO influences the culture and reputation-enhancing behavior of the organization they lead.

Following Our Moral Compass

There is a simple way and a more complicated way to get people to comply with the vision and values of the company and its strategy to create outstanding value for its key stakeholders. Let me start with the traditional, more problematic approach. Then I'll describe an approach we occasionally used at the *Australian Graduate School of Management* that actually seemed to work.

The Problematic Way

After the corporate scandals of the early part of the twenty-first century, many companies experimented with the appointment of a new member to the C-suite, namely, a chief ethics officer or a chief reputation officer. The role of these people was to take an organization-wide view of reputation management. To do this, they promoted the company's statements of moral intent and values to all managers and employees. They worked closely with the CEO and the corporate affairs group. They were happy to talk on the business conference circuit. One of the most prominent examples of this approach was *FedEx* after it transformed itself from an express carrier of parcels to a broader-based transportation powerhouse. For many years Bill Margaritis, vice president of Global Communications & Investor Relations, helped the company adopt the "workplace to marketplace" approach to reputation management noted in chapter 1.[3] The essence of this philosophy was that good reputation management must first be practiced inside the company before it can be effectively demonstrated to people outside the company. On a number of occasions I heard Bill Margaritis talk about the time and effort his company devoted to developing the institutional standards of behavior that would build a strong values-based reputation. This was a good complement to the company's high-quality suite of services offered to its customers. At this time the company was performing well. For a number of years the *Reputation Institute* used *FedEx* as an example of best practice of this values and quality service led approach to reputation management.

Having had my interest aroused by the *FedEx* example, I started to look at how other companies were implementing this style of reputation management. The problem I encountered with a corporate reputation officer (CRO) guided approach to reputation management was that in the meetings that really matter like strategy, treasury policy, operational planning, promotions, and budgets, these senior managers were often excluded or largely ignored by many line managers. Line managers were focused on bargaining for resources, setting their operational targets, and advancing their careers. And they knew that their company's "soft" statements of intent didn't have any meaningful sanctions imposed if they were ignored.

For example, I once asked a CRO of a *Fortune 500* company if his CEO was held responsible for being seen to abide by these statements. The answer was a definite yes. However, it turned out that the maximum loss the CEO could suffer for violating the intent of these statements was to lose 1 percent of his considerable pay package.

I also encountered two other problems with a values-led approach. One occurred when an employee achieved a very successful outcome for the company without due regard for some aspects of the corporate statements of intent. Often they were handsomely rewarded financially but only mildly rebuked for their ethical lapse. The signal this type of response sends inside the company is clear—hit your operational targets first and try not to damage our reputation in the process. The second problem was that as soon as a company nominated a senior manager as the company's reputation champion, many employees thought that the problem had been taken care of and they could get back to doing what they were really being paid for. And because the CROs had no direct input into creating value for the company's main stakeholder groups, their role was often seen as that of a police officer. More often than not, they would tell a line manager what he or she should not do rather than what would create added stakeholder value. Because of this the CRO inspired reputation initiative often had the opposite effect that was hoped for, namely it passed reputation management to a senior manager rather than creating a deep commitment to reputation-enhancing behaviors throughout the organization.

Because every big company involved in a scandal over the last decade or so had a suite of statements of moral intent and produced reports about what a good citizen it was, I am now skeptical about the potential effectiveness of this approach as a way to avoid major reputation damage for an organization. Yes internal statements can show the moral compass of a company, and yes they are useful in the recruiting process, and yes they can signal to outsiders that some people in the company take these things seriously, and yes they might provide some guidance during a small crisis, but they were powerless to stop the big corporate scandals of recent years. And yes some CROs and their CEOs have said that living their values did help their company survive a crisis. But there is no reliable evidence that this style of reputation management did stop any major corporate disasters.

Thus my argument is that the best role for statements of morals, values, ethics, and the like, is to show true north on the moral compass of the company. In this way they provide guidance and they might also help provide moral support for people who want to work in a "good" company. Political correctness now means that public companies need to write a suite of these statements and make them available on their websites. And if a company appoints a CRO who has earned the respect of the line managers, he or she may be able to help these people identify and avoid some of the annoying practices identified in the next chapter that corrode an otherwise good reputation. However, it will take more than some soft statements and a CRO to ensure that employees, C-suite managers, the CEO, and board members do not significantly damage the desired reputation of their company. There has to be visible, significant evidence that reputation-enhancing and reputation-destroying actions will be appropriately rewarded and punished. In this respect corporate reputation management is like many other forms of management: if there is no direct line of sight to the promotion and financial incentives of the key people involved in running the company, then a good corporate reputation it is only of background concern.

A More Straightforward Way

In chapter 1 I introduced the German notion of managers being *untreue* to their company. Translated into English this means to be disloyal or betray the company. The other side of this notion is *treue*, that is, to be loyal and faithful to the company. The general idea behind (*un*)*treue* is that if an employee does something to enhance or damage the reputation of the company, then he or she should be rewarded or punished in some way appropriate to the severity of the outcome. For example, in September 2015, when Volkswagen was exposed for deceiving US regulators about the emissions of its diesel cars, the CEO Martin Winterkorn was the first person to resign. This idea stands in sharp contrast to the culture in many Asian companies. For example, in many Japanese companies people show loyalty first to their managerial clique and second to the company.[4]

Companies could use such a simple rule to encourage and dissuade behavior that had a direct impact on the desired reputation of the company. All it would take is to identify the set of such behaviors in question and the type of evidence required to verify each one. These could be incorporated into the key performance indicators of every employee. Each company would establish its own "zone of tolerance." My last business school had such a rule. It was informally administered by the senior members of staff who would privately chastise a colleague's undesirable behavior. And occasionally it was formally administered in performance development and appraisal reviews. In an academic environment where freedom of expression is highly valued, it proved to be a useful way to curb how and where some negative things were said to outsiders about the institution. As an academic institution we did not seek to dissuade our colleagues being critical, what we tried to do was to frame this in a constructive way and channel it to where decisions could be made. Our major failing in this area of reward and punishment was not to spend enough time to publicly recognize good employee behavior. This would have helped identify people who made outstanding reputation contributions to the institution. Such role models help personify the institution's reputation.

My recommendation is that the best way to motivate employees to actively enhance their company's desired reputation and to refrain from actions that might damage this is to implement an *(un)treue* rule. To couch this rule in the language of corporate reputations, I'd simply call it a "reputation rule." While it would be stated in exactly the same way for every person in the organization, the points of proof of reputation enhancement and damage would differ. And it would become a key part of every employee's performance review. I think that this would "work" because it is simple and people tend to have a good understanding of the notion of reputation.

Managing Stakeholders

On a number of occasions I have noted that managing stakeholders is a fundamental aspect of creating a strong corporate reputation. The only problem is how to do it! In this section I will describe four key stakeholder management issues, namely (1) understand their needs, (2) prioritize the groups, (3) communicate what is to be expected, and (4) don't unnecessarily upset them.

1. Understand Stakeholder Needs

The thesis of this book is that the stakeholder value propositions (SVPs) offered by a company are the touchstones of its reputation. So the management of these is a vitally important part of winning the reputation game. As just noted, line managers will play a crucial role in this endeavor. They have to be rewarded for creating outstanding stakeholder value as well as making profits. Achieving a balance between short-term profit and longer term reputation is crucial. The best way to do this is to really understand the needs of each important stakeholder group. This then allows the company to effectively "price" its offer to each group. When people think that they get a good economic deal from a company, they are more likely to admire and respect it. However, research continually reveals that in regard to customers, many companies have only a vague idea of who they are and what they want. Let me illustrate this problem with two examples.

By all accounts the mass-circulation newspaper industry is in decline. This has come as a shock to many media owners and an affront to many journalists. How could all their good work fail to be appreciated and paid for by their readers? One reason is that both groups don't seem to understand who their readers are and what they want from a newspaper. For example, *The Australian* newspaper is one of Australia's biggest dailies. Like many broadsheets around the world, it is struggling. Until recently the advertising section of the paper's website contained the following description of its readers: "primarily a male AB audience, comprising a large amount of business decision makers" (theaustralian.com.au). To interpret this description, you need to know what an AB male is. He is actually two types of person described by a demographic classification of the community developed in the United Kingdom many decades ago to classify readers of the print media. "A" stands for upper middle class and "B" for middle class. (The other classes are C1, C2, D, and E). More recently the newspaper described its target readers as "all people 25–54."[5] Yes, *The Australian* newspaper and many others still refer to their readers by reference to their sociodemographics. So why does this occur? It is traditional in the newspaper business. Of course, this is not the only means by which they understand their customers—they do other research. But this is how they "sell" their readers to their primary stakeholder group, namely advertisers. It is a sterile description of a group of people that has almost no relationship to why they will read and sometimes pay for a mass circulation newspaper. Sociodemographics are an out dated description of the multitude of customers who might read content and notice the advertising contained in the paper.

Now contrast the description above with that provided by a recent editor of *The Economist* newspaper. *The Economist* is "a Friday viewspaper, where the readers, with higher than average incomes, better than average minds but with less than average time, can test their opinions against ours."[6] To me, this is a much more insightful description of both the newspaper and its readership than that provided by *The Australian*. It also has two unique features in the mass media world that distinguish it from most other newspapers. Its articles are written by "many hands with a collective voice." And unlike most newspapers, no article is identified by its author. Given that many people hold journalists in low regard, this might help mitigate some of the potential negative image effects that journalists impose on their outlets.

The difference between these two newspapers is success and focus. *The Economist* has a circulation of 1.4 million and growing. And it clearly focuses on trying to be the best for "people with better than average minds who want to test their ideas." There are few other papers that directly compete with its coverage of politics, economics, business, finance, science, and technology. In contrast, like most broadsheets *The Australian* is struggling to hold its readers and its advertisers. It wants to be a traditional newspaper that is widely read. It wants to offer "a large and desirable audience" to its advertisers. It seems lost in terms of its focus on being either "best for somebody with specific needs" or "best at something newsworthy that people will pay for."

As noted in the earlier discussions, employees are also crucially important to a company's success and to building its reputation. So again, the challenge is to understand what they really want from the organization. Previously I noted that a good starting point for this inquiry is that employees come in two main varieties; they either predominantly "work to live" or "they live to work." Thus the relationship that each group has with the organization is profoundly different. For example, employees who live to work use their employer to form a part of their own personal identity, and thus the reputation of the organization is much more important to them than their counterparts. They are also more likely to respond favorably to a Reputation Rule like the one described earlier. So the features of the employee value proposition designed for this group need to reflect their special relationship and identification with the organization. For example, many academics are notorious "live to workers." For these people the formal affiliation signified by their title and tenure are two extremely important value-creating features of their job. And the protocols that are used to award these positions are often used as points of proof of reputation quality. Thus a deep understanding of the latent needs of employees is needed to guide the design of a stakeholder value proposition that will engage them with their employer.

So reputation management via the SVP route requires two difficult things to do. One is to continually invest in understanding stakeholder needs. The second is to demonstrate or communicate how the company that stands behind the SVP enhances the functional, psychological, and economic values delivered to stakeholders. The discipline of marketing is the home of intellectual thought and practice for doing both these tasks.

2. Prioritize Stakeholders

While a large number of papers have been written by the academic community about which groups of stakeholders really matter, I think they have run into a dead end. The reason is that most scholars provide advice that is difficult to implement because the underlying criteria for judging the importance of a stakeholder group are difficult to measure. Also there is no rule to help managers make trade-offs across groups in a crisis situation. Hence the criteria many academics put forward are not readily implementable. For example, one of the leading scholarly contributions suggests that each group of stakeholders be assessed along three criteria:[7]

- Power—the potential of a group to impose its will on the company.
- Legitimacy—the right of the group to directly benefit from the company as determined by law (e.g., shareholders), the business model of the company (e.g., people who bear some of the risks of its success or failure), and the moral compass of the company (e.g., its predisposition to be a social enterprise, owner capitalist, or sustainable enterprise).
- Urgency—the degree to which stakeholder claims call for immediate action.

At first glance the strength of this scheme is that each criterion seems both sensible and equally important. And sometimes it leads to a clear outcome of who really matters. For example, large institutional shareholders would rate high in power, legitimacy, and urgency when they seek attention. However, the weakness of the scheme is that in many situations each criterion is very difficult to measure. For example, how would a company measure the relative potential of some disgruntled small shareholders versus an important large customer to impose its will on the company? Which party would claim to have greater legitimacy? And which party is actually more urgent to the company's prosperity? The difficulty of measuring each of these criteria across stakeholder groups provides a lot of ambiguity for the people tasked with implementing the scheme and the people who will judge the quality of the decisions made.

In contrast to this scholarly approach, in chapter 1, I noted *Macquarie Bank*'s scheme. Here shareholders and employees were stated to have equal priority. The alignment of the interests of both groups was thought to be a key driver of the company's success. In chapter 2, I noted the *Southwest Airlines* approach to this problem. A sort of "happiness" rule led to the rank ordering of employees first, customers second, and shareholders third. Again, the underlying logic was to focus on what drives the company's commercial success. As their base case or business as usual situation, both companies used a quite simple and transparent commercially focused decision rule. This allows all the company's stakeholders to accept this or reject it and take their custom elsewhere.

What troubles many boards and CEOs is how to make decisions that affect multiple groups in a crisis situation. The *Qantas* aircraft grounding case is the type of difficult situation where reputation damage can occur if managers make poor decisions or if the good decisions they make are poorly understood by those affected. What follows is an approach adapted from the study of leadership that could help work through this issue.[8] It uses a decision tree composed of a series of questions the answers to which lead to actions to be taken. The questions appear in figure 7.1.

Questions

A Do we know what information we need from each stakeholder group to calibrate the effect of our decision on their corporate reputation?
B Do we have sufficient information to make a good decision?
C Is acceptance of our decision inside the company crucial for its successful implementation?
D Will consultations with stakeholders provide relevant information?
E Is acceptance of our decision among the disaffected stakeholders crucial to limit reputation damage?

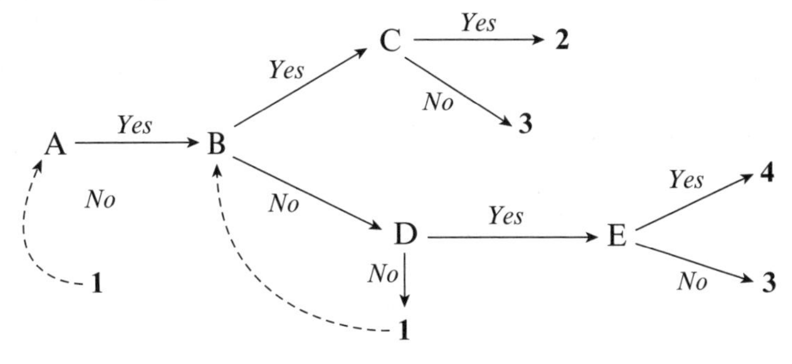

Figure 7.1

Prioritizing stakeholders

The numbers in the decision tree in figure 7.1 are the following actions to be taken:

1 Get outside help to gather the necessary information.
2 Share the problem with relevant managers and other employees, and seek their suggestions for how to handle stakeholder backlash. Try to make a "collective" decision.
3 Inform relevant managers, other employees, and stakeholders about what the company will do and how it will handle stakeholder discontent. Then make the decision.
4 Consult collectively with all affected stakeholders. Get them involved in designing a joint solution that shares the costs and benefits of the company's intended actions.

Many companies assume that they know enough about their various stakeholder groups to answer yes to question 1. This is often a mistake. In the *Qantas* case mentioned earlier, senior management assumed that the key group of federal government politicians understood what the company intended to do. They did not, and feigned considerable surprise and anger about the decision to ground aircraft and strand Australian citizens in airports around the world. This political criticism helped undermine the legitimacy of the airline's actions. *Qantas* also probably assumed that most people would judge that their actions were a legitimate use of their authority as managers. What was revealing here was an omnibus poll of 1,075 Australian regular air travelers conducted by *Essential Media Communications* a week after the lockout.[9] It indicated that 42 percent believed that the company's reputation was damaged by management actions, 27 percent believed it was damaged by the previous industrial action of employees that led to the lockout, and 26 percent believed that both parties were at fault.

Qantas also assumed that the answer to question 5 was yes, namely that most passengers would understand their decision and accept the inevitable inconvenience of being stranded with thousands of other frustrated passengers. Not so. Most passengers were hostile, as much by the decision as for not being warned in time to make other arrangements. Also there were tens of thousands of family, friends, and other people who were affected by the nonarrival and departure of the stranded passengers. *Qantas* probably also assumed that the answer to question 3 was yes. However, many frontline employees were embarrassed by the company's decision and the secretive way it went about implementing it. In effect *Qantas* answered yes to a number of questions when it should have answered no.

Managing stakeholder expectations and their subsequent behavior is much easier if the company states its priorities and the type of relationship it wants with each stakeholder group. This does three things. It tells people what to expect and this helps them understand and acknowledge corporate actions. It also makes the company accountable for what is said. Together, these conditions foster trust. The danger here is that management is not honest about "who really matters."

3. Communicate with Stakeholders

Some years ago when I was interviewing members of the boards of directors of major Australian companies not one of them was prepared to give me a definitive rank ordering of stakeholder priority. At best, they were prepared to say that "it depends on the circumstances." What this typically means is that at the annual general meeting shareholders are told that they are the most important group; when talking to customers, they are most important; when talking to employees, they are the company's most valuable resource; and so a variety of stories are told, not all of which can be true.

When one group is told it is extremely important, it goes without saying that every other group is not as important. A company might be able to get away with this subterfuge if the groups never talk to each other or if they don't see how another group is treated better than they are. But Internet-based media now makes this almost impossible. Thus CEOs should assume that sooner or later each group of stakeholders will figure out who is more important than them.

One of the lessons from marketing, particularly in the area of customer service, is that it is best to set the expectations of people rather than let them set their own. There are two reasons for this. First, when a company does this, it knows what these expectations are and thus it is better able to manage its performance to meet or exceed these expectations. Second, if stakeholders do this, then there is an overwhelming tendency for them to inflate their own self-worth and thus have raised expectations. As the figure in chapter 3 suggests when expectations are not met and people grumble in public, corporate reputations suffer.

So what should CEOs do to protect the reputations of their company? As just noted, they should be honest about who really matters and if there are any circumstances where priorities might change. When people know the roles and needs of others, it is easier for them to appreciate the trade-offs that companies inevitably have to make across groups. It is like a family. When the grandparents, parents, and siblings all know "their place" in the family, life is much easier.

While all this probably sounds sensible, the way that many companies go about communicating stakeholder priority to the various groups is often misguided. If each group is talked to separately, then it is easy for each group not to appreciate the needs of others. However, if the opinion leaders or representatives of the various groups come together to have a frank discussion with each other, then greater understanding often eventuates. I have seen this approach adopted at a prominent business school. Representatives from the faculty, administration, current students, alumni, and corporate sponsors all talked with each other about their needs and how the school could jointly accommodate these. The school established an intra-stakeholder conflict decision rule, namely "select the option that creates the maximum net benefit across all the groups." The discussions were also guided to focus on the future not the past.[10]

A final trap involving stakeholder communication is to think that the new media will become the company's engagement strategy. Many consultants, advertising agencies, public relations firms, and market research firms are pushing the line that companies must engage with their stakeholders via these new media and actively monitor what is said about them in these media. There is a large dose of self-interest in this advice. Michael Porter makes the point that these media are a facilitating mechanism for two-way communication, and that their adoption does not constitute an engagement strategy. He has recently advised his employer, the *Harvard Business School* not to use these new media to significantly disrupt the design of the core value propositions offered to students by the faculty.[11] Cohorts of students grappling with cases via an instructor-led discussion should not be replaced by online courses. The key issue here is to find out what information stakeholders want and how they would like to receive it. For example, research by the *Gallup* organization has discovered that online banking has lowered the overall engagement levels of employees and their customers.[12] Hence it is more profitable for the bank, but at the price of degrading the customer relationship.

4. Get Rid of Thoughtless Stakeholder Policies

Many companies have one or two policies that seem designed to annoy their stakeholders. I call them thoughtless policies because with a little reflection most managers quickly realize that what they are doing can easily upset some people. Here are some examples. All can have a negative affect on a corporate reputation.

- Don't be seen as fair—in the way that people are dealt with (procedural fairness) or the way that rewards are shared (distributive fairness). Both these types of fairness were at the heart of the *Qantas* dispute noted earlier. Perceptions of procedural unfairness are often shown on the media when an aggrieved customer is treated poorly by the company. Perceptions of distributive unfairness occur when a company's loyal customers see an advertisement that offers new customers a better "sign on" deal than they currently receive. Many telecommunications companies and banks use this type of tactic.

- Don't recognize loyalty—especially among employees, customers, and business partners. For example, many long-term customers appreciate having their loyalty recognized, sometimes with a discount and always with some personal communication. Long-term service awards recognize the continued contribution of employees. When loyalty is ignored, it signals that the company doesn't really care.
- Don't be opportunistic—some types of behavior will nearly always damage a company's reputation, for example, by putting prices up during the holiday period, or by levying excessive fees for minor breaches of the terms and conditions of a contract.
- Demonstrate waste—allow people to see extravagant corporate entertainment. For example, many named corporate-sponsored seats at sporting venues remain empty.
- Show customers you don't really care—many bank, car rental agency and airport customer service points are not manned during peak periods.
- Confuse customers—have a pricing policy that is difficult to understand or contains "hidden" terms and conditions. Many mobile phone plans, insurance contracts, and financial planning schemes still have such features.
- Treat employees like mushrooms—only tell them what they need to know in order to do their job. Many employees would like to know more about the strategy, business model, and finances of the companies they work for.
- Make customers pay for product features or a service they don't use—for example, most mobile phones come with about 70 features that are about 50 more than most people use.

It is hard for people to admire and respect an organization that signals its indifference to them. Sometimes the little things really do make a significant difference. Many years ago when reading a student satisfaction survey at the *AGSM* I was somewhat surprised to find that one of the things that made their experience at the school most satisfying was the people at our reception desk. It turned out that when somebody was "lost" or "in trouble," the first point of contact was at reception and the way they were treated here was always with concern and respect. Our people at reception who were the lowest paid employees were one of the most important touch points for the stakeholder value we offered.

The Roles of the CEO

One of the most important roles and biggest reputation challenges a CEO faces is to talk his or her company into being passionate about its reputation. Selling this message to the board of directors and members of the executive team is seldom a problem. They know the value of their personal reputation and how the good reputation of their company will enhance this reputation. Many senior managers also buy into the idea that in some way or other a good corporate reputation will lead to enhanced peer recognition and better corporate financial performance. The real challenge lies in getting most employees to actively buy into the reputation game. Three initiatives can help with this task. One is to explain why reputation is important to the company and to them personally. Another is to show how each person can contribute to enhancing the reputation of their company. The third is to link reputation-enhancing behaviors to employee recognition and reward, via something like the reputation rule noted earlier.

The role of the corporate story in selling the importance of reputation was described in chapter 7. Here the CEO needs to become the scriptwriter and chief storyteller. There is nothing surprising here. However, how the CEO is perceived can influence the effectiveness of the story told and the engagement of stakeholders. For example, CEOs come in the guise of business-as-usual, turnaround, celebrity, tyrants, heroes, quiet achievers, imperialists, place sitters, and White Knights hired to rescue the company. Each of these castings provides a different type of moral authority for asking employees to become reputation champions and outside stakeholders to believe in the company's reputation. Consider the case of the celebrity CEO.

During his tenure at *GE* Jack Welch developed such a high profile that it helped him to talk the company into becoming a world class enterprise. He was relentless in his message, both inside and outside the company. He backed this up by setting stretch targets and holding people accountable for their actions. By some accounts, he was not universally liked for his personal approach. But he was admired and respected for his results. And for many years in the *Fortune* opinion polls *GE* was one of America's most admired companies.

Walter Isaacon's biography of the late Steve Jobs paints a similar picture. In his last period at *Apple* he was a visionary that drove employees to solve problems that most technical people thought were impossible. He also drove them to create products that only he could imagine. His personal style was that of a tempestuous, selfish, mean tyrant. A clinical psychologist would call him narcissistic.[13] George Bernard Shaw would call him an "unreasonable man."[14] His message was that *Apple*'s DNA was the fusion of technology and the humanities that together produced a range of products that were simply better. Because of his success and the success of *Apple*'s iProducts his character flaws were tolerated by his board and many employees. Even though some journalists criticized his personality, few customers ever became aware of the real man behind the company. What they saw at product launches and other media events was a passionate, geeky leader. Like *GE*, *Apple* was highly regarded in the annual *Fortune* reputation polls and on the share market.

Through a relentless focus on driving corporate performance and financial earnings growth, Jack Welch and his peers created the cult of the all-powerful CEO. Then with some clever self-publicity, they became celebrity CEOs. They personified their companies—especially its corporate character. They were lauded in the business media such as *Fortune*, *Forbes*, *CNBC*, *Bloomberg*, and *CNN Money*. But sooner or later most of these celebrities became targets for inquisitive business journalists. Sometimes this was the result of a personal indiscretion, and sometimes it was because the performance of the company was too good to be true. For example, in a turbulent economic environment how did Jack Welch engineer *GE* to produce an unbroken twenty-year streak of earnings growth?[15]

It seems that CEO celebrity is both a benefit and a burden for a company's reputation. The benefit is that the CEO's reputation helps define the company's character. Warren Buffet once noted that many people vote in the *Fortune* reputation poll for the artist (CEO) not the painting (company).[16] For example, when Lord John Browne was head of *BP*, his boldness was often noted by the business press as a key contributor to the company's success. In contrast, the burden of celebrity occurs when the CEO's reputation becomes tarnished, and it takes some off the gloss of the company reputation. Later in his tenure at *BP*, when Browne became known as the Sun King because of his publicity seeking behavior, this image began to tarnish that of the company. Also it was a personal indiscretion that triggered his departure from *BP*. As the business press then regaled the story of his tenure at *BP*, it exposed all manner of questionable CEO decisions and company practices. Thus a CEO's indiscretion often tarnishes a company's reputation by exposing some poor internal practices. Here a lack of internal controls or a dysfunctional organizational culture or some poor judgment by the CEO or his or her board of directors comes to public attention.

A second role for the CEO is to put in place the protocols necessary to highlight, reward, and punish behaviors that enhance and degrade the company's desired reputation. The first part of this process is to define what the desired reputation should be. That is, what does the company want to be known for and how does it make a meaningful difference to its stakeholders? My recommendation is stakeholder value first and corporate character and competence second. The second part is to select some measures of success. The discussion in chapter 8 suggests that these should be customized rather than "off the shelf" measures. The key here is to ensure that the responsibility for achieving target outcomes that drive these measures is diffused throughout the company.

A third role for the CEO is to be the front person for the company in times of crisis. While every company has its own way of dealing with a crisis, and most of these involve the CEO as principal spokesperson, sometimes they do not front up early enough or be seen to take personal responsibility. For example, after the *Exxon Valdez* oil tanker ran aground in 1989 and spewed oil into the Alaskan waterways, it took Lawrence Rawl a week to comment on the incident and longer for him to visit the scene of the accident. This episode added to *Exxon*'s public reputation damage. Given the bad publicity it has received ever since, it was surprising to see something similar happen on July 6, 2013, when a train operated by *Montreal, Maine and Atlantic Railway* crashed in the Canadian city of Lac-Mégantic killing at least fifty people. CEO Edward Burkhardt arrived at the scene four days after the crash. While the company did have senior managers at the crash site during this time, they were not the people the local residents and the media wanted to see. Also it is often the small things that a CEO does at the site of a disaster that influence the company's reputation. For example, during *BP*'s Gulf of Mexico oil spill disaster, CEO Tony Hayward made the throwaway remark that "I want my life back." This made him seem insensitive to the lives lost and the damage caused by the oil spill.

My final role for CEOs is for them to take charge of their company's reputation risk management process. The job here is to identify and highlight the key reputation disaster points in their organization. By this I mean that some companies have disasters waiting to happen. They operate in a risky business or in a risky environment. For example, all the big oil companies are exploring for oil in hostile natural environments. When you do this, it is only a matter of time before something goes wrong. Also most large banks have a trading room staffed with young people whose job is to take bets on bonds, equities, and currencies. Without adequate risk controls, someone inevitably loses a lot of money. This has become known as the "rogue trader" problem. For example, in 2011 the Swiss bank *UBS* announced that it lost over $2 billion dollars due to the unauthorized trades performed by Kweku Adoboli, a director of one of its trading teams. UBS's CEO resigned as did some other senior managers. Adoboli was later found guilty of fraud and false accounting. The UK financial regulator fined *UBS* £29.7 million for the failures in its control systems. This is just one of a long list of such rogue trader incidents in the global banking industry.

In most organizations CEOs need to manage four operational lead indicators of reputation risk, namely unrealistic growth or financial performance targets, a significant deviation from budget, low employee engagement, and ethical drift.

- *Unrealistic growth*—Some CEOs like to motivate their companies by setting so-called "stretch goals." If meeting these is highly rewarded and they are not accompanied by an appropriate level of resources, then they invite people to make risky decisions and/or to cut corners. *BP*'s relentless pursuit of financial growth during the John Browne era was later discovered to be a major contributor to the company's cost-cutting approach, which in turn led to the major operational disasters noted earlier.
- *Budget variance*—When an operational division is tracking well below its budget forecasts, there is a temptation to do something drastic to address the shortfall. At this point the CEO should meet with the division to ensure that what is planned does not create

unacceptable reputation risk. For example, a medical supply company may launch a special sales incentive program to get sales up to the budgeted level. However, if this involves "entertaining" doctors or hospital staff, then the company may leave itself open for a dose of negative publicity.

- *Employee engagement*—What really makes companies great is the ability to attract, retain, and engage employees who are proud to work for them. What makes them reputation ambassadors is their pride in working for the company. While most big companies regularly measure employee turnover and engagement or one of its variants such as "climate" or "culture," it is surprising to find that so few employees are engaged. For example, a recent Gallup State of the Global Workplace survey found that worldwide, only 13 percent of workers were engaged at work. While this was an average score, even countries with the most highly engaged workforce only achieved levels in the 30 to 40 percent range.[17] What these surveys also found was that a large percentage of employees were actively disengaged. This often signals that they can't cope, don't care, or don't like their employer. In extreme cases employee engagement can turn negative and result in strike action. A subtle signal that employees are cynical about the company is the prevalence of *Dilbert* cartoons circulating among employees. Often these cartoons use cynical humor to highlight the discrepancies between stated company values and the actual values that its systems reward. It is hard for a company to have a good reputation when its employees are cynical, disengaged, or threatening strike action.
- *Ethical drift*—There are four types of ethical drift. One occurs when short-term management incentive schemes involve considerable amounts of money. This is what Frank Partnoy calls "infectious greed." Some people will do almost anything to get their bonus because even if they are kicked out of the company, they will leave with a big bag full of money. Another type of ethical drift occurs when a company puts its obligations to customers second to the ambitions of the senior managers. This was the root cause of many of the audit firm *Arthur Andersen*'s problems prior to its demise.[18] Too many partners were willing to compromise the firm's professional standards in order for them to keep their clients and their fees. Another type of ethical drift

occurs when there is a conflict of interest. A good example of this was revealed during the global financial crisis by the way the ratings agencies *Moody's, Standard & Poor's,* and *Fitch* were paid to rate company debt. They were paid by the organizations they rated rather than by the clients and investors who were dealing with these organizations. The financial incentive here was to rate the payee nicely in order to ensure ongoing fees for future favorable ratings. The fourth type of ethical drift occurs when a company deals with customers who have a poor reputation. The problems here are twofold. One is that the ethics of customers may penetrate the company. The other is that companies are often judged by the company they keep.

Because the board of directors is the ultimate authority, in most companies there is another type of ethical risk that they need to monitor. It involves the personal and professional lives of the CEO. Many corporate scandals have arisen because the board of directors allowed the CEO's right to privacy to trump disclosure to them and shareholders as long as the CEO kept meeting his or her performance targets. This situation is exacerbated when the CEO is intimately identified with the company's fortunes. The saga of Steve Job's illness while CEO of *Apple* is a good example. His refusal of standard medical advice is considered by many people to have caused his premature death. And his refusal to acknowledge the severity of his illness and reveal his odd treatment regime to his board and shareholders may well have compromised decisions taken by the company and its shareholders.

Many business people, lawyers, and journalists subscribe to the principle that in business the private life of the CEO should be considered "private." And in most cases involving family matters it is. However, when it crosses over into the company and involves things like serious ill health, sexual harassment, personal drug taking, the favoritism of an employee, or the use of company resources for private purposes, it sends a bad signal inside and outside the company. Larry Stonecipher of *Boeing*, Mark Hurd of *Hewlett-Packard,* and Paul Wolfowitz of the *World Bank* have been casualties of this type of transgression. Here I am out of step with many colleagues and business commentators. I believe that the personal integrity of the CEO is vitally important to the integrity of the company they lead.[19] Their personal integrity gives them the moral authority to make difficult decisions. This complements their formal positional authority to make these decisions. Wouldn't it be nice if more CEOs attracted comments like the following?

I respect him and believe his integrity is unmatched. This is a man whose values permeate every decision he makes, every interaction with people and every piece of counsel he shares.

Anne Mulcahy, then CEO of *Xerox*, describing Warren Buffett[20]

Like *Virgin* reflects Sir Richard Branson's rebelliousness and *Apple* reflected the genius of Steve Jobs, [Warren Buffett's] Berkshire Hathaway has brand equity around trust, stability and integrity.

Oscar Yuan, Partner, *Millward Brown Vermeer*[21]

I hope that highlighting Buffet's personal reputation does not invoke the "commentator's curse."[22]

8

Measuring Corporate Reputations: Keeping Score

What is measured improves.
Peter Drucker

and also

A firm becomes what it measures.
John Hauser and Gerald Katz

To prime the material in this chapter, I will illustrate how to measure whether an organization has a better corporate reputation than its rivals. The task I assume is to find a "best–worst" measure of the corporate reputations of a number of long-haul airlines that fly out of Australia. As I will elaborate later in the chapter, this measure is in fact a more scientifically valid way to measure the relative corporate reputations of a group of companies than any opinion poll approach such as that adopted by *Fortune* magazine to produce their annual ranking of the World's Most Admired Companies.[1]

For this task I have chosen seven competitor airlines. My evaluation of these airlines was done after *Malaysian Airlines* had suffered two major catastrophes, namely, Flight MH370 that went missing from Kula Lumpur to Beijing and Flight MH17 that was shot down over east Ukraine. If you follow the instructions in the question below and put in your choices, you would see how your evaluation differs from mine. The airlines are:

- Qantas
- Emirates
- British Airways

- Singapore Airlines
- United Airlines
- Thai Airlines
- Malaysian Airlines

In the question below you need all seven airlines because this measure is based on an experimental design for seven airlines. (The same can be done for any number of companies, but it requires a different experimental design for each number.)

Question

Please evaluate the overall corporate reputations of the seven airlines listed above in accord with the admiration and respect you hold them in at the present time. This evaluation should be based on what you know about the airlines. You may have gained this knowledge by flying with them, seeing their advertising, listening to what the media is saying about them, or talking to other people.

Your Task

For each of the sets of airlines below please select the one with the best and the one with the worst overall reputation from each set.

Set 1	*Best reputation*	*Worst reputation*
Qantas		
Emirates	✓	
British Airways		✓
Set 2	*Best reputation*	*Worst reputation*
Qantas		
Singapore Airlines	✓	
United Airlines		✓
Set 3	*Best reputation*	*Worst reputation*
Qantas	✓	
Thai Airlines		
Malaysian Airlines		✓
Set 4	*Best reputation*	*Worst reputation*
Emirates		
Singapore Airlines	✓	
Thai Airlines		✓

Set 5	*Best reputation*	*Worst reputation*
Emirates	✓	
United Airlines		
Malaysian Airlines		✓
Set 6	*Best reputation*	*Worst reputation*
British Airways		
Singapore Airlines	✓	
Malaysian Airlines		✓
Set 7	*Best reputation*	*Worst reputation*
British Airways		
United Airlines		✓
Thai Airlines	✓	

Scoring

Step 1. Add up the number of bests and worsts for each airline and then compute a net score (best to worst).

Qantas	Bests: 1	Worsts: 0	Net score: 1
Emirates	Bests: 2	Worsts: 0	Net score: 2
British	Bests: 0	Worsts: 1	Net score: –1
Singapore	Bests: 3	Worsts: 0	Net score: 3
United	Bests: 0	Worsts: 2	Net score: –2
Thai	Bests: 1	Worsts: 1	Net score: 0
Malaysian	Bests: 0	Worsts: 3	Net score: –3

Step 2. Rank the companies from highest to lowest scores—remember that the bigger the negative score, the worse the reputation.

1. Singapore (+3)
2. Emirates (+2)
3. Qantas (+1)
4. Thai (0)
5. British (–1)
6. United (–2)
7. Malaysian (–3)

And that's it. You have a scientifically valid rank ordering for you and me of where each airline's reputation sits against these six competitors.

Why this process creates a valid and reliable measure of corporate reputation is that it is based on a formal theory of choice where people prefer the best over the worst option. And if corporate reputation is to drive competitive advantage, the measure needs to reflect this. In this case choosing an airline is a better indicator of competitive advantage than rating the airline on a scale ranging from say "highly preferred" to "not at all preferred." The measure is also based on an experimentally designed set of alternatives to consider.[2] These are called balanced incomplete block designs. In the design above every company is compared once with every other company, which means that it appears in three choice sets.

The other advantage of this measure is that it is really easy for most people to do because they have an intuitive notion of what a good or bad reputation is and because most times, when they fly, they choose one of the airlines from the set of those going to that destination. The disadvantage of this type of measure is that it is not diagnostic because it does not provide any information about why the respondent thinks that each airline has a good or bad reputation. However, a couple of follow-up questions can gather this information.

The diagram of corporate reputation formation in chapter 3 suggests that a company's reputation is based on the salient beliefs people hold of the organization. To help discover these, most big companies routinely analyze the media in which the company is reported. The corporate affairs department and the CEO receive a regular flow of media analysis reports. Many companies also mine their qualitative customer research to discover this group's beliefs about the company. Customer satisfaction surveys are often used as a surrogate for reputation.[3] For employees, the annual climate, culture, and satisfaction surveys can be helpful. For other stakeholders, most companies rely on ad hoc surveys and episodes of hostile feedback to gain insight into the strength of the reputation. Sometimes companies will commission specific reputation research from an organization like the *Reputation Institute*. This organization will do "deep dive" analysis of the company's scores on the twenty attributes or belief statements used to profile its reputation. And if asked, it will use the same measure across competitors. If this mixture of data across the company sounds a bit ad hoc, it is because it is!

On the academic side of the measurement ledger, the situation is not much better. Naomi Gardberg and I spent a year reviewing a variety of scholarly measures of corporate reputation only to conclude that while they are improving, a lot of work still needs to be done in order to produce a valid and reliable measure of corporate reputation.[4] Because most of these measures are designed around a specific research question, they are not flexible enough to provide a good measure of the corporate reputations of rival companies across multiple stakeholder groups.

While this is a fairly bleak picture of the current state of affairs, it need not be. In this chapter I'll describe what a good measurement landscape should look like. And I'll identify who can help gather the data and develop sound measures of corporate reputation. Because nearly all companies do media analysis, I'll start here. Then I'll describe how to develop a set of customized measures of corporate reputation that are useful for diagnostic purposes and for determining if the company has won or lost the reputation game.

What the Media Is Telling You about Your Corporate Reputation

This section is based on my association with Warren Weeks, the founder of *Cubit Media Research*.[5] Our collaboration grew out of Warren's frustration with many of the media summaries given to CEOs. Most consisted of counts of positive and negative mentions of the company and its products tagged against different media, and sometimes incidents involving the company. This is a crude form of sentiment analysis. Through the lens of corporate reputation it is only marginally helpful.

To put media coverage in context, it is useful to note that the business media where companies are talked about have developed their own vernacular and way of framing issues. Of importance here is their focus on share price and events that "move markets." Moreover many outlets are ideological and will push the idea of free-market capitalism or sometimes social responsibility.[6] Within this context, there are four major roles that the traditional media serve when they report on firms:

- To report on significant events that occur in the business and economic environment. As we saw during the global financial crisis, the way that these events are reported and dramatized can affect public perception about the role and contribution of business.

- To report about the strategies, financial performance, employee layoffs, new product introductions, and the like, of specific companies. The positive and negative mix of these can taint a company's reputation. And it can help position the company as best at something or best for somebody.
- To act as an independent investigator. Here journalists are creating news and acting as a watch-dog for society. Many of these stories have a negative tone of voice and thus may adversely impact the corporate reputations of the companies targeted.
- To provide a platform to publicize the views of a group of external stakeholders. Here they act as a messenger to company leaders. They also provide a degree of extra legitimacy to the message and the groups involved.

The rise of the Internet media has added a few new twists to reputation monitoring. Now it is not uncommon to find hate sites, spoof and parody sites, NGO sites, and anti-corporate sites. For example, *Greenpeace* helped orchestrate a campaign against *Shell*'s Arctic oil drilling campaign. The campaign had a fake video, a fake press release, and a fake website. A few months after its creation, it had attracted 785,000 views and 1,600 comments.[7] What actual effect this site had on *Shell*'s behavior or its reputation is hard to determine. While the number of views and comments look impressive, it is difficult to know if *Shell* took them seriously and/or made any changes to its fundamental operations that it otherwise would not have carried out. The reason for this assessment is because Tom Bower describes *Shell* as a very hard-nosed and arrogant company. Thus its reputation suggests that one episode of public screaming would be unlikely to significantly affect its plans.[8] Sometimes funny and not-so-funny videos featuring a company or its products will be uploaded to *YouTube*. These websites can also attract a large number of followers, and occasionally they spark a viral social network campaign. Some media-monitoring firms specialize in tracking these sites. There is a wonderful irony here. The successful Internet sites are often monitored by journalists who then go on to introduce the issues they find to the more mainstream media. This provides the original story with more credibility.

One of the reputation problems with social media is that this medium generates a lot of noise. That is, as the volume of social comments increases, so does the amount of chatter between people arguing with each other rather than generating commentary that is focused on the company and its reputation. Thus it becomes more difficult to distinguish genuine concern, or signal, from argumentative chatter, or noise. As the ratio of signal to noise falls, it becomes harder to get a clear picture of the company. Paradoxically, this makes it easier for poor companies to hide in the morass of social chatter.

Over time media coverage defines what is important for many people to believe about companies and what aspects of corporate character and performance are being used to evaluate them. For example, some years ago one of the big European technology companies wanted to project an image as a technology leader, but its press coverage consistently portrayed it as selling stylish products. One of the reasons for this discrepancy was that the business journalists thought that while the company had good technology, which they framed as "stylish," they also thought that it was slow to get its products to market. Hence it was not a "leader." Thus the company developed a media reputation for product design rather than innovation. Not bad, but not what they wanted.

To understand the nature of a company's media reputation requires two things. The first is the type of story the journalist is pursuing. For example, is this a story about a company that:

- is on top, or
- perched for a fall, or
- struggling to survive, or
- in a turnaround situation, or
- in the middle of a crisis?

And is the journalist a self-proclaimed reporter or do they have an agenda, such as being a "professional destroyer of reputations" as one journalist described himself on a *YouTube* segment.

The second issue is to analyze the words and phrases used by the journalists and bloggers to describe the company and its competitors. Because the words used by people are the ones that have real meaning to them, the number of times a word is used will be a good guide to its importance. Some of these words will fit neatly into the natural language of reputation and how the company would like to be evaluated. Other words will be new and insightful. And sometimes the writer will reveal the values that he or she is using to judge the morality of the company's behavior. For example, during the extensive media coverage of the *Qantas* industrial dispute referred to earlier, the CEO was frequently referred to by his name Alan Joyce, not his role as CEO. Thus the story became personal. It was often framed as Alan Joyce of Irish heritage who was leader of an Australian icon company fighting with his Australian workforce and the person directly responsible for the hardship to Australians Mary and Peter Traveling Citizens stranded in a foreign country. You can imagine the emotion charged watercooler conversations about how to fix the *Qantas* dispute. And from then on for many people the reputation of *Qantas* is affected by the reputation of Alan Joyce the Irish-born CEO.

As the previous examples illustrate, the analysis of words and phrases should be done to reveal the themes, contradictions, expectations, and values in what is said. This is important not only to highlight any misalignment between a company's desired and media reputations but also because people seldom unconditionally like or dislike a company. Discussion about the company can now move along from "we have a good or bad reputation," to "we are known to be good at this and not so good for that." The contradictions between good and bad aspects of a company are insightful because they demand an explanation.

To illustrate these ideas, consider an article about *Apple* published in *Business Week* titled "A bruise or two on Apple's reputation."[9] The article contains several elements:

- *Business Week story line*—"Is the company's stellar service keeping up with its hyper growth? Some customers don't think so."
- *Journalists' themes*—as *Apple*'s new products (iPod, iPhone) become more successful, they are being purchased by customers who are less devoted to *Apple* and who are often less "tech-savvy." "The vitriol of complaints on some *Apple*-related blogs and websites is approaching that usually reserved for cable TV." Positive endorsement from a long-time customer Nigel Ashton. Negative endorsements from two new customers Catherine Temple and Michael Levin accompanied by their forlorn photos.
- *Apple's position*—Timothy Cook claims that an array of internal metrics show service has never been better.
- *Contradictions*—Cook versus the two new customers and the blogs. Cook versus an academic expert who endorses the claim that as the customer base becomes more diverse it becomes harder to satisfy.

- *Comparisons*—"Even small cracks in a pristine reputation can be a sign of larger problems. Just ask Dell." Table of customer satisfaction scores from an independent research firm shows *Apple* (79 percent down from 83 percent), *HP* (76 percent up from 75 percent), *Gateway* (75 percent up from 73 percent), and *Dell* (74 percent down from 78 percent).

The rich content of this three-page article is lost if it is classified as either a mostly positive or mostly negative or a mixed piece of journalism. However, if it is examined through a multi-focal lens, then we see strategic issues (market expansion), industry issues (all competitors have 75 percentage scores on satisfaction), and product and service issues (new multi-function products make it harder for some customers and company service people to get these products to work). Some of these issues support the *Apple* corporate story of great product design and some challenge aspects of it. Also we see conflict—Cook contradicting the journalists' evidence in the article. This "you say" versus "we say" piece of journalism is likely to be noticed by employees. Hence it will require a clear response to them from senior management.

When journalists and bloggers write about a company, they expose their mental model of what is important for success in an industry. For example, John Gapper states that "when a company is doing noticeably better than competitors in its industry, there are three possible explanations: skill, luck, or edge."[10] Media coverage often reflects the journalist's view about which of these is operative for the company in question. These mental models can be better understood by interviewing the people who follow and talk about a company. For example, reading the financial press suggests that a company will be respected if it is a good exponent of the strategy of exploration or exploitation. Exploration is based on innovation, whereas exploitation is based on becoming more efficient. However, to fully understand how a journalist calibrates a company's implementation of either strategy requires understanding which corporate behaviors they focus on to signal each strategy. To launch innovative new products may signal a good explorer company. Cost cutting, restructuring, and the adoption of modern management techniques may signal a good exploitative company. Understanding these mental models then helps the company to tailor its communication to these opinion leaders.

Based on the analysis of tens of thousands of media pieces, *Cubit Media Research* has discovered that most can be classified into one of eight broad macro themes. These are shown in figures 8.1 and 8.2. The business themes tend to be described with reference to "hard numbers," while the social themes are often written about in terms of corporate behaviors that impact on specific types of stakeholders. The business themes tend to occur more in weekday media, while the social themes in weekend media. Each macro theme is comprised of a number of micro themes. For example, financial performance may be discussed in terms of earnings, profit, strategy, growth, and the CEO. Social themes often contain human interest stories and product themes such as new products. In the "old media" journalists tend to specialize in industries.

These two figures summarize the numbers behind the media coverage. They act as starting points for a discussion of a company's media reputation. Figure 8.1 shows company salience, namely which companies are getting coverage. The media play an important role here. Who they select for attention and what they say puts these companies' reputations in play. This figure also shows whether all the companies are being talked about in the same way. For example, our company's products and services are not nearly as noteworthy as those of our major competitor.

Figure 8.2 shows the risk profile of the media coverage—what topics are attracting positive, mixed, or negative stories. Here we see that regulatory issues seem to be attracting too much negative attention. Having a public argument with a regulator or being put under investigation are common causes of such media activity. They may also trigger a values-based discussion of the company about its ethics or moral responsibility. Another worrying feature of this graph is the negative commentary about stakeholders. Here stories about disgruntled stakeholders can infect other people. The field of word-of-mouth and viral marketing suggests that negative commentary can be more damaging than the boost provided by a similar amount of positive coverage.

The numbers in the two figures are invitations to unpack each macro theme into its micro themes. For example, do the product and stakeholder themes focus on the superior or inferior value offered to these people? Also, when journalists focus on strategy and governance, one micro theme that has proved troublesome for many companies is the profile of the

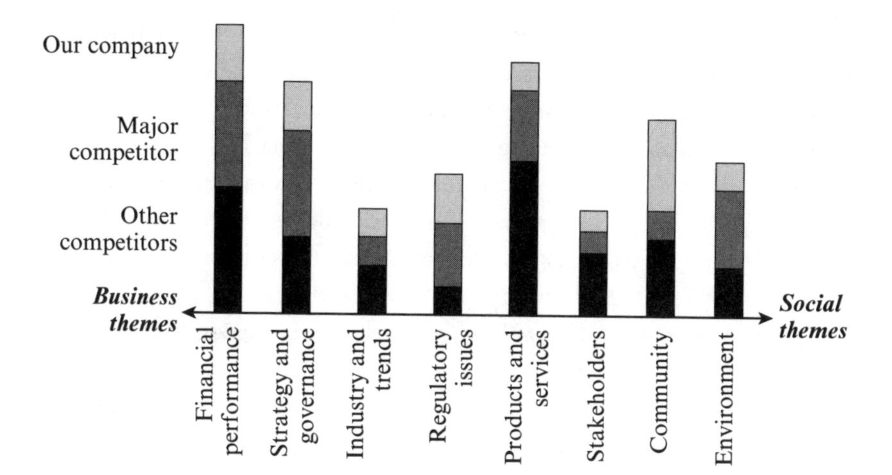

Figure 8.1

Media salience

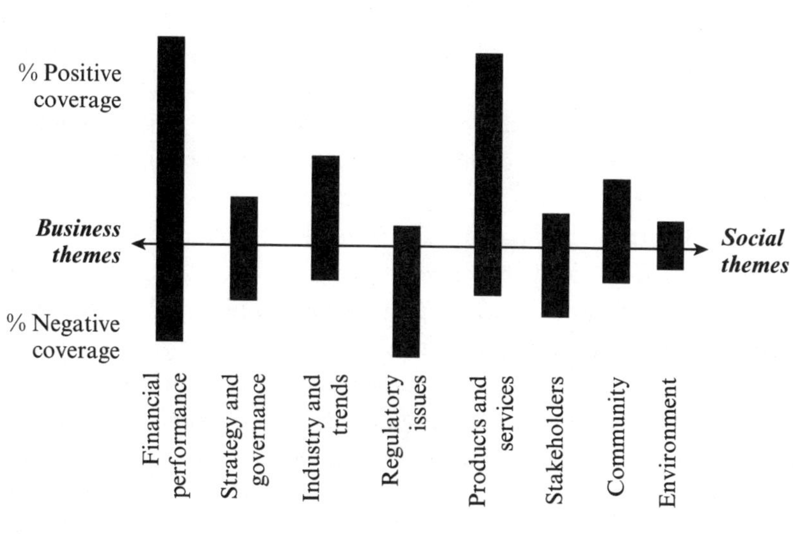

Figure 8.2

Our company's profile

CEO. In some countries, charismatic leadership is a positive theme, while in others, it is tainted with celebrity. In either case, when a high-profile CEO is called to account in the media, their reputation and that of their company is in play. The effects of this can be particularly damaging inside the company. After a series of such encounters with the media one high-profile CEO of a US company was chastised inside her company with the chant of "ditch the bitch." She was eventually ditched by the chair of the board who soon after suffered the same fate!

The next part of media analysis is to relate each macro theme to the language of corporate reputations. Are values-laden words used? Are stakeholder value words used? Are reputation words such as admiration, respect, trust, reliability, credibility, confidence, honesty, status, fairness, and legitimacy also used when discussing corporate issues? And why is this language used? For example, a company will lose credibility when it breaks a promise. It will be judged as unreliable if it fails to meet expectations. It will lose its moral authority if its behavior doesn't fit with the values of its stakeholders. In essence a company needs to know if the media is talking about its reputation. Very few conventional media studies are structured to highlight the links between what journalists and other opinion leaders say about a company and its reputations.

The final part of media analysis is to think about how to act on the information uncovered. For example, positive message themes need to be protected, and other "missing" positive themes need to be advanced. Often a well-known theme can be used to provide credibility for a missing theme. As noted earlier, *GE* has two such positive message themes. One is its well-touted record of profitability, and the other is the company's less talked about environmental (Ecomagination) initiative. By setting specific financial targets for its Ecomagination products and services *GE* could link its profit story to its environment story. For a negative message theme, two options are available. One is to fix the underlying issue or to communicate how it is being addressed. The other is to seek to correct the misconception by providing new information or briefing selected journalists. For a mixed message theme, the task is to understand whether this results from a contradiction of what the company is saying or inconsistent messages. Then the task is to promote your side of the story.

Developing Customized Measures of Corporate Reputation

I now shift attention to describing three quantitative measures of corporate reputation. As noted in the quotes at the beginning of the chapter—"If you can't measure it, you can't manage it." Hence we need some measures. BUT!! It is important to understand the nature of any measure chosen to calibrate a corporate reputation. In the following discussion I'll avoid a technical discussion of this because it is a bit complicated, but I'll highlight some of the commonsense aspects of reputation measures.

The three measures described below are interrelated. The role of the first measure is to calibrate the rank order of a company's reputation against its rivals. This will indicate the potential for the company's reputation to lead to a competitive advantage. The role of measure 2 is to discover the basis by which people evaluate the company's reputation. The role of measure 3 is to calibrate how much a good reputation is worth in a specific situation. The central idea of this measure is to determine the relative importance of a good or not so good corporate reputation relative to the other attributes people use to make their choices about which companies to engage with.

Measures That Matter 1: Is a Company Better or Worse Than its Competitors?

Recall the best–worst measure of reputation in the introduction of this chapter. This is a good example of a quick and psychometrically valid measure of how one organization's reputation compares with its competitors. As noted earlier, measures of different numbers of organizations will require different experimental designs. Any market research firm that does choice modeling can design these.

A critical part of this style of measure is to explain what you mean by the concept of corporate reputation to the people rating the organizations. The failure to do this is one of the biggest problems with the most prominent measure of corporate reputation in the scholarly literature. It is *Fortune* magazine's measure of the World's Most Admired Companies. In this measure each respondent is asked to rate a number of companies on nine attributes, namely ability to attract and retain talented employees, quality of management, social responsibility to the community and the environment, innovativeness, quality of products and services, wise use of corporate assets, financial soundness, long-term investment value, effectiveness of doing business globally. However, nowhere in the instructions to respondents is the notion of reputation explained to them.[11] Hence each respondent is free to interpret each of the nine attribute rating scales as they wish. Thus when you add up these nine scores, each rated on an 11-point scale to get an overall evaluation, what you get is a very messy, or as some have labeled this type of measure as "junk."[12]

One of the critical advantages of the best–worst type of measure at the beginning of this chapter is that it forces the researcher to define what reputation means before asking people to rate the reputations of a set of competitive companies. And because the choice options for each set of companies are best reputation and worst reputation, the question format captures the semantic understanding of reputation that most people have. Thus reputation is a much more commonsense construct to measure than something like "the wise use of corporate assets."[13]

Measures That Matter 2: What Makes a Company Good and Bad?

A number of times I have mentioned that people seldom unconditionally consider a company to be all good or all bad. And as explained earlier, this is more likely to be the case for people who are better informed about the company. The insight that can be gained from knowing what is good and bad about a company, however, is lost in most quantitative measures of corporate reputation, both those of academics and practitioners. The reason is that they create single-number summary measures that are easier for the media to report and much easier for the statisticians to correlate with other variables. For example, in the table of 2012 RepTrak™ winners in chapter 10 it is easy to see that *Rolls Royce* has a better reputation than *Specsavers*. In the report where these numbers appear each company's score is correlated with the "percentage of respondents who would recommend that company." The correlation is 0.79, which is very high. But what does this mean?

This correlation can mean either that

- as a company's reputation increases, so does the percentage of people who will recommend it increase, or that
- as the percentage of people who recommend a company increases, so will its reputation increase.

Each interpretation is equally valid because a correlation tells you nothing about the direction of causation. And in this case it can be argued that a good reputation causes positive recommendations about the company AND that positive recommendations by people enhance the reputation of the company in question.

These *Rolls Royce* and *Specsavers* reputation numbers are the aggregate scores of 20 questions, each measured on a 5-point scale. However, what these total scores hide is that fact that two companies with the same score can have very different corporate reputations. This will occur in the middle of the range of scores, precisely where most companies will be located. Figure 8.3 illustrates this point. To keep it simple, I present three companies whose reputation is measured on four 5-point scales. Each has a very different reputation profile yet each has the same overall reputation score. Thus the way that the measure is communicated in the polls camouflages the structural differences between the reputations of these companies. When this happens, the overall reputation score really is junk.

Throughout the book I have described three competing models of reputation formation, namely the stakeholder value proposition (SVP) model, the character and competence model, and the corporate social responsibility (CSR) model. Now which of these is adopted will

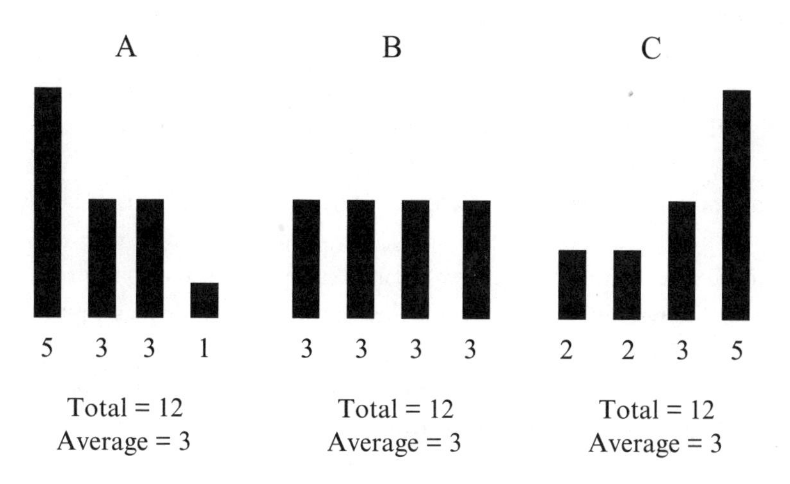

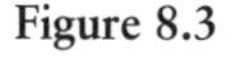
Figure 8.3

Similar scores but different corporate reputations

determine what is included in a measure of corporate reputation. For example:

- The SVP model assumes that being evaluated as best at something and/or best for somebody is the most important driver of a strong and distinctive corporate reputation. Thus SVP-based measures of corporate reputation would be made up of questions about the attributes of the value proposition offered to each particular group of stakeholders, such as those in the "onion diagrams" described in chapter 6. The typical way of doing this is to get respondents to rate the importance of each attribute's contribution to having a reputation for being known as best at something and/or best for somebody. Five or seven-point Likert-type rating scales could be used. The problem with this method, however, is that if prior research has been used to help identify the important attributes, then one should expect that most respondents will rate most of the attributes as important. And they do tend to do this. Hence this approach is not very helpful as a way to find out what really matters. A better approach is to ask respondents to rank-order the attributes from most to least important.

The SVP approach to corporate reputation measurement would result in a different measure for each stakeholder group. Because each is composed of a different set of attributes, these reputation measures would not be comparable.[14] By this I mean that from a measurement theory perspective, it would not be meaningful to state that the company has say a better reputation among its employees than its customers. These SVP measures provide a fine-grained understanding of the corporate reputations of various stakeholders groups, but this comes with the restriction that they are noncomparable and they can't be added together to get a measure of the company's overall corporate reputation. For many companies this will not be too burdensome because they are interested in their corporate reputation in different markets, such as the market for employees or the market for customers.

If a company does want to compare its SVP-based corporate reputations across groups, it could nevertheless do this by asking each group to also rate the overall reputation of the company as follows:

Please evaluate the overall reputation of Company X. By corporate reputation, I mean the admiration and respect you hold this company in at the present time. You can rate Company X as predominantly good or bad, or if there are significant elements that are both good and bad, then please rate it as mixed. If you don't know much about this company then please tick the "don't know" option. If for whatever reason you "don't care" about this company or its reputation, then please select this option.

Good			Bad	Don't know	Don't care
+2	+1	−1	−2		

There are a couple of important elements of this measure. One is that there is no midpoint option on the answer scale such as a 0. This is to get the respondents to make a judgment. If a zero is included on the scale, research has shown that many people will select it.[15] A second element is that the "good" and 'bad" answer options are coded with positive and negative numbers. This is to signal that good is "good" and bad is "bad." Had the scale been numbered say from 5 to 1, then this would signal that "bad" is really just "not so good." A third element is that things are explained to the respondents. Corporate reputation is defined in the question and what is meant by "mixed", "don't know," and "don't care" is also explained. This is done to minimize the chance that each respondent will interpret the question differently.[16] Finally a "don't care" answer option is included because it is important to know if the respondent simply doesn't care about the company. When the general public is asked to evaluate a disparate list of companies, this is a very important inclusion. It tells the researchers about the relevance of each company to the sample of people polled for their opinion. Before a company bases its reputation management on the responses of a group of people, it would be nice to know if they are both knowledgeable about it and care about it.

- The character and competence model assumes that a set of these attributes define the identity and reputation of the company. Because these speak to all groups of stakeholders, only one set of these need to be assessed, and hence only one measure is needed.
- The CSR model assumes that being evaluated as a good corporate citizen is the most important driver of a good corporate reputation.

> Here the relative contribution of various attributes of CSR to the reputation of the company would be measured. Again, because the same attributes of CSR would be meaningful to all the groups of stakeholders, only one measure of corporate reputation would be needed.

Some researchers use what I call a "mixed measure" of corporate reputation. Because they are not quite sure exactly what contributes to the overall reputation of a company, they combine SVP attributes, organizational identity attributes, and CSR attributes in the same measure.[17] This is the style of measure adopted by *Fortune* World's Most Admired Companies measure and the *Reputation Institute*'s RepTrak™ measure. These multi-attribute measures are typically composed of between nine and twenty rating scales. Here the company is assumed to have an overall reputation based on the evaluation of a very broad array of its characteristics. These measures also assume that the respondent knows a lot about the companies being rated.[18] And, because the scores on the rating scales are added together or averaged to get an overall score, it is further assumed that the good aspects of the company can compensate for the bad aspects. This may not be a sensible assumption if people form their evaluations primarily by judging a company on only one or two criteria. For example, if a person decides that any company that is involved in tax avoidance is bad, then it does not matter what else it does.

These different measures highlight a fundamental difference in the way that scholars, and possibly managers, think about what a corporate reputation is. The SVP measure focuses on being good for somebody. The character and competence model focuses on being good at something. The CSR-based measure focuses on being a good corporate citizen. In contrast, the mixed measure is unfocused. It assumes that a company has a "meta" or "halo" reputation that makes it on average an admired and respected company. As noted in chapter 1, the academic community has yet to reach a consensus about which model and measure of reputation is best. However, what can be said about the four approaches is that the first three are much clearer about how a strong and distinctive corporate reputation is formed and should work than the third approach. And because of this it should be easier to measure these effects and easier for managers to decide if they want to invest in creating a better corporate reputation.

Measures That Matter 3: Is Your Corporate Reputation Worth Anything?

The answer to this question is revealed if people place a monetary value on the company's reputation when they make decisions about whether or not to engage with it. Surprisingly, few studies of corporate reputation actually measure this effect. They measure many things that are related to the effect, but not whether people are actually prepared to pay for the privilege of being associated with a company they admire and respect. For example, a typical empirical study will search for statistically significant correlations among (1) various corporate characteristics and the company's overall reputation; (2) corporate reputation and trust, admiration, respect, and the like; and (3) corporate reputation and stakeholder behaviors such as customer loyalty. These relationships are important, but they don't tell the company if its reputation is more financially valuable than those of its competitors.

What would be ideal to know is how much money a person would be willing to pay in order to deal with a company when all other aspects of their relationship are held constant. If this amount of money is larger than the amount they are willing to pay to deal with the company's rivals, then it is winning the reputation game. It turns out that it is possible to estimate these amounts. Let me explain.

A couple of years ago my colleagues and I did a study that focused on how companies can win the war for talented employees.[19] In this study we estimated that for MBA students about to enter the workforce, the value of a potential employer's good corporate reputation was $12,388. We did this by asking each student to evaluate 16 pairs of hypothetical job contracts that were made up of features such as contract length, reputation of the company, pension contributions, promotion opportunities, salary, and travel demands. Across the contracts, each feature was varied across a number of levels. For example, the MBA salaries ranged from $90,000 to $150,000. The corporate reputation levels ranged from being in the top 25 percent globally, as named by the *Reputation Institute*, to not listed by the *Reputation Institute* but known to receive negative media coverage from time to time. For each pair of contracts the student chose the one they most preferred. From the 16 choices each person made we statistically estimated the relative value (aka utility) of each feature. When one of the features is stated in a dollar amount, as done here with the starting salary, then with some further statistical estimation, it is possible to put a dollar value on all the other features that is anchored to the average dollar amount (of the starting salary in this case). This is where the $12,388 dollar value of corporate reputation comes from. If the salary range was different, then the value of the reputation would also be different.

The research technique we used is known as a "discrete choice experiment." In these experiments people are not asked to rate things, they are asked to make a choice—in this case it was for a job contract (or employee value proposition) where one of the features is reputation. This is exactly what people do when seeking employment. And it is exactly what other key stakeholders such as consumers, investors, business partners, and local communities do when they engage with companies. They make choices that involve trade-offs across the features of the overall offer the company makes.

The greatest strength of this way of measuring the value of a corporate reputation is also its greatest weakness. It is far more complicated to design, administer, and produce the statistical estimates of utility than the traditional opinion poll style of research. But, after we did our employment study with the MBAs, we repeated it with samples of white-collar, medical, legal, public service, and manual employees. And they all survived the experience!

To summarize, measuring corporate reputations is not straightforward. Off-the-shelf measures like Rep Trak™ have severe limitations while customized measures mean that they have to be developed with the help of a good market research firm. My argument is that if trading on the company's reputation is going be a key part of its strategy, then the company can't afford not to develop a suite of customized measures. To demonstrate that this really is a simple decision, I provide a thought experiment in appendix A to show how to estimate the worth of doing customized research.

Context Matters

Probably the most overlooked issue regarding the measurement of corporate reputations is that of context. By this I mean:

- type of stakeholder or spectator,
- situation in which the person is considering engaging with the company, and
- the way questions are asked.

Each of these contexts can have a profound effect on the measured scores of the people chosen to evaluate a company. Hence each must be considered or controlled for in any valid measure of corporate reputation. They seldom are. Let me elaborate.

The beauty contests opinion poll measures of corporate reputation are essentially context free. The instructions to respondents seldom ask respondents to specify their knowledge of and relationship with the companies under evaluation. Also they seldom ask them to consider the reputation of each company as they would if they were going to say, buy a product from them for a specific use occasion, or change jobs within the next three months to advance their career, or invest $10,000 in their shares to add to their superannuation fund. Each such context can trigger a different set of salient beliefs about the company; it can change the relative importance of these beliefs, and it can evoke different values against which to judge the company. When a large number of people evaluate a company with reference to many, many different contexts, the scientific properties of the resulting measure are questionable.

Rupert Younger, currently the director of the *Oxford Centre of Corporate Reputations,* illustrates the importance of considering context by noting that many MBA students consider that the investment bank *Goldman Sachs* has a good reputation for the first job after graduation—because of the intense and varied on-the-job training if offers; but the company has lousy reputation for a long-term career—because of the intense and varied work required. So this company has both a good and a bad reputation as an employer among the same group of people—which one depends on the situation.

One final example of how context affects reputation was recently published in the journal *Science*.[20] It deals with the ratings many of us use on social network sites like *Trip Adviser*. Here we rely on digitized, aggregated opinions about companies to make decisions. Based on a series of experiments, it was found that if the initial evaluation of a business issue people saw was positive, then this created a significant positive social influence bias (+ 25 percent) that persisted over a five-month time frame. If it was negative, then no such bias was observed. Hence companies would do well to manipulate their online reputations by making sure that the first evaluation people see is positive.

9

Keeping Out of Trouble

What follows are some corporate behaviors that routinely tarnish and sometimes damage an otherwise good reputation. The discussion is organized around the building blocks of a good corporate reputation discussed in the previous chapters. I start with stakeholder value because this is the touchstone of a strong, commercially valuable reputation. This can then be undermined by the mindset of the company and the coverage it receives in the media.

Stakeholder Value

Designing value for stakeholders is not an easy task. With customers, some companies like *Apple* adopt a market-driving approach. They create new products that are functionally better than those of their competitors and then launch these into the market. They succeed or fail. This is a fast failure approach to new product testing. While it is risky because of the investments made prior to launch, in *Apple*'s case they have had more successes than failures (remember the Newton PDA). In contrast, most other companies adopt a market-driven approach to innovation. Here research is done to help understand customer needs and to help design the new product or service. More research is then done to test the new products prior to launch. In this process customers have more chance of having input into what is offered to them. Success here depends on good research, good interpretative skills, and skilled marketing to tell consumers that their expressed needs have been catered to. Either approach can lead to simply better products and services.

The trap with the design of stakeholder value propositions involves which group's value proposition should anchor the design of those offered to the other groups? As an old marketer, I like the idea that customers are a company's most important group of stakeholders. If they don't buy your products and services at a price that provides a profit, then sooner or later the company becomes an historical footnote. Hence customer value is what gets designed first. However, my thirty years in a business school taught me that engaged employees are the key to a company being customer focused. These people directly or indirectly design and deliver the customer experience. Disengaged employees are a dead-weight cost to the company and often the source of reputation-damaging activities. Thus the employee value proposition must engage these people to create value for customers. Their employment contract needs to reward activities that directly or indirectly touch the customer and/or enhance the capabilities of the company to do this.

A second trap with creating a good corporate reputation on the back of the customer and employee value propositions is that there needs to be a sharp focus on what really matters to these two groups. When such a focus is achieved, it can then be communicated succinctly. Consider the following examples in table 9.1. They are companies that have caught my attention or that of other people because they are well regarded for being best at something or best for somebody. They have not been used as examples earlier in the book. I present them as additional "food for thought."

The most difficult part of building a strong reputation on the back of stakeholder value is being realistic about the organization's capabilities and its target customers. For example, at the *Australian Graduate School of Management* we targeted two primary groups of students and one primary group of academic faculty. Because we were a small, largely self-funded school, we could not afford to overreach. Hence we set our sights on becoming one of the best second-division business schools. Because the very best students tend to go to the United States for their MBA, we wanted to attract the best of the leftover Australians and the best of the European and Asian students that wanted a US-style education in a great world city (Sydney). Our reputation signal to these groups was our *Financial Times* business school ranking. Our point of proof was getting the students a better job on graduation. For academic faculty we wanted to attract the best Australians, some of whom were working overseas and wanted to "come home." We also wanted to attract good US-trained

Table 9.1
Companies that are best at something and/or best for somebody

Company	Best at	Best for
Louis Vuitton	Luxury leather products (aka soft luxury)	People who want a sample of European sophistication
Lego	Colored plastic bricks	Parents who want their children to enjoy learning to become more creative and solve problems through play
Novo Nordisk	Insulin and insulin pens	Diabetic patients and health care professionals
Volvo Trucks	High-quality road lorries	Long-haul truckers
Ecolab	Traditional laundry and cleaning products and related services	Hotels and hospitals that can't risk having dirty linen and surfaces
Cochlear	Hearing implants	Profoundly deaf people
CSL	Vaccines and plasma protein biotherapies	Hospitals and patients who require quality blood-based products
AP Møller Maersk	Shipping containers	
Intuit	Personal computer accounting software	People and small businesses that struggle with their household finances
Walt Disney Studios	Making people happy	Children who want a great 30 minutes in their day
Garmin	Mobile GPS devices	People who need to know where they are and how to get from A to B
Academi (the remade Blackwater)	Private armies (protection and security)	Companies who need to protect their employees in hostile environments
Singapore Airlines	International air travel	Travelers who want a civilized long-haul flying experience
Mayo Clinic	Health care	People who need specialist health care
Zara	Fast affordable fashion	Young people who use the latest fashion clothes to express themselves
Cirque du Soleil	Circus entertainment	Adults who want a grown-up circus experience

Table 9.1 (continued)

Company	Best at	Best for
Wikipedia	Up-to-date knowledge	Curious people
BBC	News and documentaries that project British culture	Anglophiles
Incat	High-speed ocean-going ships	Passenger and vehicle ferry operators
Kone	Building lifts and escalators	Builders and users of multistory buildings
IDEO	Design thinking—designing things that people touch	Manufacturers who want better designed products
Dyson	Engineering products involving air flow such as vacuum cleaners and fans	People who will pay a bit extra for a better designed and performing appliance
RollsRoyce	Gas turbines and reciprocating engines	Aircraft manufacturers and shipbuilders
Deer & Co	Agricultural machines	People who cultivate and harvest the land
McKinsey & Company	Strategic advice	Boards of directors and CEOs of the world's leading businesses, governments and institutions

faculty that did not quite fit in with the US timetable of promotion. We became a good second-chance school for some mid-career faculty and a good first-chance school for young faculty who wanted more time to build their career. Our location and our resources realistically confined us to being "the best of the rest," although we seldom referred to ourselves in this manner.

Now consider *Harvard University*. To feed their world-class reputation, they need a lot of money, only so much of which can come from tuition fees. So they seek to raise a considerable amount of money each year from alumni and other benefactors. But how should they use their reputation to help secure these funds? First, the university's good reputation helps convince a potential donor that their money will be used for something important, that it will make a difference, and that it will be well managed. Most philanthropists want to be convinced of this. But as a *Harvard* fund raiser noted to me, now they need a dose of realism in order not to overstate their case for funding. They are competing with two other worthy causes that will nearly always take precedent over their cause. The most important of these is the benefactor's family (children and grandchildren). The next most important is this person's favorite cause. This can be anything that they believe in at the time. So *Harvard* must settle for being "the best third choice." In this way it is realistic about its position in the line of worthy causes. This also suggests that seeking small amounts of money from a lot of donors is a good way to capitalize the *Harvard University* reputation.

The Company Mindset

The Fish Rots from the Head

Bob Garratt wrote a book on developing effective boards of directors with the title *The Fish Rots from the Head*.[1] What might be surprising, given its title, is that it was read by many board members. The proverb means that bad leadership affects the body corporate. But what does this actually mean in the context of corporate governance and reputation?

One interpretation is that "boards are designed to fail." The complexity of the modern corporation is such that given the limited time able to be devoted to this job, no individual director can ever be fully informed about their company's operations. And this problem is exacerbated by relying on management for much of the processed information they receive.[2] Also few directors have a broad enough set of skills to really understand all the items on the board's agenda. This means that most board members have at least one "blind spot." Thus boards are too easily led by the CEO, a couple of "expert" directors, and the invited external consultants (who will make money if their project goes ahead). A second interpretation is that boards often make poor decisions that are based on some uninformed assumptions about the role of their CEO.[3] Two are that the chief executive epitomizes the company and that he or she is predominantly responsible for its success or failure. Often the CEO will acquiesce to this view and business journalists will propagate it. When a CEO is put atop a pedestal at the expense of others in the organization, it is an engaging story in the business press but often a depressing one inside the organization.

A third reason why boards might offer bad leadership is that they become dysfunctional. In chapter 6 the saga of *HP* introduced Carly Fiorina. Let me continue this story to illustrate how poor corporate governance can damage the reputation of a company among its employees and shareholders. As noted earlier, Carly Fiorina was brought into *HP* as a White Knight savoir. Press reports at the time said that her strategy was "to reinvent *HP* from the ground up." However, after much turmoil in 2005 she was asked to leave. One issue that bedeviled her time at *HP* was the acquisition of *Compaq* computer. There was dissent in the company boardroom about this, and a board member leaked sensitive information to the media. At this time *HP*'s media story focused on Fiorina's stewardship of the *Compaq* acquisition. And this controversial story trumped *HP*'s own innovation corporate story. Subsequently as the company struggled to reach her publicly stated financial targets, Fiorina became a tragic figure in her own story. She was fired by board chairwoman Patricia Dunn.

Time would reveal that the dismissal of Carly Fiorina was the prelude to a nasty story about the governance of *HP*. It started when Patricia Dunn decided she needed to find out which board member leaked information to the media. A two-phase investigation, characterized as a spying operation by the media, identified the culprit, who when initially exposed refused to resign. At this point the nature of the investigation prompted the resignation of another director. And it was his attempt to get the company to acknowledge the reasons for his resignation that brought the internal investigation and some deep animosities within the board into public view. What soon followed was the resignation of the "leaky director" and the termination of Patricia Dunn.

And then *HP*'s story went from bad to worse. Carly Fiorina was replaced by Mark Hurd in 2005. Under his reign he restored *HP* to its leadership position in the personal computer market and doubled the company's share price. However, he was booted out in 2010 for ethical lapses. He left with a golden handshake worth $12.2 million. Hurd was replaced with Léo Apotheker the former boss of *SAP*. He lasted 11 months before he was replaced in 2011 by Meg Whitman the former boss of *eBay*. Her first major hiccup was paying $11.1 billion for the acquisition of *Autonomy*, a British software firm. It seems that *HP* did not do adequate due diligence for this acquisition. The net result of this was paying far too much for the company. After writing off $8.8billion of this investment, the company was sued by three of its shareholders. These suits were settled via mediation in 2014 at which point *HP* engaged the lawyers who were involved on the other side of these shareholder actions to pursue the management team of *Autonomy*. And while this was happening, Meg Whitman was in the process of cutting *HP*'s workforce by 50,000 people. Spare a thought for *HP*'s employees during this period of corporate governance disasters. As the primary ambassadors for the company's reputation what story could they credibly tell about the virtues and quality of their company?

Be Careful How You Play the Corporate Growth Game

Consider the case of *Johnson&Johnson* one of the largest health care companies in the world and one America's most admired companies for many years. An article in *USA Today* spelt out the problem facing the company.[4] The economy grows maybe 3 percent a year and Wall Street wants, say, 7 to 12 percent earnings growth. The question is how to grow earnings by considerably more than the economy? The options are to grow by acquisition, improve profit margins by raising prices or cutting costs, introduce innovative products, enter new markets, or make manufacturing more efficient. Many big companies pursue all these strategies. For example, in 2010 *J&J*'s profits grew to a record $13.3 billion. But in the process it suffered considerable financial and reputation damage caused by taxpayer health care fraud claims ($751 million), foreign bribery fines ($70 million), being sued by consumers for faulty hip replacements, and having one of its manufacturing plants shut down because it did not meet federal government safety standards. In his letter in the annual report CEO William Weldon responded by stating that "We are deeply committed to the people who use our products, to our employees, to the communities in which we live, and to you, our loyal shareholders." Nothing in this statement hinted at how he would play the share market growth game. Hence it would not be unreasonable to expect more missteps as *J&J* tries to meet the expectations of the market and keep customers, employees, the community and shareholders all as the number one priority.

To further illustrate the difficulties of growth, consider the challenge Sam Palmisano set for *IBM* in 2004. He announced a target that required *IBM* to grow by the size of a new *Fortune 500* company each year. The problem with big companies seeking to grow even bigger is that the economies of scale that may come from such growth are often offset by the diseconomies of complexity. Also competitors try to put a break on what can be profitably gained in most established markets. Thus growth has some natural limits.

A serious growth-based reputation trap is to enter markets that have different mores and protocols for doing business. For example, when Saddam Hussein was in power in Iraq, many companies paid "commissions" to various people in Saddam's regime to facilitate their project bids and to fast-track various approval processes. Sooner or later these were exposed and the reputations of the companies and the managers involved were tarnished. There is a well-known list of countries that present this type of reputation risk. When dealing with them, most managers would do well to abide by the principle that sooner or later everything will become public.

One of the biggest growth-related reputation challenges facing many companies is to grow by implementing a new program of major innovation. Both the academic and business literatures proclaim that innovation is an important corporate capability and a key driver of growth. So it is quite common to see companies signal their intention to become significantly more innovative. For example, here are some innovation corporate slogans from a quick search of the web:

- *3M*—innovation; innovative technology for a changing world
- *HP*—invent
- *Toray*—innovation by chemistry
- *NEC Corporation*—empowered by innovation
- *GigaLane*—innovation and excellence in RF and microwave
- *Datel (C&D Tech)*—innovation and excellence
- *Plantronics*—sound innovation
- *Silicon Graphics*—the source of innovation and discovery
- *Poclain Hydraulics*—driving innovation
- *Pak Innovation*—innovation beyond thinking
- *MSI*—innovation with style

- *Fujifilm*—value from innovation
- *Daihatsu*—innovation for tomorrow
- *Hatachi*—social innovation, it's our future
- *BAE Systems*—innovation for a safer world
- *Texas Instruments*—technology for innovation
- *Diamon Fusion International*—innovation that ignites business

Now radical innovation is a lot like exploring for oil—it is expensive and risky. And it is plagued by myths like being first to market with a radical new product is the key to success.[5] It is also bedeviled by the uncomfortable fact that many, some say most, radical new products will not meet the expectations of the company or its target customers. So a company that is seeking growth objectives like "making 50 percent of profit from products that did not exist five years ago" is more than likely exposing itself to failure on a regular basis. If these failures are not managed well, then the company is putting its reputation at risk. For example, this damage will be more severe if the company adopts a Branded House strategy where all these products carry the company name rather than if it adopts a House of Brands strategy where they each carry a different brand name.

Apple and *Singapore Airlines* are two companies that have built their reputations by being innovative, but in very different ways. *Apple* has been successful with a number of radical customer-interface innovations most of which rely on existing technology. The key to their success was the vision of Steve Jobs and the fact that *Apple* had many more high-profile successes than failures. In contrast, *Singapore Airlines* has brought many firsts to the civil aviation industry. Some of which like being the first international airline to fly the *Airbus A380* were commissioned by its central product innovation department. Others that deal with the face-to-face customer service experience were suggested by employees. The key to the *Singapore Airlines* approach is that it does not try to be the best in every aspect of customer service but rather they try to deliver a better overall customer experience.[6]

Manage Shareholder Expectations

Probably more CEOs have been fired for not meeting their short-term financial targets than any other single cause. Yet CEOs still make specific earnings forecasts. Share analysts love these, and so do many boards, because they are seen to be setting stretch targets for their companies. Specific forecasts set expectations and as noted earlier, when these are not met, reputations suffer, in this case for both the CEO and his or her company. So what can be done?

First, most stock exchange listing rules do not require earnings guidance, although they do require the reporting of "earnings surprises" and any information that is likely to materially affect the share price. So, in uncertain times, the approach adopted by Niall Fitzgerald, the chairman of *Reuters,* is noteworthy. He said that his company will "seek profitable growth within an acceptable risk profile."[7] This statement is usefully vague in the sense that it does not state a specific profit forecast, nor does it benchmark the company against its peers such as outperform some share market index, and it avoids the tone of a "grand gesture." And yes, it will require some explanation about what uncertainties preclude more specific target setting.

Another initiative is to present some evidence as to why taking a longer-term view is preferable to focusing on the short term. For example, *Harvard Business Review* has launched an initiative to promote focusing on the long-term performance of companies.[8] Their idea is to publish a scorecard of the performance of CEOs over their complete tenure at a company. Other publications like *The Economist* newspaper support such an endeavor.[9] Both publications lament that one of the prime reasons for the focus on short-term financial performance is pressure from the board of directors.

In recent years excessive executive compensation packages and huge severance payments to long-serving or underperforming CEOs have riled many shareholders and generated negative publicity for the companies and the executives involved. Instead of selling their shares and doing what the US calls the "Wall Street Walk," many shareholders are sending the board a protest vote about the size and shape of executive compensation packages. Some big shareholders are even targeting the chair of the compensation committee as being personally accountable for what they see as excessive generosity. Switzerland, it seems, has had enough of such behavior. Billed as the "the people's initiative against fat-cat pay," on March 3, 2013, 68 percent of the Swiss electorate voted to require listed companies to offer shareholders a binding vote on senior managers' pay. Failure to comply will result in large fines or up to three years in jail.

A big part of the reputation problem here is that many people see the size of executive pay packages and frame this as "greed." They do not understand the logic behind the size and structure of the package. To improve the reputations of all the parties involved in setting these packages requires explaining to shareholders the structural aspects of the principal–agent problem that underlies executive compensation and how this is to be expected to motivate executives to behave in the long-term interests of the company. Performance might then replace greed as the benchmark against which executive pay is gauged. But, the usual response to this problem is for the board and CEO to mount a "charm offensive" to win shareholder support at the next annual general meeting. Hum!!??

Another form of reputation-damaging activism in the boardroom occurs when hedge funds, self-styled socially responsible funds, private equity partners, pension funds, institutional investors, or the occasional wealthy activist shareholder publicly agitates for better short-term financial performance and sometimes a change in corporate governance. Poorly managed these incidents can expose boardroom tensions and lead to more transparency than the company wants.[10]

Be Clear about the Role of the Company

Earlier I was critical of the ability of bolt-on CSR programs to meaningfully enhance a company's desired reputation. My reason is that most people will either see through the reasons why this is done or they will simply ignore the programs. Yes, it often makes employees feel better about themselves and their companies. And yes, the recipients like the benefits they receive. But, as Michael Edwards says, business could do a better job in helping society if they paid their taxes, obeyed regulations, ended monopolies, and stopped lobbying the political system.[11] I would add to this list that they help produce a strong and vibrant economy. This is the primary role of business. Done well, it would really help improve collectively corporate reputations in America, Australia, Canada, and elsewhere.

At the heart of any activity like bolt-on style CSR that extends the basic role of business is the fundamental issue of who really pays for such activity. A Dilbert cartoon sums up this problem.

"We need to show corporate social responsibility" an employee tells the boss. "OK" says her employer. "I'll cut your salary and give the extra money to poor people." The worker is taken aback. "I was hoping we could hose the stockholders, not me."

The big danger with corporate activities that are not aligned with the strategy of the company is that someone will make the trade-offs explicit. This will then open up the opportunity for an emotional debate about winners and losers. For example, every time a company makes a sizable donation to a group affected by a natural disaster, the company gets praise from the politicians and social commentators and a silent rebuke from many of its shareholders. For example, after the 2005 Asian tsunami a spokesperson for the *Australian Shareholders Association* criticized companies for donating money to the victims of this disaster.[12] In this type of situation the argument from the shareholders is that if they wanted to make a donation, they would have, and they would have received praise from their friends, and the tax benefit. Also, if shareholders know that a company has such a philanthropy policy, this fact can be taken into account in their buy or hold decision. Otherwise, it is a case of managers donating shareholders' money without their consent.

Don't Pay Your Fair Share of Corporate Tax

For many years *General Electric* prided itself on its ability to avoid paying corporate tax on its US profits. It didn't publicize this cost saving, and few people outside the top echelons of the company knew the full extent of its tax avoidance. Inside the company the practice of tax avoidance, which was and still is perfectly legal, was labeled fiscal responsibility. But in 2011 David Kocieniewski of *The New York Times* published an investigative piece about *GE*'s tax-paying behavior.[13] Overnight *GE* became the Poster Child of Bad Corporate America. Here is the story.

Based on a review of *GE*'s statutory company filings Kocieniewski reported that during 2009–10 *GE* made worldwide profits of $14.2 billion of which $5.1 billion was made in the United States. After submitting its 57,000 page tax return the company paid no tax in the United States.

It also made a claim for a potential reduction of its future tax liability of $3.2 billion. While Kocieniewski's interpretation of these figures was not independently verified, *GE* did not provide any other estimates to counter them.

As subsequent news commentary about this episode revealed, *GE* achieved this position through a wide variety of legal tax avoidance schemes. In the business community *GE*'s tax department, which employed 975 people at that time, gained a reputation for being "the world's best tax law firm." Inside *GE* the tax department was the company's best performing profit center. During this period *GE* also paid $41.8 million for lobbying and political campaign contributions.

Corporate tax avoidance then became such a big issue that parliamentary inquiries were held in the United Kingdom and the United States, and it was included on the agendas of both the G8 and G20 summits in 2013. Even *The Economist* newspaper labeled the practice of massive tax avoidance as "inexcusable."[14] The following prominent companies were outed for their tax avoidance behavior: *Amazon, Apple, Bank of America, BHP Billiton, Boeing, Cadbury, Chevron, eBay, Exxon Mobil, Google, HSBC, IKEA, Microsoft, News Corporation, Hewlett-Packard,* and *Starbucks*. When *Starbucks* subsequently tried to pay some tax to the UK government, it was roundly criticized for its hypocrisy.

What happened was that an entrenched and very common corporate practice was reframed by the media and then the politicians. Tax avoidance went from being seen as financially responsible corporate behavior to socially irresponsible corporate behavior. And when it became clear that the US was losing corporate tax revenue of between $50 billion to $170 billion annually, many people became angry.

My examination of the practice of corporate tax avoidance revealed two things: [15]

- There is a fundamental ethical divide between Corporate America, Australia, Canada, and "Corporate Elsewhere," and advocates of CSR. Multinational companies and their tax advisers believe that paying tax is amoral; that is, it is neither right nor wrong. It is a legal issue. In contrast, CSR advocates believe that it is a moral issue. It is a fundamental and easily measured example of a company's citizenship behavior.

- Whether tax avoidance is socially irresponsible hinges on the issue of what is meant by abiding by the law. As was noted in chapter 2, abiding by the law is one of the fundamental rules of the game of corporate reputations. A company can't be seen to be breaking the law and hope to have a good reputation. Now the issue becomes whether a company should be seen to be abiding by the "letter of the law" or by the "spirit of the law."

It turns out that "the spirit of the law" is a fuzzy idea—even among the legal community. One interpretation is that it is the popular and political understanding of the legislation. Thus, if legislation says that companies should pay tax on a reasonable determination of their profits, then they should. Another interpretation is that there is no spirit independent of the language of the law used in the legislation and interpreted by the courts. Thus, if the tax law allows companies to organize their affairs so that they can avoid paying tax, then why shouldn't they do this?

The problem here is that what might be considered as abiding by the law inside a company may not be perceived in the same way by outsiders. Hence companies need to explain their stance and the reasoning behind behaviors such as tax avoidance and political lobbying.[16] To date, each of the companies accused of immoral tax practice noted above has meekly claimed that they have broken no tax laws. And while this is generally true, it has not diminished the perception by many sectors of the community, politicians, and tax authorities that they are poor corporate citizens.

Tarnish Your Industry Image

Earlier in this book I mentioned some "sin" industries. The usual list includes alcohol, gambling, tobacco, nuclear power, military weapons, civilian firearms, adult entertainment (porn), and genetically modified organisms.[17] The shadow of these industries tarnishes the reputations of all the companies in them. The paradox here is that despite their poor reputations among the general public, many of these companies survive and prosper. They are either too big or too important to government revenue to be hounded out of business. And many shareholders like their financial performance. This is not to say that they would not prefer to have better reputations—a look at the social reports on their websites suggests that most would.

In recent years a number of other industries have become much less reputable than they once were. Advertising and public relations, print and television media, forestry, mining, petroleum, processed food, fast food, pharmaceuticals, government and politicians, and Wall Street financiers have all seen their overall standing in the community diminish. One reason is that too many people and companies in these industries have done things that eroded the trust they once enjoyed. Generally, this was a gradual process highlighted by some signature events such as the global financial crisis or a major oil spill or a corporate collapse.

Another reason for the fall from grace of many of these industries is that they stopped demonstrating their worth to society. Consider the advertising industry. It is hard to have a good reputation when most people think that the product you produce is an unwelcome intrusion into their enjoyment. It also doesn't help that social critics often accuse advertising of trying to manipulate children and take advantage of other vulnerable sections of society. To add to this, many of the business managers that pay for advertising believe that half of what they spend is wasted, but they can't work out which half.[18] This is the environment in which the modern advertising industry operates.

It is interesting to think about how the advertising industry might improve its reputation. An attempt to do this by the *Advertising Federation of Australia* is informative. Their idea was to manage an accreditation system for their members and link this to the professional development of staff and compliance with the various codes and laws that affect advertising. Will this work? No, because it is voluntary and it is a self-regulation initiative that will lack credibility in the eyes of many people. Also it has no real sanctions for noncompliance and doesn't address the key causes of the reputation problem outlined above. Advertising needs to become more entertaining and thus less intrusive, and also more informative and thus useful if it is to enhance the reputation of the industry and the companies that use it.

What is curious about the degradation of the reputations of these new "sin" industries is that there were many warning signals that reputation trouble was brewing. Max Bazerman and Michael Watkins have called this phenomenon "predictable surprises."[19] A company has all the data it needs, but it fails to connect the dots. The obvious data are significant episodes of negative publicity. As was noted in chapter 8, media play two roles here. One is the investigative nature of company reporting. David Kocieniewski's article exposing the tax avoidance of *General Electric* was a good example. His peers rewarded him with a *Pulitzer Prize* for this reporting. The other is the platform the media provide for disaffected groups. The *Occupy Wall Street* movement was a good example of this. Even though they were largely leaderless and had a muddled message, they received considerable media attention that focused on the financial practices of big corporations.

A less public sign that reputations are eroding can often be found in social and public opinion research. There is a vibrant industry of these researchers in most industrialized countries that many companies ignore. Some that do invite these researchers into their management conferences generally find that the story told about the evolution and current state of social attitudes is interesting. But they don't know what to do with this information. It doesn't fit neatly into any part of the business or reporting line or budget plan. So it is pushed to the background and soon forgotten. Thus, when issues "blow up," many companies are surprised. And they are doubly surprised if they become the focus of negative publicity. The offshoring of work has been one such issue. Many people are disconcerted that companies don't make things at home and employ local people. Thus they are receptive to negative information about how these companies treat the workers in their overseas factories. Obesity is another issue. *Unilever*'s CEO publicly admitted in early 2013 that his company missed the growing concern over obesity, although you would think that by just looking at the people on the street this would seem obvious.[20]

It is easy for companies that focus on short-term performance to be surprised or blindsided by issues that have their origins in slowly changing social attitudes. What should have been anticipated and planned for manifests itself as a reputation crisis. Sometimes these are handled well, but often not! This reactive approach stands in stark contrast to the occasional company that tries to get ahead of the public debate. For example, the outdoor clothing company *Patagonia* has tried to lead its consumers to be more responsible environmental citizens and been applauded for its efforts. In contrast, *Chevron* has launched a public relations initiative called "Human Energy" that discusses a range of issues relating to the use fossil fuels. This effort has been challenged by

Greenpeace and others as "greenwash". The reputation trap here is captured in the old saying—"you can't be a part of the solution if you are a cause of the problem."

One final place to look to see how the reputation landscape is changing is after an economic crisis. As I write this chapter, the PIGS countries of Europe (Portugal, Ireland, Greece, Spain) have been and still are going through such a crisis. We can see on the nightly news the social turmoil that poor economic management inflicts on a country. We can also see which groups are blamed and who is held to account. In effect many such crises change the nature of the implied social contract vis-à-vis government, business, and society. And this means that one of the macro rules of the reputation game in chapter 2 has changed.

Honesty is the Best Corporate Reputation Policy

Many companies damage their reputations when they cut costs as a way to enhance their profitability. They suffer a customer backlash when it is discovered that they have substituted a cheaper ingredient into a product or offshored production to a lower cost country. Employees also often react negatively to such cost-cutting endeavors. For example, in 2001 in an effort to cut costs, *Dell* outsourced its product support to India and reduced the number of technicians who provided on-location service to its customers. Yet it continued to sell in-person service plans to its customers. Complaints from customers increased dramatically.[21] This is an example of product dishonesty because on the basis of past delivery customers have come to expect a certain level of quality service. Over the last decade many companies have made similar decisions. Paul Midler's book *Poorly Made in China* catalogs the risks involved in using China as a manufacturing source. He notes that many Chinese manufacturers engage in "quality fade."[22] In order to save costs, very small changes are made to the design or manufacturing or materials of the products exported. Often the importers suspect that this is occurring but do nothing until a product fails in the hands of a consumer.

Over the last two decades schools and universities have been particularly troubled by the accusation of intellectual depreciation. The claim that the language and numerical skills of graduates are insufficient to meet the needs of the modern workforce is an example of this. In the school system it is now difficult for teachers to stop children progressing through the system with their cohort regardless of their intellectual capability or their achieved knowledge. In the university system there has been the problem of "grade drift." Here and there we learn that every student gets an A or at worst a B. Nobody seems to fail a subject, especially when they have paid fees for their course. So we see depreciation in the basic quality expected, and the schools and universities singled out for attention should not be surprised to discover that they are not as admired and respected as they once were.

Honesty in its various forms is hard to enforce inside an organization. It is much easier to allow it to erode, often being eaten away in small pieces. For example, recall my story of the *Australian Graduate School of Management* in chapter 6. One of our key honesty issues involved the signaling power of our student grades. Was an A student really better than a B student? And had both students mastered the subject? The companies that recruited our students wanted to know the answer to these basic questions. In the early era when student fees were modest and faculty teaching was not evaluated by student satisfaction scores, most lecturers graded each student against a body of knowledge that was considered appropriate to the level of the course. In subjects like statistics, finance, and accounting, it was easy to judge whether a student had mastered the concepts. In subjects like marketing and leadership, it was more difficult.

Over time three things happened to challenge the intellectual honesty of this approach. One was that student fees increased significantly, and with them the expectations of the students that they would be taught everything they needed—as opposed to their learning what was required. The second was that the intellectual quality of the class increased—as measured by their average GMAT scores. The third was that the faculty was evaluated in part by student satisfaction scores. Their salaries and career prospects were now officially tied to their teaching. The three forces combined to put pressure on the distribution of grades to drift up. It soon became clear that more students were getting higher grades in every class. If this trend continued, the *AGSM* would begin to look like many US business schools where nearly every student got an A or at worst a B. We stopped this grade drift process by grading to a distribution in each subject. That is, only *X*% could get an A, *Y*% could get a B, and Z% could get a C or fail. All except the very best students hated it; many faculty disliked it, and most employers loved it. We needed such a rule because we couldn't trust ourselves to be intellectually honest.

The trouble with policing honesty inside an organization is that it is hard to define and enforce. There has to be a set of principles that guides behavior. Principles define what it means to be honest. Then there have to be some enforceable rules and sanctions. For example, for a time I chaired the examinations committee at the *AGSM*. When a faculty member submitted a distribution of grades that did not conform to the norm, the committee would not approve them for release. Arguments ensued. People got upset. I was sometimes abused. The committee held its ground. Honesty was maintained. Our desired reputation was tested. Feedback from recruiters was positive. Our reputation was validated. And now more than a decade later, I can still recall some of the arguments.

Respecting Employees and Customers is the Second Best Reputation Policy

A signal of employee recognition and respect is when a CEO talks about how "we" achieved certain results as opposed to how "he" or "she" achieved such outcomes.[23] The use of the plural rather than the singular is always well received by employees and often respected by outsiders. Another way in which senior managers respect their employees is to share sensitive financial information with them. This helps them understand how the company business model works and their role in the corporate ecosystem. In contrast, many managers subtly devalue the worth of their employees by calling them a human "resource" or a "strategic asset" or "human capital"—to be managed by the HR department. If people are a resource or an asset, then the language and modus operandi of business suggests that just like other assets and resources, they should be used, exploited, made more productive, and made less costly. This mindset soon permeates the organizational culture, and being a reputation ambassador can easily become an afterthought.

Another way that companies undermine the ambassadorial function of their employees is to put in place performance appraisal systems that force them to compete with each other rather than focus on creating value for stakeholders. The most vicious of these schemes have been called "rank and yank" or "stack-ranking" schemes. In such a scheme, employee performance is graded along a "vitality curve." Those at the top get the bonuses and those whose performance is in the lowest category are dismissed. Under the direction of Kenneth Lay *Enron* used this scheme. Every six months 10 to 20 percent of employees left the company. Another version of this is practiced by the best consultancy firms. Here, a large number of people are hired for a relatively few permanent positions. Nothing does more to de-motivate teamwork than such a practice. And in some cases an employee will stand back and let another person make a career-limiting mistake that might well damage the reputation of the company.

The way to overcome these problems is to get employees to value the future of the company and to feel that they are helping create this future. The sometimes ridiculed academic tenure system in universities does this. First, it is an incentive for the non-tenured faculty to work hard. Then it formally recognizes an outstanding contribution. It binds the recipient to the university and allows people to take make long-term investments in their research, teaching, and service, all of which enhance the reputation of their institution. Yes, it does have the downside that some older faculty can go to sleep on the job, but this is easily remedied by things like peer pressure and a significant salary adjustment.

In many organizations employees regard customers as more of a nuisance than a joy to serve. This might sound harsh, but employees often feel that customers fail to appreciate all the effort that a company makes on their behalf. Hence it is not uncommon to hear certain groups of customers referred to in derogatory terms. When this occurs and they are given unflattering code names, it is a sign of disrespect that can often flow into the customer service experience. The reputation trap here is to implicitly accept the frustration that employees express rather than search for and fix the root cause of the problem. One solution practiced by some American companies is to start calling their customers "partners," or "guests," or some other name that supposedly enhances their social status. To many non-Americans this just seems contrived and superficial, especially when the title is used during a service failure. It is better to fix the stakeholder value proposition than paper over the cracks with pages from a dictionary.

The Media

The media, both old and new, present some interesting challenges to managing corporate image and reputation. I will outline two. One focuses on the image presented in the media and whether or not this reflects the desired image of the company. I call this is the mirror trap. The other focuses on how companies publicly react to bad news rather than focus on its underlying cause. I call this the PR trap.

The Mirror Trap

An article in *The Economist* newspaper provides a good example of how companies can look into their corporate mirror and be pleased with what they see while the media and other people are looking into an industry mirror and are seeing a different image.[24] The article opens as follows:

> The barons of high-tech like to think of themselves as very different creatures from the barons of Wall Street. They create cool devices that let us carry the world in our pockets. They wear hoodies, not suits. And they owe their success to their native genius rather than to social connections.

Then comes the Steve Jobs quote about these people:

> ... the crazy ones, the misfits, the rebels, the troublemakers, the round pegs in square holes.

This portrayal is the desired self-image of many firms that inhabit Silicon Valley. However, the article then goes on to paint a different picture of this industry. This one is based on being just another group of capitalist companies that engage in tax avoidance, have a need to maximize growth and profits, have offshored most manufacturing jobs, have links with the military, and reap the sometimes huge personal financial rewards from the money trees they planted in the Valley.

The reputation trap here is to fail to appreciate how the perceptions and evaluations of some key opinion leaders are deliberately trying to change the reputation landscape. Being a member of the Silicon Valley club of companies was something that often conferred a dose of admiration and respect on each member. But articles like this one in *The*

Economist are trying to shatter the image of the Valley. If Silicon Valley becomes more like Wall Street, then the back story for each of these companies will have changed dramatically. No longer will customers, employees, investors, regulators, and local communities be as willing as they once were to tolerate the sometimes aberrant behavior of these special companies.

The interesting thing about a media attack on an industry or a group of like-minded companies is that it is hard for one company to effectively respond to the criticism, especially a company without a high-profile founder. It is more likely that each company will ascribe any blame to the others in the group and then proceed to get on with business as usual. Over the past few decades industries like education, pharmaceuticals, and processed food have followed this path. And many of their members have been guilty of not understanding and appreciating the emotional reaction of how some of their actions infuriated people. As a consequence they were slow to rectify the situation and apologize. Some reputation damage followed because of the next trap.

The Public Relations Trap

Each year many companies make some missteps that receive negative comment in the media. Often the business press focuses on how the events will impact the financial performance of the company. Its impact on employees, customers, and society tends to be appear in the weekend media. As the former *New York Times* and *Wall Street Journal* reporter Ryan Chittum notes, because the nature of professional journalism is to dig up a story, run it, and then move on to something else, most one-off stories rarely leave a large impression. To do so usually requires a drumbeat of reporting that pounds information into the collective consciousness and sometimes puts it on the agenda of a regulator.[25] Hence there tend to be two types of negative corporate stories, one with a short life span and the other with a broader and long-lasting impact. The conundrum is how to tell early on if a story will have a short or a long life cycle? And then what type of response is appropriate. For example, is a "we are sorry for …" type of response all that is necessary?

Consider the case of the *Commonwealth Bank of Australia (CBA)*. It was savaged in the press for having given bad financial advice to 12,000 of its customers. The delivery of poor financial advice happened over a number of years. The bank admitted that it was caused by a sales-driven organizational culture embedded in a flawed compliance structure.[26] The incident surfaced in a parliamentary inquiry and then in the media, via the efforts of a former employee whistleblower.[27] Because the bank had been the prime subject in the parliamentary inquiry, the press and the opposition party in the Australian Parliament called for a Royal Commission into the bank and its senior management. The chair of the parliamentary inquiry was scathing in his condemnation of the bank's financial advisory practices and of its callous attitude to rectifying the losses of its customers. Anybody who watched the nightly news was aware of the bank's behavior. This included all their customers.

This incident raises two interesting questions. First, how should the bank respond? Second, how did it respond? Before answering these questions, it is worth noting that the *CBA* is one of the biggest and most profitable companies in Australia. It has also been afforded special status by government fiscal policy as one of the "four pillars" of Australian banking. (There are four such big banks.) All these banks offer a similar array of financial products and services, and while switching banks is quite easy, there is a general perception that there is no significant gain to be made by making the effort to change banks. With this in mind, some media commentators suggested that most of *CBA*'s customers would stay with the bank regardless of how it responded.

Now how should the bank respond? It is easy to build the case that this incident exposed some serious shortcomings in the bank's culture and compliance systems and that these need to be addressed. Also the customers affected should be proactively identified by the bank rather than wait for them to complain. Then there are all their financial hardships resulting from this bank failure that should be rectified. Various blogs and newspaper stories outlined such a remedy. A quick "we are sorry, we will fix the internal problems, and we will ensure that all affected customers are fully recompensed" style of response was expected by both the media and the bank's customers. This was not how the *CBA* responded.

Following the revelation about its misdeeds, the bank was slow to respond and defensive in its attitude to both the victims and the media. Initially, the incident was framed as a "rogue employee" problem by the bank. And later still, it was discovered that nine of these rogue employees were still working for the bank. The CEO was slow to front the media and apologize to the affected customers. In the process he announced the formation of review committee with independent oversight to deliver fair and consistent outcomes to the affected customers, with the proviso that the restitution would be limited to money lost as a result of bad advice. There was no mention of financial compensation for emotional distress. And he expected that the total amount of compensation would not affect the company's share price.

A few months after the media storm subsided, the real contrition of the *CBA* was revealed when it rewarded the senior manager in charge of the troubled division at the time a significant performance bonus. He received remuneration of $5.6 million, which was a rise of $1.1 million. He later resigned. And as expected, the media and affected customers were incensed.[28] The bank's actual response reveals two reputation insights. One is that the bank thinks that its corporate reputation is probably not very important to its commercial success, be that with the general public, the regulators, or its customers. The second is that the people who really matter in the *CBA* are the core group of senior managers.

Only time will tell if the *CBA*'s framing of this crisis as a minor PR problem was correct. Unless its customers defect in numbers that are large enough to reduce its profitability, we should expect to see the bank continue to seek profit, sometimes at the expense of its corporate reputation. Such customer defection will only occur if two things happen. One is that customers place more value on the reputations of their banks than they currently do. The other is that if one or more of the bank's competitors are perceived to have a significantly better reputation that the *CBA*. To date, there is no obvious sign that either condition is emerging. For example, a short time after the *CBA* was exposed for providing poor financial advice, its biggest competitor was exposed for doing a similar thing.

The media play an interesting and as yet poorly understood role in the formation and destruction of corporate reputations. In many cases, their influence seems large, but in many other cases, their influence is far less significant. The problem is that when asked, media representatives will always say that it a significant factor in the process of reputation formation and destruction. And as new forms of media emerge and jockey for prominence, the potential role of each one becomes more uncertain. Michael Porter's observation about new technology, noted earlier, seems worth repeating here as a corporate reputation trap, namely don't confuse a new technology with a company's strategy.[29]Indeed this would occur when managers think that the new media must become the anchor point of the company's reputation strategy rather than it being an enabler of this strategy.

10

Distracting Reputation Myths

The business school where I spent most of my academic life was small and focused on trying to do a few things well. We developed a reputation for quality in these areas, and over the years we periodically had to protect this reputation from some of our deans. The ones who were past academics tended to focus the school on achieving academic excellence while the ones from the city periodically tried to get us to expand in any direction that the advisory board thought was fashionable at the time. Many of these strategic redirections would have forced us to put our current reputation at risk. The classic example occurred when one dean suggested that we open an office in Asia. To do so would require committing our best resources to this venture. Our size meant that these resources would no longer be available to support our current operations. As one old professor explained to the dean in a faculty forum, "we are about to become a small, late entrant into a highly competitive market where the institutional arrangements are opaque, where nobody is making any money, and where we have no obvious comparative advantage." Widespread passive resistance across the faculty effectively scuttled the venture.[1] But incidents like this taught us that it is easy to be distracted by current events and fashionable management ideas.

In this chapter I will describe a number of ideas that distract the attention of companies from creating a reputation for excellence. I call these ideas myths because their popularity far exceeds conclusions that should be drawn from the available evidence. Some of these myths have been challenged by the global financial crisis, some have been challenged by scholarly research, and some by examining the assumptions on which they are based. And yes, there is some truth in each myth, but adhering to their claims very often diverts attention from creating a winning corporate reputation by being simply better.

Evidence for the first myth comes from an extensive research program undertaken by my colleague Timothy Devinney and his research team. Over the last decade they have surveyed thousands of people around the world. Their findings challenge the views held by disciples of corporate social responsibility (CSR) who believe that these activities necessarily underpin a good corporate reputation. Devinney's research gives comfort to many scholars and managers who are skeptical of the value of engaging in CSR programs that are unrelated to the core strategy of their company.

Evidence for the second myth comes from a thought experiment and the lack of systematic evidence that suggests that companies that are more transparent generally have better corporate reputations. And as illustrated below, transparency should only be expected to enhance a desired corporate reputation in some very specific circumstances. These comments stand in contrast to the advice proffered by many social commentators who suggest that sunlight is the best disinfectant for unprincipled corporate conduct. This piece of folk wisdom confuses transparency with telling the truth. As two of the biggest examples of corporate fraud in Europe and America demonstrated, *Parmalat* and *Enron* disclosed massive amounts of information required by the regulators, but neither told the truth. While there may be a link between honesty and transparency, the latter does not guarantee the former.

Evidence for the third myth comes from the global financial crisis and some major corporate disasters. This really showed us that some companies are too big to fail regardless of their corporate reputations, before, during, or after a crisis. This evidence also suggests that many misdeeds do not accrue the reputation penalties that the conventional wisdom suggests they should.

Evidence for the fourth myth comes from accounting and the descriptions of corporate reputation provided earlier. Saying that a good corporate reputation is an "asset" is really the wrong concept for the stock of goodwill created by having a good reputation. Rather than being an intangible asset, this stock of goodwill is more like the equity in one's house. The house is the asset and the equity is what the homeowner actually owns net of the bank mortgage.

Evidence for the fifth myth comes from understanding how reputation rankings of companies are created and how they can and should be used. Some of these are better constructed than others and some more useful than others.

Belief in any of the five myths can easily distract a company from investing in the activities most likely to create a reputation of distinction. They have also distracted much scholarly inquiry into the nature and nurture of corporate reputations. These are intriguing ideas that can be put aside when thinking about how to create a corporate reputation designed to create a competitive advantage.

1. *Adding a Bit More Corporate Social Responsibility*

Over the last decade CSR developed its own industry. Codes of conduct were developed and some became recognized, specialist CSR report writers emerged, ratings agencies evaluated companies for their CSR contributions, consultants specialized in helping companies develop CSR programs, NGOs sometimes bullied companies into adopting animal welfare and fair work practices for their overseas contractors, a conference circuit emerged, and academics did specialized research. There were enough social and environmental disasters to feed this industry with examples of poor corporate practice. For many companies, displaying their CSR activities became politically correct. For others, it became a passion of top management—sometimes as a strategic imperative, sometimes as a whim, but often as a public relations exercise. And as the public relations industry took hold of CSR, this area of endeavor earned a reputation for flakiness among many business people.

Earlier I noted some concerns about the veracity of a CSR approach to building a reputation that will offer a commercial advantage. Here are two more concerns. The first is that to be perceived as a very good corporate citizen, the company must also be seen to be socially legitimate. Here the comparison point is a set of broad social and commercial standards of performance.[2] While some of these standards are decreed by regulation, many others are contested. This debate is called the "grey areas" of reputation. Thus, to win, a company must use its CSR practices to be seen as more legitimate than its competitors in some "grey areas" of morals and ethics. This is quite a difficult task to accomplish, especially when a social critic can identify a single aspect of the company to criticize.[3] As the saying goes, "the moral high ground is really expensive real estate."

The second issue with CSR is convincing CEOs and shareholders that a CSR-based social reputation really matters to the commercial success of their company. As noted earlier, business gurus such as Michael Porter say that it should, if not in the short term then definitely in the longer term. And CSR, especially of the sustainability version, should ultimately pay off in terms of better financial performance. But empirical evidence of such a general effect is mixed. For example, two studies published in 2013 challenge the notion that CEOs should guide their companies to be more socially responsible. One study conducted by the *Harvard Business Review,* which has repeatedly published Porter's advocacy, found that the correlation between the financial performance and social and environmental performance of 3,143 worldwide companies was ZERO.[4] Another study by Marc Mazodier and Amir Rezaee found that the stock market returns to philanthropic sponsorships were slightly negative.[5] These findings are not good news for CSR advocates, especially the new breed of US benefit corporations that are designed around providing a specific type of social contribution.[6] They also do not support the idea that a CSR-based reputation will provide a company with a competitive advantage.

Two studies that I could find where CSR helped a company to achieve a better commercial outcome examined how consumers care about the public responsibility of the companies they buy from. For example, one large opinion poll study found that a company's reputation for CSR mattered to consumers, but not nearly as much as the company's reputation for fairness toward consumers or its leadership and success.[7] Another study of US undergraduates found that a company's CSR reputation had a small positive effect on the evaluation of one attribute of the company's new product. Here again, the company's reputation for its market leadership and R&D capability had a much more significant effect on the evaluation of the new product.[8]

Notwithstanding this evidence, the corporate reputation-enhancing potential of CSR is defined by two factors. The first is what David Vogel called the market for virtue.[9] If there is sizable demand for CSR inside the company by employees wanting to engage, and outside the company by customers and investors, then serving this market is a sensible reputation-enhancing activity. Sadly what Vogel and many others have discovered is that the market for companies seen to be "doing good" is quite limited.[10] Readily available evidence of this is the low market shares of the companies that adopt CSR as their primary competitive or differentiation position. For example, I can't think of any case where such a company is a market leader in its category.

To further illustrate this effect, Timothy Devinney's research team conducted a study of the reputation-enhancing effects of a good social reputation on winning the war for talent.[11] This was a proposition advanced by global HR consultancies like *Hill & Knowlton* and *Kelly Services*. We asked people to choose among job contracts that were made up of functional attributes such as time demands; motivational attributes such as opportunities for promotion; social attributes such as organizational culture; financial aspects such as salary, and reputation attributes such as the social reputation of the potential employer. Now a good social reputation would be valued if a potential employee was prepared to trade off some of the other aspects of the job offer for the opportunity to work for a company of good social standing. We surveyed 2,035 people who were in the job market and found that without exception, social reputation mattered but only very marginally. If job offers had similar financial and functional attributes, then a better social reputation might act as a tie-breaker. In no case would it substitute for good basic terms and conditions of employment. The HR policy implications of these findings are profound. If a company wants to win the war for talent, then it should first offer the best working arrangements.

The second factor driving the ability of CSR to enhance a company's desired reputation is the fit between CSR and the core activities of the company. In essence CSR can be a management whim (lose fit), an important community service obligation, a part of the company's values, or an integral part of the company's strategy (tight fit). In the most extreme lose fit case, CSR usually has no relationship to the core activities or the DNA of the company. And because of this many people who are not the recipients of the CSR don't care very much about this aspect of the company's activities. In fact, as I noted earlier, some research has shown that companies that engage in financial earnings manipulation or that have poor product and environmental performance are significantly more likely to engage in whimsical types of CSR.[12] While this is somewhat rare, the next example is quite common.

Many companies seek to deflect attention from parts of the organization that might not be well respected by engaging in a well-publicized CSR program. In effect they bolt-on various CSR activities to their core activities. For example, in the United States, in 2000, when *Philip Morris* spent $150 million on television advertising to publicize the $115 million it had contributed to support shelters for battered women, it was pillaged in the press.[13] In Australia the Big Four retail banks (*ANZ*, *CBA*, *NAB*, and *Westpac*) have all used a variety of CSR programs to deflect attention among the general public from how they achieve their record-breaking profitability.[14] At the heart of this antagonism are the high interest rates and fees charged to consumers.[15] To help counter their poor reputation, all the big banks implemented CSR programs. But many of these activities had no relationship to either the core business of banking or the primary cause of their poor reputations. For example, at the time of writing, on its corporate website the *CBA* bank proudly proclaims its support of Community Cricket (developing this sport among the community), raising funds for breast cancer research, and Clean Up Australia Day (an annual environmental cleanup event). *Westpac* bank has community partnerships with surf lifesaving, the Melbourne Heart Foundation, the Salvation Army, and two football clubs. The other two banks have similar diverse CSR engagements. All the banks are lauded by the recipient community groups for their largesse—and often given awards for their efforts by the CSR industry. However, while these are all worthwhile causes, they are really nothing more than the sugarcoating of the unpalatable fact that it is the interest rates on loans and customer fees and charges that help make these retail banks some of the most profitable in the world.[16] While the reputations of the big banks continue to languish below many other companies in the economy, no single bank suffers a reputation disadvantage to its rivals because they all have similar product and service offerings and thus reputations.

Because I referred to *Apple*'s CSR earlier, I will add it again to this discussion. When Steve Jobs returned to the company, one of the first things he did was to cut the company's philanthropic donations. When I wrote this chapter, I searched the US corporate website for the company's philanthropy using this word in their internal search engine and got "no results were found." Their website does have a set of environmental reports, but these do not compare the company to any benchmark such as a competitor nor are they audited. And as mentioned elsewhere, *Apple* is one of many large US companies that actively practice tax avoidance.[17] So it seems that the social responsibility aspects of the company do not play a significant part in shaping its overall reputation.

While all these examples illustrate that a company's CSR actions or lack thereof don't seem to materially affect its overall reputation, there still might be some situations where CSR is a valuable addition to one's reputation. My best guess is that where this may occur is for the infrastructure companies that provide services that are fundamental to economic efficiency and social development. For example, the big telecommunications companies build and maintain the information superhighways that facilitate commerce, provide entertainment to the masses, and enable people to connect with family and friends. The big oil companies provide the raw material for energy, plastics, chemicals, and many drugs. The electricity companies light and power the world we live in. The health care companies look after our health. All these types of companies have a profound community service obligation because they each touch many of the fundamental aspects of the lives of the citizens of the countries in which they operate. My suggestion to them is that they would be better corporate citizens, and respected for this, if their primary focus was on doing a better and more efficient job before sponsoring other needed social causes.

2. *Running Naked through the Markets*

The idea that companies should be transparent has been fashionable for a long time. The following quip and quote put the case well.

What you see is what you get and what you don't see gets you.

Anonomous

Sunlight is said to be the best of disinfectants.

Louis Brandeis (1913).

Watchdogs like *Transparency International* study publicly available information to gauge how big companies are committed to abiding by the law, anti-corruption, and providing information about their internal workings. Charles Fombrun, the major academic and consulting guru in the corporate reputation field has advocated that companies engage in voluntary disclosure of information about themselves.[18] However, the paradox of the notion that more information means more transparency was noted by the Nobel economics laureate Herbert Simon who suggested that a wealth of information often leads to a poverty of attention.

After the global financial crisis the push for more transparency gained further momentum. One argument was that if taxpayer dollars were required to bail out companies, then surely the public had the right to look inside these organizations—and then roundly criticize what they did not like about their morals, protocols, and behaviors.[19] Another line of argument is that greater transparency will lead to better corporate governance—having decisions scrutinized by all manner of critics will help improve the ethical nature of the company's key decisions. The constraint on this line of argument for improving the reputations of companies is that there are existing corporate laws and regulations, ratings agencies, and institutes of accountants and directors that proscribe what good corporate governance entails for public companies. Hence most people may be excused for thinking that most of these companies are already adequately governed. In the case of private companies the paradox is that they are private because they want to remain private. And as *The Economist* newspaper recently noted, the number of public companies in Britain and the United States is falling and the number of private companies and other forms of enterprise that have opaque governance is increasing.[20]

Another issue with the argument that more transparency will lead to more ethical decisions is that your ethics are likely to be different from mine.[21] In a corporate context this is the issue of moral agency—the ability of the company, as opposed to its officers and employees, to make ethical decisions on behalf of its shareholders and other stakeholders. This boils down to the two questions of (1) who counts, and (2) what interests held by those who count, count?[22] A common situation where this issue plays out for companies is in the area of bribery. When operating in many countries bribes to government officials are the ethical norm, and as some recent research has discovered, these are generally an economically solid investment.[23] A classic example of this issue emerged in the investigation of the *Australian Wheat Board* (AWB). They, like approximately 2,000 other companies, were found guilty of paying kickbacks to the regime of Saddam Hussein. In *AWB*'s case this was to secure large wheat contracts. The ethical problem was that even though *AWB* had a transparent code of ethics, the group of managers responsible for securing these wheat contracts would not sign it. They practiced their own code—do whatever it takes. Their approach was justified by the claim that "everyone's doing it."[24] Their code of ethics helped them secure about 90 percent of Iraqi's wheat market. Thus, while there was a public uproar when this fact became public knowledge and the Australian government was embarrassed, many wheat farmers and investors were not so publicly outraged. This type of issue highlights that what employees, investors, consumers, business partners, journalists, and the local community consider good corporate behavior will often differ considerably. Hence, whom should managers placate?

The dilemma here is that what investors, regulators, and the civil society want is information about how a company is run—its assets and liabilities, its risks, and its future prospects—that is truthful, understandable, relevant, standardized, and public. And this is also precisely the type of information that competitors would appreciate. So what should companies do? Let me outline five types of transparency. The first type is practiced by company analysts and seeks to fully understand the business model of a company. Sometimes what is found here leads to a loss of confidence in the company and will damage its reputation. The second is an internal practice that is thought to lead to better quality decisions, better corporate outcomes, and ultimately a better reputation. The other three types are different forms of external transparency, of which the latter two seem to describe contemporary practice. Here the idea is that companies that are more transparent are more credible and accountable and that these factors lead them to have better reputations. However, I am aware of no research that verifies this claim.

- Forensic transparency—company analysts use the information available about a company to understand how it operates and how it makes money. For example, for some major airlines the frequent-flyer program and the treasury function are more profitable than the operational side of the business. So while the airline accrues its primary reputation from its operations, it makes most of its money from its non-core activities. There is a touch of schizophrenia about this.

- Internal transparency—company managers present their reports in a forum where other managers challenge and debate them in face-to-face meetings. Sometimes these forums include the people who are affected by the decisions. Interestingly, this was the culture in the early years at *Enron* when it was effectively run by Richard Kinder. It also characterizes the internal culture of *Macquarie Bank*.
- Fish bowl transparency—a company would operate so that any interested person could scrutinize all its decision making and actions. Now this really would be a "public" company.
- Voluntary transparency—a company provides information that allows people to understand its mission, morals, strategy, and the incentive schemes of senior managers. Companies that adopt this approach will also practice compliance transparency.
- Compliance transparency—a company abides by the disclosure requirements of the regulators and stock exchanges on which it is listed. The guiding principle here is would a specific piece of new information influence the decision of a person to buy or sell securities in the company at its current market price?[25]

The problem with forensic transparency is that you can spend hours on the website of a big company trawling through mega bites of information. Pretty soon you realize that much of it has been written by the corporate lawyers or the public affairs department and is so spin-doctored that it is futile. Often the issues that are crucial to reputation and performance are not reported, such as intellectual property, the value of brand names, levels of customer satisfaction, and the capabilities of the workforce. Companies know about these factors, but they are reluctant to create measures and report them. Other important information is difficult to interpret. For example, fully understanding the financial engineering, treasury practices, tax policy, and accounting reports of a large company is a real challenge for most people. And consider the plight of the tax assessors at the US *Internal Revenue Service* when *General Electric* submitted 57,000 (electronic) pages of tax information in 2009. When is enough transparency enough!

The problem with internal transparency is that it remains internal. Seldom do the debates become public, and often unexpected outcomes are inadequately explained. For example, when the highly respected private company *Seventh Generation* fired Jeffrey Hollender, one of the company's cofounders, neither he nor the board was forthcoming about the reasons for his departure. And this is despite transparency being one of the founding principles of the company.[26] In a public company this would be a classic corporate governance failure.

The problem with fish bowl transparency is that it is unrealistic. It is noted to help draw a contrast with the other types of external transparency. The problem with voluntary transparency is that there is little agreement among the purveyors of best practice as to what best practice should be.[27] Laundry lists of desirable information produced by organizations such as the *Global Reporting Initiative* often encourage companies to pick and choose to report where their company excels rather than where it is deficient. And the diversity of reports produced each year makes it difficult to compare performance across companies and across time. Two other problems with voluntary reporting are that most reports are not audited by a credible outsider and there are no penalties for noncompliance with best practice. Hence how this information is supposed to enhance the reputations of the stakeholders who really matter to a company's success is unclear.

The problem with Compliance Transparency is that it sets up an environment in which reputations can be easily tarnished. Companies are motivated to practice what is called "rules lawyering" or "creative compliance." This involves exploiting the complexity, technicalities and loopholes in the law rather than trying to comply with the spirit of the law.[28] Consider this proclamation by a member of one of the largest UK accountancy firms:

> No matter what legislation is in place, the accountants and lawyers will find a way around it. Rules are rules, but rules are meant to be broken.[29]

Thus, when corporate practice is seen to subvert the intention of the government, it is motivated to introduce more rules and regulations. The environment in which companies operate becomes more complex, and the compliance costs of both parties increase. And there is ample opportunity for a company to receive negative publicity for its exploits in abiding by the letter of the law rather than the spirit of the law.

It is little wonder then that reliable, widespread evidence for the beneficial effects of more transparency on corporate reputation is hard to find. However, counterexamples where companies that lack transparency still have good reputations are abundant. For example, in the beauty contest myth, as described below, *Google* is a standout performer in the reputation polls and yet it is known for its secretiveness. Also most people are blissfully unaware of the tax practices of the companies they admire. And a look at corporate websites suggests that many companies are happy for them to remain this way. While their social reports extol their philanthropy and other CSR activities they seldom boast about how their effective tax rate is lower than the statutory rate of corporate tax. The point of this example is to illustrate that often hiding potentially controversial information in a complicated document such as the company's annual report is an effective way not to intentionally damage one's reputation.

Where increased transparency makes sense from a reputation-building perspective as opposed to, say, a corporate governance perspective is when the salient beliefs of some key stakeholders about the company's good attributes or behavior are unknown or incorrect. This situation provides an opportunity for a company to enhance its reputation. Figure 10.1 suggests that this is a somewhat rare situation—the bottom right quadrant. In the two cases where the company knows it is poor, then being more transparent is likely to create a worse reputation. In the case where people think that the company is good and the company knows

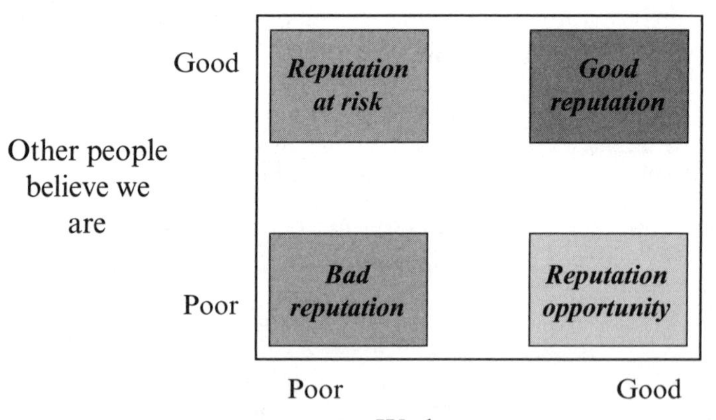

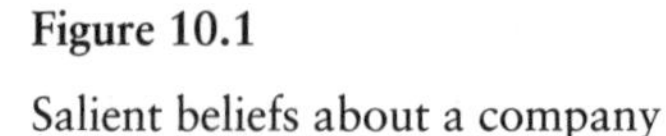

Figure 10.1

Salient beliefs about a company

that it is good, then becoming more transparent is redundant. Hence in many circumstances being more transparent is likely to result in reputation damage.

Another time when more transparency is better than less is when the company is involved in a crisis. At the time of writing this chapter, my former university is being accused of hiding a case of academic misconduct. The university's response is that it has run two inquiries into the matter, one internal and the other involving external reviewers, and both have exonerated the accused professor and his laboratory. The problem is that the university, which is a publicly funded institution, will not release the reports for public scrutiny. Thus last night's five minute lead item on the national television news made the university look as if it was trying to hide something. As one media critic said, often rumors about an organization have an odious smell of truth.

3. *To Operate in Society We Need to Be Good*

The global financial crisis (GFC) of 2007 to 2009 is considered by many people as the worst financial crisis since the Great Depression. Economies were put at risk of collapse and trillions of dollars of corporate and private wealth were destroyed around the world. The *US Financial Crisis Enquiry Commission* reported in 2011 that the crisis was avoidable.[30] It was caused by among other things, the widespread failures in financial regulation, dramatic breakdowns in corporate governance, the incorrect pricing of risk, and *Wall Street* practices that created a shadow banking system that few people really understood. In effect the crisis was caused by some of the key factors that underpinned the good financial performance of Corporate America and thus its good reputation!

Because of regulatory failures and the international nature of finance, what started out as a designed-in-America financial crisis soon morphed into an economic crisis that spread around the world, and then became a social crisis for people in America and other countries whose economic circumstances were damaged.[31] Apart from firms like *Lehman Brothers* `that were sacrificed on the altar of public opinion, few of the top people who were directly responsible for the crisis paid much of a personal price for the damage their decisions and lack of oversight caused others. Yes, many people in the financial industry lost their jobs, but a few years after the crisis, it was business as usual with huge salaries and bonuses being paid to these captains of industry.

The GFC finally put an end to the proposition that a good citizenship reputation underpins a company's social license to operate. For example, the *US Treasury* invested about $200 billion through its Capital Purchase Program to support hundreds of American banks. It invested $60 billion to bail out *General Motors* and *Chrysler*, some of which it may not recover. Ironically, because both *GM* and *Chrysler* were struggling financially at the time, the GFC gave them a chance to reinvent themselves. Another irony here is that the *Occupy Wall Street* movement and many opinion polls at the time were strongly against these bailouts. These polls reflected the poor reputation of many of the companies that asked for, and received government assistance.

Before the GFC it was widely known that some companies were too important to government revenue generation to stifle. For example, the companies involved in the alcohol, gambling, and tobacco industries contribute billions of dollars annually to government revenue. Government simply can't afford for these companies to go out of business. What became blindingly obvious during the GFC was that the major financial institutions and some other companies were also "too big to fail"[32] and "too big to jail."[33] However, this should not have been the surprise that it was. Governments of all political persuasions routinely offer industry assistance to companies that employ large numbers of workers in key electorates.

4. *A Good Corporate Reputation Is an Intangible Asset*

The editors of the recently published *Oxford Handbook of Corporate Reputations* state that one of the few uncontested principles of corporate reputation scholarship is that a good corporate reputation is a firm-specific, rent-producing asset.[34] To help substantiate this idea, the scholarly literature has sought to ground the construct in the more developed theoretical domain of corporate strategy. Here the resource-based theory of the firm has been used to suggest that a good corporate reputation is one of the intangible assets that companies use to help create a competitive advantage.[35] This theory posits that a company invests in acquiring and deploying tangible and intangible resources (assets) that allow it to exploit market opportunities and/or minimize threats. To provide a competitive advantage, an asset must be difficult to imitate, durable, appropriable, nonsubstitutable, and superior.[36] In the case of a good corporate reputation, this means that it is difficult for competitors to build, it lasts a long time, it offers its owner a benefit, a competitor cannot deploy a substitute for a good reputation (e.g., a high-technology manufacturing process or a celebrity endorser), and it is significantly better than those of competitors. In combination, this is a tough test for most intangible assets including a corporate reputation to pass.

This intangible asset test becomes even harder to pass when one considers that corporate reputations are evaluations of a company held by its stakeholders and other people. Because these evaluations are only ever partially controlled by the company, reputations are quite a fickle construct—they are good or bad and are strong or weak. They are at the behest of different groups of stakeholders. Yes, companies try to manipulate them, but they are really owned by each stakeholder and are in effect "rented" by the company. Hence they can't really be an "asset" or "liability" of the company. These terms have a common business meaning where it is assumed that assets can be bought and sold and liabilities have to be paid off. And in the discipline of accounting, they have specific meaning, mandated measures, and statutory reporting requirements.

In accounting, intangible assets like reputations are usually regarded as goodwill.[37] If one company purchases another, the difference between the book value of the acquired company and the amount of money paid is called purchased goodwill. This is required to be amortized in the Profit&Loss statement over a definite period of time. This type of goodwill has a market value that is written off. The accountants also recognize internally generated goodwill like the value of the corporate brand name. In contrast, and somewhat peculiarly, this is not permitted to be recognized as an asset of the company. The expenditures that generate the intangible assets that underpin internal goodwill are recorded as expenses, but the total asset is never given a specific value. Thus, from an accounting perspective, both types of goodwill appear in the Profit&Loss statement as direct or indirect expenses that decrease earnings per share, and thus the share market value of the firm. In essence the accounting treatment of goodwill, like the company brand and reputation, is the opposite of what one would expect from the reputation literature!

Another problem with regarding corporate reputation as a quasi-accounting asset has been outlined by Frank Partnoy.[38] If reputation is regarded as an asset, then it should be expendable—otherwise, why invest in it? Thus, once a company has a stock of reputation, it should be considering how to use it—by charging higher prices, shirking on its expected commitments, defrauding others, or engaging in illegal behavior. These are all rational commercial ways to use a good reputation. The question now becomes at what rate to invest in and monetize the stock of reputation? In this line of argument a good corporate reputation has shifted roles—from being a private mechanism to encourage and reward good corporate behavior, or measure success, or regulate dubious behavior, or punish bad behavior, to being just another asset to exploit. Thus the metaphor of reputation as asset can easily lead to a different corporate mindset from that used by many reputation advocates. An example of this use of reputation was discussed earlier when examining how the Australian airline *Qantas* engineered a crisis and then monetized a part of its good reputation as a way of paying for the resolution of a dispute with its workforce.

Given the quite different natures of reputation, intangible assets, and goodwill, it is confusing to talk about reputations as "assets." It is even more confusing to try to put a specific dollar value on them such that they might appear like other accounting assets in the balance sheet of a company.[39]

5. *Winning a Beauty Contest Is Not the Same as Winning the Reputation Game*

The Economist newspaper has a regular column authored by a group called Schumpeter. On April 17, 2012, Schumpeter was invited to a presentation of the *Reputation Institute*'s annual RepTrak™ corporate reputation survey. The *Reputation Institute* is a scholar-led consultancy that has been studying corporate reputations since 1997. It is supported by a number of academics and large companies around the world. It has its own proprietary measure of corporate reputation that is used to rate and then rank companies in a number of different countries. After attending the presentation, Schumpeter did the unthinkable— wrote a piece in *The Economist* that was skeptical about corporate reputations.[40]

Schumpeter had three criticisms of the advice proffered by their hosts and their measure of reputation. First, reputation measurement conflates too many different things. The RepTrak™ measure is made up of twenty different scales in the areas of leadership, performance, innovation, the workplace, ethics, citizenship, and products and services. Second, the reputation industry overplays the power of reputations. The mantra at the presentation was that what the company stands for matters more than the products and services it sells.[41] Third, a central conceit drives the industry. The message was that to have a better reputation, work harder at managing your reputation.

What probably set Schumpeter off against the corporate reputation industry was the reputation ranking of companies in table 10.1. The raw numbers give a false sense of precision. Many senior managers and business commentators like Schumpeter regard such lists as beauty contests. And as I noted in chapter 1, many CEOs and Schumpeter don't see the commercial relevance of these lists.

As you would expect, the *Reputation Institute* disagrees with this argument—vehemently! They argue that a company's reputation is formed across the wide variety of factors that they measure, and by analyzing peoples' perceptions across these factors, they can see where a company needs to improve. There is some merit to this argument if the people who rate the company matter to its success, and they know what they are

Table 10.1
2012 Rep Trak™winners

Global winners	UK winners
BMW (80.8)	Rolls Royce Aerospace (84.03)
SONY (79.31)	Dyson (83.67)
Walt Disney Company (78.92)	Alliance Boots (83.61)
DAIMLER (78.54)	Marks & Spencer (82.18)
Apple (78.49)	John Lewis (81.82)
Google (78.05)	Jaguar / Land Rover (80.35)
Microsoft (77.98)	Mothercare (79.94)
Volkswagen (77.04)	Selfridges (79.05)
Canon (76.98)	William Grant & Sons (78.99)
Lego (76.35)	Specsavers (78.89)

Note: Numbers are each company's Rep Trak™ score out of 100.

rating. And herein is a problem for RepTrak™ and other opinion polls that survey members of the general public. First, the opinions of most of the people surveyed don't really matter to the companies rated. They are not major investors, key account customers, employees, important business partners, journalists, community opinion leaders, or government regulators. Most are merely spectators. And most of these people don't, and can't know about many of the factors they are asked to rate. For example, how many members of the general public know about whether the companies listed in table 10.1 "pay their employees fairly" or have "potential for future growth" (which are two of the questions asked).

There are, however, four reasons why RepTrak™ and other reputation rankings that poll members of the general public might be useful. I say might because we need research to test these hypotheses.

- Victories in certification contests help legitimize companies by relying on the taken-for-granted axiom that the winners are better than the losers.[42] And so this status might embellish some of the attributes of a winning company's products and services.
- Sometimes the opinions of a disparate group of people, also known as a "crowd," can provide an informed view of a company. Here, a crowd will be "wise" when (1) there is a diversity of opinion, (2) people's opinions are not determined by the opinions of those around them, (3) people draw on their local knowledge, and (4) there is some mechanism (like the Internet) that exists for turning these private judgments into a collective action.[43]When these conditions hold, we have a "wise crowd." And in such situations a poll like RepTrak™ might act as an early warning signal about the state of a company's reputation. For example, it is not unusual to find that managers tend to believe that their company has a good reputation if there is no indication that it is bad.[44] Often these polls suggest that the company has either no strong reputation or that some aspects of its reputation are not as good as managers think. Alternatively, if the polls signal that the company is respected and liked by a wide range of people, this may translate into an increase in confidence and trust by some key stakeholders—if they believe that the admiration of the general public is important to the continued success of the company.

- ublicity surrounding these rankings gets people to think about corporate reputation as something to consider in their decision to engage with companies. Thus, if more people insist that companies act in ways that enhance their reputations, then companies will respond to these demands.
- Some celebrity CEOs like to bask in the prestige of a good ranking. When this happens, corporate reputation may take on a more important role inside the company.

However, all these reasons obscure the more cynical role of these polls, namely to gain publicity for the host organization and lubricate its business opportunities. And this is where Schumpeter's criticism hurt. It directly challenged the legitimacy of the *Reputation Institute* and its measure.

As I noted earlier there are some reputation polls that do matter to the organizations rated. One group of these polls rate business schools. Three prominent ones are conducted by *Business Week*, *The Financial Times*, and *The Economist*. They use a variety of measures of reputation and gather data from the people who really matter to the success of a business school, namely students, alumni, and recruiters. The business schools actively try to improve their ranking, alumni bask in the glory of a good result, and prospective students use the ranking to help decide where to go. Notwithstanding the considerable academic criticism about how these measures of reputation are constructed, this is a game that the business school deans feel they have to play in.[45]

Before a company becomes concerned about any type of reputation ranking, it should ask three questions:

1. Is the ranking based on the salient beliefs of key stakeholders about what really matters to them?
2. Does the ranking provide a useful template for change?
3. Is the ranking a legitimate device for promoting the company's reputation?

Only positive answers to these questions will render a ranking useful.

11

Frequently Asked Questions

This chapter is for managers. The following questions are the ones that business school students and attendees at management development programs often ask that I have not addressed earlier. Because there is little research that directly addresses each question, my answers will be based on a blend of scholarship and intuition. And occasionally I will note that an answer is my best guess.

When do organizations need a good corporate reputation to secure a social license to operate?

Put simply, most companies don't need a formal social license to carry on their current operations. It has already been implicitly granted because they are successfully operating. Companies providing products and services in fields such as the arts, banking, education, energy, entertainment, food, clothing, housing, medicine, telecommunications, and transport are welcomed by the societies they serve. Modern society can't do without them. And as the global financial crisis demonstrated, when some of these companies wantonly abuse this invitation, they are reprimanded but not hounded out of business.

However, some companies are forced by the nature of their business to invest in a good reputation as a precondition to operate in new fields. For example, mining and energy companies must go to wherever the earth yields up their valued resources. Often the location of a new mine is controlled by a demanding government. And to get access to the resources the company must dig up the terrain, build transport infrastructure, and sometimes move communities. These activities require a social license to operate. And a good corporate reputation can be helpful here.

Peter Firestein describes how *BP* tackled such a task when it built a thousand mile pipeline through Azerbaijan, Georgia, and Turkey.[1] It consulted thousands of land tenants to determine the least disruptive route for the pipeline and the locations of power stations and other infrastructure. *BP* then gave $30 million to NGOs to invest at their discretion in hospitals, water systems, schools, and other social assets along the route. These pragmatic reputation-building activities helped minimize risk from social disorder and support its business case.

Two general situations where a good corporate reputation can help a company operate are when it provides basic infrastructure and when it innovates. When private companies take over "public" assets such as airports, roads, trains, electricity generation and delivery, health care, and water systems, they are often perceived to be more powerful and influential in people's lives. This expanding social footprint is often accompanied by the responsibility to act honestly and fairly across diverse groups of people because, when these companies were owned by the government, each had an explicit community social obligation. For example, it was expected that the postal service was equally available to everybody. The second situation involves innovation. Often it poses risk to society. So society's tolerance for the inevitable failures and mistakes that accompany this endeavor can be enhanced if the company involved is highly regarded.

Does a company have to be liked to have a good reputation?

The world of branding suggests that great brands are liked and often loved by their devotees. To show this attachment, many people are proud to wear a company or product logo on their clothing. And sometimes employees and customers even tattoo themselves with the brand name or symbol (e.g., *Harley-Davidson*). Brand consultants say that it is this emotional attachment that gives brands much of their market power. Many corporate reputation consultants agree. For example, the RepTrak™ measure of corporate reputation includes a variable that measures emotional appeal. Thus being liked is good. But is it always necessary?

Recall the story about *Exxon* in chapter 2. *Exxon* preferred to be feared rather than liked because this acted as an entry barrier to competitors who knew that they would pay a high price to compete head to head with this giant company. It also encouraged them to appeal the fine imposed for the *Exxon Valdez* oil spill. The result was a saving of billions of dollars. In the Darwinian world of finance, many firms would rather have a reputation for opportunism or predation than be liked.[2] And especially when they are on mission, the armed services would probably prefer to be feared than liked.

So, in a corporate context, companies can be liked or feared and still be respected. What it will strive for will depend on what it needs to succeed. For example, many law firms want to be feared more than loved while many cosmetics companies need love not fear. When companies want to be loved, the price they pay is that they have to show love in return. Hence the people who love the company must be recognized for their love. If you have millions of customers, this is not an easy thing to do. Many companies try to use their customer loyalty program to do this. The trick here is to make sure that the program is designed to foster a deep relationship not just a longstanding one. When people fall out of love, the outcomes can be both messy and nasty. As the old saying goes "be careful what you wish for."

Can an organization survive and prosper if it has a mixed corporate reputation?

One high-profile organization with a mixed reputation is the *Roman Catholic* Church. Some people like it; others hate it. And most people would agree that the Church has a mix of positive and negative attributes. Its new CEO is being given a lot of free advice about how to fix the more unsavoury aspects of his organization.[3]

But is the mixed reputation of the Church putting it at serious risk? Are the parts of its tarnished reputation a significant liability? Is it a major problem that most people around the world don't like it? These issues might stunt the growth of the Church, but it would be a bold person to suggest that it will not survive for the next 100 years. Hence my answer to the question of there being a problem with having a mixed reputation is yes and no.

The No Case Like many contemporary faiths, the primary business of the *Roman Catholic* Church is to provide spiritual comfort for its flock. Its secondary concern is to provide charity. Across all religions, people buy into the spiritual part of the offer to a greater or less extent. Thus there will always be a significant number of people who dislike the product category (religion), some of the various brands (Christianity, Islam, etc.), and sub-brands (Roman Catholic, Protestant, etc.). Some people will give the *Roman Catholic* Church lip service, and a smaller group will be its active devotees. The majority of people around the world that are atheists, agnostics, and followers of another brand of religion will never be convinced to become a follower of this Church whatever its reputation. So outside of the beliefs of religious fanatics who are focused on destroying the *Roman Catholic* Church, the Pope can simply ignore the beliefs of most non-Catholics about his Church. As one of the world's largest membership organizations, his Church is too important in most countries to be persecuted.

The Yes Case A good reputation is necessary to reassure the faithful—both of the lip service variety and the active followers. Here its role is to provide reassurance that the choice of this brand of religion is correct. A good reputation helps to legitimize Church doctrine and provides a degree of extra moral authority to Church elders and lay people. However, where a good reputation could have an immediate affect to help overcome the Church's current problems would be if it was made a nonnegotiable standard against which its members' behavior is judged. If any officer of the Church does anything to damage the desired reputation of *Roman Catholicism,* he or she would be proactively excommunicated. Had this standard been enforced in the recent past, then far fewer of the Church's current problems would have gained the time to fester to their present damaging state.

Again, the key issue here is to identify who really matters to an organization's survival and prosperity. Good reputations matter for the people who matter. But keeping a watching brief on the others is a good idea.

Is it true that corporate reputations take a long time to develop but only a short time to destroy?

These twin ideas have been floating around for decades. They were immortalized in the following attributed quotes by Benjamin Franklin and Warren Buffet:

> It takes many good deeds to build a good reputation, and only one to lose it. (Benjamin Franklin)

It takes years to build a reputation and five minutes to ruin it. If you think about that, you'll do things differently. (Warren Buffet)

Advocates for the cause of reputation management love these quotes. In fact they have been repeated so often that this idea has become a fundamental tenet of reputation management.

The notion of slow-to-build is founded on the idea that it is demonstrated past performance over a period of time that is the principal way that reputations are created. The notion of fast-to-destroy is founded on the idea that trust is easy to damage and that being seen as untrustworthy immediately undermines a good reputation. But are these ideas true?

Business people started to question the idea that corporate reputations take a long time to develop when companies like *Amazon*, *Google, eBay, Twitter, Facebook,* and *YouTube* burst onto the business scene and grew at a fantastic rate. In the space of just a few years these companies built very strong corporate reputations. They were based on each company's technical innovations and how these helped change people's definition of, and often participation in, a market. In the jargon of the technology industry, each company developed a "killer app." In other words, they did a simply better job of meeting the current or latent needs of a group of people than the existing products and services. Another key aspect of the reputation-building process was the widespread public attention each company received as a leader in its new field. It was current performance, leadership, initial growth, and a lot of favorable social chatter that made them household names. Thus the media amplified the deeds of these companies. Soon they were appearing in the top stratum of many of the annual corporate reputation polls. However, the fickle nature of this reputation creation process became apparent during the dot-com bubble (1997 to 2000) in the saying "dot.come – dot.go."

Why did so many tech companies fail in the dot-com bubble? The principal reasons were that their business models were not strong—many simply ran out of cash. The business model many of these companies ascribed to was summarized as get big fast, and hope that the winner takes all. Another reason for failure was that a company with a better or more reliable technology came along that allowed it to offer a better deal for customers or a better quality service. In this case the media chatter amplified the difference between the incumbent and the challenger. As we now see, in many of these markets the company with the best offer was the one that persisted and then won the reputation game.

However, to confound the issue of fast-to-destroy we sometimes see a well-respected company involved in a major crisis that emerges with its reputation largely undamaged. An old example of this was when *Johnson & Johnson*'s Tylenol brand of pain tablet was tampered with in 1982 and again in 1985. In both cases people were poisoned. And in both cases the company was not blamed for the incident. Their communications and product recalls were seen as a concerned and dutiful response to this unfortunate situation. In contrast, in recent years *J&J* has been savaged in the media for Medicare fraud, the illicit marketing of off-label drugs, and having to recall some high-profile drugs and products used in hip replacements. Despite these home-grown disasters, the company still ranks highly in many reputation polls. For example, in 2014 it was ranked first in the pharmaceuticals category of the *Fortune* poll and 19th overall.

More recently the relationship between corporate irresponsibility and reputation has attracted academic scrutiny. This is a "grey area" of corporate ethics. It is inhabited by activities like tax avoidance, which is legal, as opposed to tax evasion, which is illegal.[4] Here a company occupies an ambiguous or contested zone of social judgment. In a study of US firms during the period 2006 to 2012, Gregory Jackson and Stephen Brammer could not find any systematic evidence for sharp reputation penalties associated with many "grey area" instances of corporate irresponsibility.[5] This finding and specific cases like the poor recent publicity of *J&J* noted above, run contrary to the conventional wisdom expressed in the quotes by Benjamin Franklin and Warren Buffet. They also question the veracity of the role of the loss of reputation as a social form of corporate regulation or private governance.[6]

So how do these examples speak to the question stated above? My suggestion is that it is about time to consign this assertion to the dust bin. There are simply too many counter examples to blindly believe that corporate reputations are like fine china—difficult to craft and easy to smash.

Can a company fully recover from a crisis that damaged its corporate reputation?

A reputation once broken may possibly be repaired, but the world will always keep their eyes on the spot where the crack was.

Joseph Hall, English bishop (1574–1656)

While Bishop Hall's observation seems reasonable, I am aware of no major scientific study that provides definite support for it. The problem with designing such a study rests on the issues of defining the size of reputation damage, what level of change would constitute "recovery," and over what time frame should the study be conducted?[7] Also, if there are many individual cases suggesting recovery does happen and many that suggest it doesn't, then a large cross-sectional study will tend to be inconclusive because the overall effect will be the average of a lot of positives and negatives.

However, not all is lost in terms of answering this question. There are some interesting studies about stakeholder response to a crisis, and a thought experiment can help identify conditions when you might expect full or partial recovery or long-term damage. Consider the following findings about how two different types of stakeholders responded to the same crisis.

A study conducted by Anastasiya Zavyalova found that when some highly reputed US colleges and universities suffered negative incidents (on-campus murders and basketball team rule violations) some alumni increased their donations to their school while non-alumni tended to decrease their donations.[8] The explanation for this behavior was that when an organization is held in high repute the stakeholders (alumni) who identify strongly with it can protect both the organization and their personal identities by actively supporting and defending its actions. The other group was happy to punish the organization for its misdeeds. Thus, when an organization has a lot of people who use it for vicarious self-enhancement, it might be insulated from severe damage and in some cases might even achieve a net positive outcome from a negative event. Now consider a thought experiment.

Crises come in many forms, and it would be reasonable to expect that the form of crisis together with the way it is reported and handled will affect whether or not people attribute the incident to be the company's fault. And it is this attribution that is likely to affect the damage to and subsequent recovery of a company's reputation.[9] Consider the following possible causes of a corporate crisis:

- An act of God
- An act of a random outsider
- Poor company procedures
- Management failure

What differentiates the first two from the others is attribution, namely the likelihood that a person will blame the company for the incident. If the company is deemed to be at fault, then its reputation is in far greater risk than otherwise.

Now consider some possible outcomes of a crisis:

- One-off financial loss to the company
- Damages to the company's operational capabilities or prospects
- Significant damage to the environment or a local community

Here the time frame and the magnitude of loss are the differentiating factors. The longer lasting and bigger the outcomes of a crisis, the more damaging it might become. Also, if the organization suffers the loss as opposed to an outside group, then the reputation damage might be different.

We would expect that various combinations of these causes and outcomes together with whether the company is considered to be well recognized (a so-called elite company), how it handles the crisis (well or badly), how the media report it (factually or sensationally), and whether the company's competitors have been involved in a similar incident will result in different levels of reputation damage and thus chances of recovery. So the answer to the question above is "it depends." Thus beware of any categorical answer of yes or no.

Is it possible to quickly establish a strong corporate reputation?

One of the fastest corporate reputation-building episodes that I can recall involved a group of academics and practitioners who established the company called *Long-Term Capital Management* (LTCM).[10] In 1993, 11 men started a small hedge fund management firm based in Greenwich, Connecticut USA. The company slogan was "the financial technology company." Consider their short biographies as listed in *Wikipedia*:

- John W. Meriwether—former vice chair and head of bond trading at Salomon Brothers, MBA (University of Chicago)
- Robert C. Merton—leading scholar in finance; Professor at Harvard University, PhD (MIT)
- Myron S. Scholes—co-author of the Black–Scholes model; Professor at Stanford University, PhD (University of Chicago)
- David W. Mullins Jr.—former vice chairman of the Federal Reserve Board, Professor at Harvard University, PhD (MIT)
- Eric Rosenfeld—arbitrage group at Salomon, former Harvard Business School professor, PhD (MIT)
- William Krasker—arbitrage group at Salomon, former Harvard Business School professor, PhD (MIT)
- Gregory Hawkins—arbitrage group at Salomon, worked on Bill Clinton's campaign for Arkansas state attorney general, PhD (MIT)
- Larry Hilibrand—arbitrage group at Salomon, PhD (MIT)
- James McEntree—bond trader
- Dick Leahy—executive at Salomon
- Victor Haghani—arbitrage group at Salomon, Masters in Finance (London School of Economics)

When *LTCM* began operations in February 1994, the firm quickly amassed $1 billion in capital from some of America's richest individuals and institutions. This can be considered a measure of the financial value of *LTCM*'s reputation. At the time of its formation, this group was seen as the best-of-the-best, or as one commentator noted—the finance team of the century. Their approach was to use complex mathematical models to eliminate risk and take advantage of small anomalies in the bond market. For the first few years of operation they were very successful and produced annual returns of 21, 43, and 41 percent. The status of Merton and Scholes as the high priests of the academic finance discipline was confirmed in 1997 when they shared the Nobel Memorial Prize in Economic Sciences for their work in pricing stock options. In 1998 *LTCM* crashed and the *Federal Reserve Bank of New York* organized a bailout to avoid disaster in the financial markets. At this time their market exposure was approximately $1trillion.[11]

Before its collapse, *LTCM* was widely regarded as best at modeling financial markets and the best place to invest for wealthy investors. After its collapse, it became a case study in the limits to using complex mathematical investment models.[12] What is also of note was that the bailout of *LTCM* by the *Federal Reserve* sent a signal to many Wall Street firms that some institutions were too big to be allowed to fail. This moral hazard would be seen to play out again a decade later in the global financial crisis of 2007 to 2009.

As noted earlier in this chapter, many Internet companies have also created good reputations in quite a short period of time. At the heart of their success was a service that fulfilled a need, was in many cases cheap to try, and that was supported by a lot of positive media hype and vast amounts of favorable word-of-mouse communication. While most of these services failed, when one really helped people to solve a problem or enhance a relationship, it became a household name. For example, the phrase "to *Google* something" is now well established in the language of many Western countries. And *Dr Google* is often the first general practitioner consulted about an ailment.

The case of *LTCM* and many of the Internet companies illustrates a paradox. For most companies, reputations are only available to established enterprises. They have to be earned through good products, services, and gestures. However, for others, they are created almost immediately. They are simply conferred. While both such types of establishment provide insight into what helps create a strong corporate reputation, the fast-track group suggests that storytelling is crucial. All these companies focused on telling a convincing story about themselves. They then supported this with some signals about the company's strategy, character, quality, and competence.

To illustrate this storytelling approach to reputation formation, consider how a new market research firm might establish its identity and signal its quality without an established track record. The starting point is the firm's name. Because names introduce firms, they can be used to set expectations and position the enterprise relative to its rivals. For example, descriptive names like *Cheap-Research*, *Customer Insights,* and *Advertising Metrics* immediately suggest what these firms do. Another popular naming strategy is to coin a catchy or clever name that has no inherent meaning to anybody other than the owners. The problem here is that for a new firm, these names don't work to position the firm as standing for something. This will take time to achieve. Another common naming strategy for a new firm is to name it after the owners. This is wonderfully uplifting for the principals but only works if they are well known and have a good reputation. Here their established reputation acts as a security bond for the engagement. This strategy can sometimes cause problems for a new firm if one of the named owners is not an engagement partner for a new client. Descriptive names tend to be the safe alternative.

A key aspect of a new firm's reputation is the sum of the reputations and status of its principals and their commitment to the new enterprise. For example, *LTCM*'s principals had lots the formal qualifications from prestigious universities, they had about 350 years of accumulated experience in the industry, and all had held highly paid positions in academe or the finance industry. Thus they had both good reputations and high status, which combined to produce a strong signal of quality.[13] Other signals of quality are the reputations of any prominent financial backers, members of an advisory board, and initial clients. For example, some of *LTCM*'s founding investors were thought to include the prominent investment banks *Julius Baer & Co.*, *Bear Sterns*, and *Merrill Lynch*. The reason for attracting well-known and respected clients is so that the new firm can "rent" their reputation by association.

Commitment can be signaled in a number of ways. One is by investing the money of the principals in the firm. In the case of *LTCM* these people had $149 million invested in the firm. Another signal of commitment is whether the firm's launch marketing is expensive or cheap. When a firm spends a considerable amount of money launching itself, it is signaling to its clients and competitors that it is confident in its ability to survive and prosper.

The new firm's head office is a signal of numerous things. Its location makes a statement of who you are and sometimes where you expect your clients to be. In the case of *LTCM* locating in the rich town of Greenwich signaled two things. One was that this was a somewhat mysterious firm with a different approach to investing. Being away from Wall Street was important to cultivate this image. The second was that what they were doing was secret. Not even their clients were allowed to know the precise suite of mathematical models used. Also, when a firm locates in an architecturally interesting building, this acts as a billboard to clients and a statement of organizational culture to employees. How the office is presented, especially the crossover areas where clients and employees meet signals the type of engagement approach to be expected. Formal meetings in a boardroom suggest something different to less formal meetings in employee–client work spaces. Advertising agencies and architectural firms tend to set themselves up quite differently to engineering firms.

Another signal is to offer a sample of quality. Sometimes signing up to a voluntary industry code of best practice can signal quality. For *LTCM* their samples of quality were the highly acclaimed academic papers of Merton and Scholes and later the Nobel Prize. Many professional service firms, even those that are well established, write thought leader articles to do this. A variation on this approach is to publish case studies of how previous situations could have been improved or some new research that provides new insights into old problems. Also the partners of the firm can give presentations at industry and client events. Some may volunteer to make presentations in university courses, such as to executive MBA students where potential clients lurk. However, the best sample of quality is to do some quick assignments for prestigious clients that show bottom-line results.

The pricing of the firm's services is another interesting signal. For most clients (and people) price is either a signal of quality or a measure of sacrifice. The same general rule applies here. However, if price is set high to signal quality, then the firm will need to offer some implied guarantee of quality. The best way to do this is to base price on benefits delivered not the cost of delivery. Most professional firms use a cost-plus approach to pricing where fees are designed around a markup of the blended head-rate hours of the people who do the work. The alternative is to set a price based on value created by the assignment undertaken. This success fee approach requires that the firm understand what this value is to the client. It can then set its price as a percentage of the value created. This type of price signals that it is in the best interests of the new firm to do the best job it can.

Another type of signal to invest in is critical acclaim. Can the new firm get some important person or publication to certify its strategy, character, and competence? Many business and finance magazines did this for *LTCM*. The idea here is to get publicity for some hidden attribute of quality that is otherwise difficult for an outsider to verify, such as a new analytic technique or database of information. The roles of critics are very important because they channel the attention of buyers to some companies and away from others. They also confer legitimacy on a company by discussing it. An added bonus occurs if they praise it.

The weakest but often the most used signal is the corporate proclamation. All new companies make statements about themselves, their capabilities and what they will do. In effect they are trying to provide a proof of service. There are two problems with these proclamations. One is that they are often poorly worded. For example, a new firm might say that it is "reliable." A better way to say this would be that "it offers old-fashioned reliability." This now links it to a widely held free-standing emotion. A second problem with proclamations is that too often they are simply cheap talk. To be effective, they must be verifiable and enforceable or be accompanied by some type of money-back guarantee. Only in this way will corporate declarations link the company's subsequent actions to its reputation.

So yes, a new corporate reputation can be engineered, but it really helps to have some substance behind the signals sent to outsiders.

Will a change of corporate identity symbols boost our reputation?

Many companies think so, and many consultants are pleased that they think this way. But will a change to the typography of the company name, the logo, color scheme, and corporate slogan help produce a better reputation? As I'll argue here, the answer is likely to be no. And occasionally a change of the corporate identity symbols will cause derision and a backlash among people on social media who consider that they are members of the company's community. This happened to the clothing company *Gap* and to the coffee giants *Starbucks* when they made a change to their corporate logos.[14]

Many corporate identities get changed after a merger or acquisition, or when a holding or investment company decides to become a more prominent operating company. Other identities get changed when a new CEO takes over, especially one from outside the company, and especially when he or she is brought in to rejuvenate the organization. If corporate identity is changed after there is tangible organizational change, then it can help signal this substantive change. However, if the identity symbols are changed prior to meaningful organizational change, this is often interpreted by employees and the media as a cosmetic response to a substantive problem. And if the changes are small, most customers won't notice. Hence a positive flow-on reputation effect is unlikely.

Another time corporate identity symbols get changed is when management gets convinced to do so by an identity consultant. One line of argument here is that good identity design reflects and demonstrates the presence of effective management.[15] However, whether a new logo is a better signal of this than higher profits is something I will leave up to you. An audit of the inconsistent use or abuse of the corporate livery is another trigger for identity change, as is the argument that the identity is simply out of date. From this point on it is easy to convince the CEO and the board that some change is required to modernize the symbols that adorn every piece of corporate hardware and communication. Because even minor changes can cost millions of dollars, it is worth thinking about when such a change might offer some reputation benefits. For example, in 2000 it cost *BP* approximately $200 million to become "Beyond Petroleum" and change its retail and corporate livery.[16]

In most organizations it is not unusual to find some inconsistent use of corporate identity symbols—even when there is a thick manual that prescribes when and where they should be used. To dramatize their inconsistent use, consultants may create a display of this muddled usage. While such a display highlights the diversity, it is not really a valid test of whether or not stakeholders are confused by the inconsistent usage. The reason is that a person seldom sees more than one version of the corporate identity at the same time. And if they do see two slightly different versions, it is unlikely that they would notice the difference. The sad fact is that most people are not very interested in your company's logo and color scheme, and thus its potential to enhance a corporate reputation is limited.

When auditing the consistency of use of corporate identity symbols, the crucial reputation issue is to determine whether inconsistent usage is a sign of sloppy administration of the company's identity policy or is it a signal of a fracturing organizational culture. In the first case, a bit more vigilance is all that is needed to rectify the problem. In the second case, when different parts of an organization are making changes to the corporate identity or deliberately not using it, they may be signaling that they want to be different from their colleagues. And this is a signal of reputation risk. For example, many years ago the package delivery company *UPS* used the corporate slogan "as sure as taking it there yourself."[17] This slogan was clever because it spoke to the essence of *UPS*, namely it could be trusted because it took as much care with your delivery as you would. For some reason the slogan was discontinued in the United States. However, in Asia the old slogan kept being used. This was a subtle signal to head office that *UPS*'s reputation in Asia was based on a different value proposition than the one used in the United States. This type of identity inconsistency is an important reputation issue because it is signaling something fundamental about different parts of the organization.

Whether making any change to company's identity is likely to pay off requires specifying the roles that these symbols should play to support or enhance the desired reputation of the company. For example, from a strategic point of view, a good corporate slogan makes the company's mission amenable to proof. Recall my redrafting of the *Bell Pottinger Private* slogan mentioned earlier—"better PR, better reputation, better results." This slogan would remind employees and clients what the firm is offering and how to judge its success. In effect it holds the firm's operations (better PR) hostage to its success. Identity also plays a tactical role. For example, a company like *McDonald's* wants to stand out to the public and do so in a friendly and inviting way. Thus its identity symbols need to attract attention in a cluttered retail environment, foster true recognition, and project an image conducive to being a "family restaurant." In both cases, for a small change in identity to impact on reputation, it must change or reinforce the desired salient beliefs about the company.

The strategic and tactical problem with many corporate identity symbols is that they are essentially meaningless to everyone other than their creators. Most are composed of a name, colorful logo, and a slogan that do not resonate with each other. Let me illustrate this problem with two sets of identity. The current *Qantas* identity is the name of the airline that now means nothing to most people. It is an acronym for Queensland and Northern Territory Air Service. This is where in Australia the company first operated. The second element is a white kangaroo on a red sloping triangular background. The kangaroo is a distinctly Australian animal. Various depictions of it have been used on the *Qantas* logo since 1944. Most travelers who see this logo on the tailfin of an aircraft know that it belongs to *Qantas*. Sometimes the company name and logo are accompanied by the slogan "Spirit of Australia." The company has made some memorable corporate advertisements using this theme. Both the logo and the corporate message reinforce each other. The dominant salient belief fostered and reinforced by these identity symbols is that *Qantas* is the Australian airline. This belief may then trigger any number of other beliefs about the company's culture, service, safety record, and so forth. Thus the *Qantas* identity signals and signifies some key aspects of the company's desired corporate reputation.

To contrast the way the *Qantas* identity works, consider the identity of *DELL* computer. I am writing this book using a *DELL* computer and monitor. As I look at the company logo on these two products, the only memory that they prompt for me is that Michael Dell is the founder. There is nothing in the way that the logo is written in upper case and a backward sloping E that triggers anything special about the company. A look on the company website reveals that their current corporate slogan is "Listen. Learn. Deliver. That's what we're about." This site also suggests that for the company "customers are at the core of everything we do." Because this sentiment and the slogan could apply to any computer manufacturer, it doesn't differentiate *DELL* from its competitors. In comparison to the *Qantas* identity, it underperforms.

The best corporate identity symbols reinforce in graphic or literary form the corporate brand promise—for both employees and customers. This promise or value proposition is the prominent salient belief that fosters a good reputation. Mediocre identities do nothing. They are boring and anonymous and unlikely to upset anyone. The worst corporate identities are confusing and set incorrect expectations. For example, one of the largest private UK health insurance and healthcare companies is called *Bupa*. It is the initials of the name *British United Provident Association*. Now the old name was fairly meaningless, and I would venture that the new name is just as meaningless. For example, if you didn't know this was a health fund, you might think it was an Indian restaurant.

Let me conclude this section with a story about *Air India* and the danger of fiddling with a company's identity symbols. Some years ago when I visited the airline, its logo was a red-and-white stylized centaur sometimes accompanied by the slogan "your palace in the sky." At 3am while driving from the airport into Mumbai, I noticed the corporate logo proudly displayed on the company's main building. Upon commenting about one of the few illuminated neon signs in this part of the city, my host advised that I not mention this logo during my discussions with the airline's management team. A previous CEO had changed the logo to signal his intention to make some significant changes to the airline. Many customers were delighted, but many senior employees were wary and some senior functionaries criticized his endeavor. The next CEO quietly reinstated the old logo. What happened here was that while everybody knew that *Air India* needed to make some fundamental change if it was to survive as India's major airline, in typical Indian fashion some senior managers and politicians really did not want significant change. They were regents in their own palace in the sky. Thus the old corporate logo became a symbol of resistance. It was like a heraldic shield, which is from where many of these corporate logos were originally derived.[18]

What is the role of head office in building reputation?

To give the discussion some context, I will introduce the issues by reference to universities. These institutions are acutely aware of the value of a good reputation for their teaching and research. And there is always debate about where investments should be made to enhance these two types of reputation.[19]

One critical debate within universities is about where to invest to get reputation gains. The usual options are in the faculty (e.g., by buying star professors), students (via scholarships), university facilities (e.g., buildings), programs (e.g., alumni), or administration (the C-suite and their support staff). A tension within many universities is about the growing size of the investment in administration. Administrators argue that a better run university generates a better reputation. However, most academics argue that the role of administration is to complement them in their generation of reputation. Not surprisingly, as an old academic I favor the second option. My argument is that administrators do not create the sources of capital that deliver the university's desired outcomes at the quality that enhances the reputations of their universities. They do not teach the students. They do not make discoveries. They do not publish research and scholarship. But their decisions affect these endeavors, so they do matter.

The problem within the university sector is the same for all companies. What is the reputation role of head office? Is it a primary source of reputation, or a guardian of reputation, or a complement to the activities of others? While the CEO has a special role to play because of his or her leadership, the point of view taken in this book is that the role of head office is complementary. Their value comes from two activities. One is to design ways in which to release the reputation benefits from the company's various sources of capital, especially to the stakeholders who really matter. The other is to design and enforce protocols to protect the organization's reputation. As many recent corporate crises have demonstrated, often this second role is not well executed.

Are social media an important source of reputation risk?

There are many people who say that the answer to this question is a definite yes—just look at any current business magazine. However, I disagree for a number of reasons. First, I don't subscribe to the argument that the chatter of spectators who use social media is necessarily important to a company's reputation. Most of this chatter occurs in an echo chamber—like-minded people share their views with other like-minded people. For most companies, few major customers, potential employees, or business partners troll these media spaces as a source of information to help them decide whether or not to engage with a company. Yes, there are some sites like *TripAdvisor* where this happens, but for most companies there is no evidence that this is a credible source of information for the stakeholders who really matter to the company's commercial success.

Second, some recent research suggests that most of the comments made about businesses on these social media have a positive tone of voice rather than being negative.[20] So the only way that bad information could cause a bad reputation is if it is regarded as much more influential than good information. We simply don't know if this effect occurs. So until then it is a good working assumption to conclude that good social media information probably dampens the bad information. The net effect is probably zero.

Third, the new broadband technologies have made it much easier for people to create a lot of noise about companies relative to the amount of new information they create. As the ratio of information to noise decreases, it becomes harder for anyone to get a clear picture of a company. And as noted earlier, by seeding these media with positive comments, it makes it easier for poor companies to parade as if they are good companies.

Fourth, because much the advice proffered by consultants about the massive influence of the Internet and social media is self-interested, I regard most such pronouncements as premature and exaggerated. There are two reasons for this. One is that these pronouncements reflect what Michael Porter says is a confusion of technology with company strategy.[21] This occurs when people think that the new technology must become the firm's strategy rather than it being an enabler of this strategy. The second reason is the vast literature on the adoption and diffusion of innovations that suggests that this new media is like most other technology innovations. It will be adopted by certain groups, some more enthusiastically than others, and ignored by many people for as long as they can (the laggards). And many of the adopters have a low capacity to affect a company, in either a positive or negative manner.[22]

There are a couple of caveats to my general opinion about the influence of the web. While most of its criticism of companies seems to have few major reputation effects, sometimes it can create significant problems. The situations of concern are twofold. One is for the so-called viral loop companies such as *Facebook*, *YouTube,* and *LinkedIn*.[23] Most of these companies rely for their success on people who are social network strivers such as artists, rappers, photographers, models, comedians, entertainers, teenagers, and wannabees. Others like *eBay* rely on communities of shared interest such as product traders. Bad word-of-mouth, or more accurately word-of-mouse, can destroy the social and interpersonal foundations of these companies. Because of this many of them design online reputation systems to help their customers determine the trustworthiness of people with whom they will associate.[24]

The second case concerns opinion leaders who start what has been called a "communication fire." And because of the persistence of content on the web and the ease of use of search engines, episodes of bad company behavior can have a long shelf life. For example, in June 2005 Jeff Jarvis, the creator of the popular technology blog *Buzz Machine* wrote a post describing his bad experience with *Dell Computer*'s customer support.[25] After receiving comments from other customers who had similar complaints, he put up additional posts and links to other bloggers. Technology and business mainstream media then picked up the story. Two of Jeff Jarvis's blogs were entitled "Dell Hell" and the "Flaming Notebook." These names lingered on the web long after the problems that caused them were rectified. And because of this, they are easy for people like academics to find.

Epilogue

To finish the book, let me state what I consider to be the biggest challenge facing companies that want to play the corporate reputation game. It is simply to get people inside and outside the company to use corporate reputation as an important determinant of their choice of which companies to work for and to engage with. If more people demand that companies be more reputable, then more companies will become more reputable, and the market for corporate reputation will grow.

On the employment side of this equation, the research by Richard Florida into the rise of the creative class of workers is insightful.[1] This growing labor market consists of people who change jobs on a frequent basis. They are less inclined to want to conform to organizational directives and group norms. Merit is a strong value orientation. These people want to be recognized for their abilities and effort. And crucially from a corporate reputation perspective, these employees identify more with their occupation, profession, and lifestyle interests than with the company they currently work for. Because they rely on themselves more than their employer to grow their skill base and define their identity, they are less likely than their forbears to be overly concerned about the reputation of the companies they work for or buy from. To capture the loyalty and respect of this new class of employees, companies will need to provide employment that taps into their values and lifestyle.

On the consumer side of the equation, companies will need to convince customers that a respected company does offer added value to the products and services it sells. This added value can enhance the identity of the customer who buys from a respected company, or it might act as a guarantee of quality for the features of the company's products and services that consumers can't reliably assess. Wouldn't it be nice if modern corporations really did stand behind what they offered to the market and took full responsibility for their actions? At present the ever-expanding morass of laws and regulations designed to protect consumers from devious sellers sets up an environment where it is easy for companies to abide by the letter of the law rather than seek to enhance their two faces—lian and mian-zi. It also makes it easy for consumers to ignore the companies that make and sell most of the things they buy. Only when something is really important does the company's reputation matter.

On the general public side of the equation, companies will need to convince people that a vibrant economy can be built on the principle of sustainability. The new style of benefit corporation is making a muddled attempt to attract custom with this reputation position—as has *GE* with its Ecomagination program. Currently these attempts are being drowned out by the master image of Corporate America, Australia, and Canada, among other industrial countries, as a group of companies predominantly concerned with making money for themselves and their shareholders rather than helping to create a vibrant economy that directly benefits the societies in which they operate. And as the global financial crisis demonstrated, governments of all political persuasions were impotent and often incompetent when faced with significant corporate misconduct.

As I write this chapter, a Federal Government Senate inquiry is questioning the tax avoidance practices of two of Australia's largest mining companies—*BHP Billiton* and *Rio Tinto*. Both companies stand accused of shifting some of their profits offshore to minimize their tax burden. Episodes like this highlight the more general reputation problem faced by most large companies, namely they often have trouble reconciling their "profit story" with their "employee story," their "customer story," and their "community story." And as I outlined earlier, this problem is underpinned by the issue of stakeholder priority—who really matters. Some companies like *Apple* seem to grapple with this issue better than others. As an outside observer, it seems to me that *Apple* makes great products for its customers and handsome profits for its shareholders. Employees and business partners get rewarded when they service these two masters. Spectators, the community and civil society groups are politely ignored. Regulators are tolerated and sometimes resisted. As a spectator, I know my position in this hierarchy.

While the emphasis of this book has been on the practices of WEIRD companies, maybe the business practices of organizations in the emerging economies of the world have something to teach their more sophisticated counterparts. Here the good name of the business trader more directly underpins its commercial success. This is summed up in the old Kenyan proverb:

Leave a good name in case you return.

Notes

Preface

1. C. J. Fombrun, List of lists: A compilation of international corporate reputation ratings, *Corporate Reputation Review* 10, 2 (2007): 144–53.

2. J. Mackintosh and J. Authers, Sin stocks pay as alcohol and cigarettes beat sober rivals, *Financial Times* (February 10, 2015). At ft.com/markets/equities. Accessed February 10, 2015.

3. W. H. Starbuck, Keeping a butterfly and an elephant in a house of cards: The elements of exceptional success, *Journal of Management Studies* 30, 6 (1993): 885–921.

4. M. L. Barnett and T. Pollock, eds., *The Oxford Handbook of Corporate Reputations* (Oxford: Oxford University Press, 2012).

5. C. J. Fombrun and C. B. M. van Riel, *Fame and Fortune* (Upper Saddle River, NJ: FT Prentice Hall, 2004).

6. Experimental psychology: The roar of the crowd, *The Economist* (May 26, 2012): 81–83.

7. This phenomenon is evident from looking where most people from developing countries go to get a business school education.

Chapter 1

1. This idea has become known as the affect heuristic. It is sometimes characterized as "the emotional tail wags the rational dog."

2. P. Roberts and G. R. Dowling, Corporate reputation and sustained superior financial performance, *Strategic Management Journal* 23, 12 (2002): 1077–93.

3. Reported in Analysis: Public company reputational crises, *Oxford University Centre for Corporate Reputation* (issue 6, Hilary Term, 2013): 3.

4. What probably happened here was that the investment community had overestimated the fine to be levied and/or it changed its collective view on how this type of risk would be better managed at the bank in the future.

5. J. M. Karpoff, D. S. Lee, and G. S. Martin, The cost of firms cooking the books, *Journal of Financial and* Quantitative Analysis 43, 3 (2008): 581–612; J. M. Karpoff, The grey areas of firm behavior: An economic perspective, *Socioeconomic Review* 12 (2014): 167–76.

6. Articles like this are typical. BP crisis: The impact on your savings and investments, *BBC News Business* (June 17, 2010); BP profit rise marks turning point, *The Guardian* (October 25, 2011); BP: A shrunken giant, *The Economist* (February 8, 2014): 53–54.

7. Schumpeter, Sailing through a scandal, *The Economist* (December 20, 2014): 96.

8. Paul Midler's book *Poorly Made in China: An Insider's Account of the China Production Game* (Hoboken, NJ: Wiley, 2009) provides a good example of such conditions.

9. In industries that most people do not respect this sets up a fascinating dilemma. How do you select respected people with enough industry experience to be trusted by outsiders?

10. See, for example, D. Vogel, *The Market for Virtue* (Washington, DC: Brookings Institute Press, 2005); D. Doane, The myth of CSR, *Stanford Innovation Review* (Fall 2005): 23–29; T. M. Devinney, P. Auger, and G. Eckhardt, *The Myth of the Ethical Consumer* (Cambridge, UK: Cambridge University Press, 2010); P. Auger, P. Burke, T. M. Devinney, and J. J. Louviere, What will consumers pay for social product features? *Journal of Business Ethics*, pt. 1, 42, 3 (2003): 281–304.

11. T. M. Devinney, P. Auger, G. Eckhardt, and T. Birtchnell, The other CSR, *Stanford Social Innovation Review* 4, 3 (2006): 32–33 and 35–37.

12. In February 2015 *Apple* became the first US company to record a stock market valuation of more than $700 billion—which just exceeded the combined market value of *Google* and *Microsoft*.

13. C. J. Fombrun, N. Gardberg, and M. L. Barnett, Opportunity platforms and safety nets: Corporate citizenship and corporate reputational risks, *Business and Strategy* 105, 1 (2000): 75–106; A. Kemper and R. L. Martin, After the fall: The global financial crisis as a test of corporate social responsibility theories, *European Management Review* 7, 4 (2010): 229–39.

Chapter 2

1. See for example, C. Brønn and G. R. Dowling, Corporate reputation risk: Creating an audit trail, in S. Helm, K. Liehr-Gobbers and C. Storch (eds.), *Reputation Management* (Berlin: Springer, 2011), 239–55; R. G. Eccles, S. C. Newquist and R. Schatz, Reputation and its risks, *Harvard Business Review* 85, 2 (2007), 104–14.

2. Reputation: Risk of risks, *Economist Intelligence Unit,* White Paper (2005); Schumpeter, The enemy within, *The Economist* (March 1, 2014), 66.

3. T. Bower, *OIL: Money, Politics and Power in the 21st Century* (New York: Grand Central Publishing, 2009).

4. These companies were *BP*, *Chevron*, *Exxon*, *Gulf*, *Mobil*, *Shell*, and *Texaco*. Together they controlled 85 percent of the world's oil reserves and fixed the world price of oil.

5. Lee Raymond, *Exxon*'s chairman stoutly expressed no shame for his company's behavior. He also seemed to dismiss the emotional and financial distress the disaster caused to Alaskans. To Exxon such fines were nothing more than the cost of doing business.

6. BP: A shrunken giant, *The Economist* (8 February, 2014), 53–54.

7. Fedex.com USA site. Accessed April 20, 2014.

8. T. C. Schelling, *Micromotives and Macrobehavior* (New York: Norton, 1978).

9. T. L. Friedman, *The Lexus and the Olive Tree: Understanding Globalization* (New York: Farrar, Straus and Giroux, 2000).

10. An example of the profitability of the iPad can be found in The boomerang effect, *The Economist* (April 21, 2012), 7. For an overview of Foxconn, see Foxconn: When workers dream of a life beyond the factory gates, *The Economist* (December 15, 2012), 56–57.

11. See, for example, Protectionism in China: Red Apple, *The Economist* (April 6, 2013), 62.

12. See, for example, E. Michaels, H. Handfield-Jones, and B. Axelrod, *The War for Talent* (Boston: Harvard Business School Press, 2001).

13. B. McLean, Is Enron overpriced? *Fortune* (March 5, 2001).

14. G. J. Benston and A. L. Hartgraves, Enron: What happened and what we can learn from it, *Journal of Accounting and Public Policy* 21 (2002), 105–27; P. M. Healy and K. G. Palepu, The fall of Enron, *Journal of Economic Perspectives* 17, 2 (2003), 2–26; P. K. Chaney and K. L. Philipich, Shredded reputation: The cost of audit failure, *Journal of Accounting Research* 40, 4 (2002), 1221–45; D. M. Boje, C. L. Gardner, and W. L. Smith, (Mis)using numbers in the Enron story, *Organizational Research Methods* 9, 4 (2006), 456–74.

15. A. Schiffrin, *Bad News: How America's Business Press Missed the Story of the Century* (New York: The New Press, 2011).

16. T. Bower, *OIL: Money, Politics and Power in the 21st Century* (New York: Grand Central Publishing, 2009), ch. 16.

17. See Roy Morgan Research, Finding No. 4888 (May 2, 2013). Accessed at www.roymorgan.com.

18. For a review of the benefits of public companies, see The endangered public company, *The Economist* (May 19, 2012), 11; see also The big engine that couldn't, *The Economist* (May 19, 2012), 27–29.

19. See G. Lakoff and E. Eehling, *The Little Blue Book: The Essential Guide to Thinking and Talking Democratic* (New York: Free Press, 2012). J. Romm, *Language Intelligence: Lessons on Persuasion from Jesus, Shakespeare, Lincoln*

and Lady Gaga (CreateSpace, 2012). Lexington, The war of words, *The Economist* (July 13, 2013), 35.

20. See, for example, K. D. Elsbach and R. M. Kramer, Members' responses to organizational identity threats: Encountering and countering the *Business Week* rankings, *Administrative Science Quarterly* 41, 3 (1996), 442–76.

Chapter 3

1. M. L. Barnett and T. G. Pollock (eds.), *The Oxford Handbook of Corporate Reputations* (Oxford: Oxford University Press, 2012).

2. K. T. Jackson, *Building Reputational Capital* (Oxford: Oxford University Press, 2004), 43.

3. C. Kobrak, The concept of reputation in business history, *Business History Review* 87, 4 (2013), 763–86.

4. G. Page and H. Fearn, Corporate reputation: What do consumers really care about? *Journal of Advertising* (September 2005), 305–13.

5. J. Macey, *The Death of Corporate Reputation: How Integrity Has Been Destroyed on Wall Street* (London: FT Press, 2013).

6. See, for example, G. Jackson et al., Grey areas: Irresponsible corporations and reputational dynamics, *Socioeconomic Review* 12 (2014), 153–218; R. W. Clement, Just how unethical is American business? *Business Horizons* 49 (2006), 313–27. See also2013 and 2014 *Edelman Trust Barometer*—results are based on an online survey of 26,000 people across 26 countries:www.edelman.com. Accessed September 9, 2013 and May 25, 2014. *Building Trust and Growth* PWC (2014) from www.pwc.com/taxceosurvey. Gallup—Confidence in Institutions—Historical Trends at www.gallup.com/poll/1597/confidence-institutions.aspx.

7. See, for example, J. B. Barney and M. H. Hansen, Trustworthiness as a source of competitive advantage, *Strategic Management Journal* 15 (1994), 175–90.

8. See, for example, M. Gosti and A. M. Wilson, Corporate Reputation: Seeking a Definition, *Corporate Communications* 6, 1 (2001), 24–30; M. L. Barnett, J. M. Jermier, and B. A. Lafferty, Corporate reputation: The definitional landscape, *Corporate Reputation Review* 9, 1 (2006), 26–38; S. Highhouse, A. Broadfoot, J. E. Yugo, and S. A. Devendorf, Examining corporate reputation judgments with generalizability theory, *Journal of Applied Psychology* 94, 3 (2009), 782–89; K. Walker, A systematic review of the corporate reputation Literature: Definition, measurement and theory, *Corporate Reputation Review* 12, 4 (2010), 357–87; S. Helm and C. Klode, Challenges in measuring corporate reputation, in S. Helm, K. Lier-Gobbers and C. Storch (eds.), *Reputation Management* (Berlin: Springer, 2011), 99–110; D. Lange, P. M. Lee and Y. Dai, Organizational reputation: A review, *Journal of Management* 37, 1 (2011), 153–84; A. Bitektine, Toward a theory of social judgments of organizations: The case of legitimacy, reputation and status, *Academy of Management Review* 36, 1 (2011), 151–79; A. Clardy, Organizational reputation: Issues in conceptualization and measurement, *Corporate Reputation Review* 15, 4 (2012), 285–303.

9. V. P. Rindova and L. L. Martins, Show me the money: A multidimensional perspective on reputation as an intangible asset, in M. L. Barnett and T. G. Pollock (eds.), *The Oxford Handbook of Corporate Reputations* (Oxford: Oxford University Press, 2012), 16–33.

10. One reason for the popularity of this theoretical perspective is that it is easy to measure the reputations of companies—you simply ask a group of people to rate the companies on a set of scales.

11. I call them "working" definitions because they are not formed to guide a particular measure of the construct. This requires making each one a bit more complicated than is needed at this stage of the discussion.

12. D. Lange, P. M. Lee, and Y. Dai, Organizational reputation: A review, *Journal of Management* 37, 1 (2011), 153–84.

13. C. J. Fombrun, *Reputation: Realizing Value from the Corporate Image* (Boston: Harvard Business School Press, 1996). In particular see chapter 3.

14. G. R. Dowling, *Creating Corporate Reputations* (Oxford: Oxford University Press, 2001).

15. J. A. Schumpeter, Hatred of bankers is one of the world's oldest and most dangerous prejudices, *The Economist* (January 7, 2012), 56.

16. In 1989 the cover story title of *The Bulletin* magazine's lead article was "Why the banks are bastards." This saying about Australia's major banks has persisted to this day. The article that coined this reputation is S. Kennedy, The unloved bank manager, *The Bulletin with Newsweek* (May 2, 1989), 42–54.

17. For example, do people allow good things a company does to offset bad things it does. This is known as a compensatory process. If they don't, then what sorts of bad things are important enough to render a reputation as bad? There are many different types of evaluation processes that research needs to explore because the way people come to an overall evaluation will affect how companies respond.

18. This is the most notable definition of values from M. Rokeach, *The Nature of Human Values* (New York: Free Press, 1973), 5.

19. D. Aitkin, Setting a values compass, *The Australian* (March 6, 2005), 32; T. Devinney, P. Auger and R. DeSailly, *What Matters to Australians: Our Social, Political and Economic Values* (2012), available from T. Devinney—T.Devinney@leeds.ac.uk.

20. D. Porritt, The reputational failure of financial success: The bottom line backlash effect, *Corporate Reputation Review* 8, 3 (2005), 198–213.

21. N. Shoebridge, We use them but we love to hate them, *Australian Financial Review* (October 9, 2006), 56; G. R. Dowling, How the tension between "good" and "bad" profits can wreak havoc with a company's reputation, *Business Strategy Series* 9, 6 (2008), 330–35.

22. Survey of the professions, *Roy Morgan Research* (April 11, 2014), available at www.roymorgan.com.

23. D. Kahneman, *Thinking, Fast and Slow* (London: Penguin, 2011), ch. 28.

24. The phrase is used by Jaques in "All the world's a stage" speech in *As You Like It*.

25. M. J. Kotchen and J. J. Moon, Corporate social responsibility for irresponsibility, *BE Journal of Economic Analysis and Policy* 12, 1 (2012), 1–23.

Chapter 4

1. L. Heracleous and J. Wirtz, Singapore Airlines' balancing act, *Harvard Business Review* (July/August 2010), 145–49.

2. T. Bower, *Oil: Money, Politics and Power in the 21st Century* (New York: Grand Central Publishing, 2009), ch. 13.

3. C. Hoyos, BP battles to clear its Augean stables, *Financial Times* (September 20, 2006), p. 21.

4. This section is based on my work with Peter Moran. See G. R. Dowling and P. Moran, Corporate reputations: Built in or bolted on? *California Management Review* 54, 2 (2012), 25–42.

5. See, for example, the contrarian Jon Entine's home page at www.jonentine.com/.

6. Downloaded from http://www.bcorporation.net/community/seventh-generation (June 10, 2014). However, some of the company's environmental and product performance claims have been challenged by *Procter & Gamble* and then quickly withdrawn by the company.

7. From the *Patagonia* USA website. Accessed December 10, 2011, and December 12, 2014.

8. "B corps: Firms with benefits, *The Economist* (January 7, 2012), 53–54.

9. This seems especially so for consumers. See, for example, G. Page and H. Fearn, Corporate reputation: What do consumers really care about? *Journal of Advertising Research*(September 2005), 305–13.

10. Accessed from the *GE* website March 3, 2013.

11. G. Haigh, Who's afraid of Macquarie Bank? *The Monthly* (July 2007), p. 4. Downloaded from http://www.themonthly.com.au/issue/2007/july/12409644771.

12. The full article is M. Friedman, The social responsibility of business is to increase its profits, *New York Times Magazine* (September 13, 1970).

13. M. E. Porter and M. R. Kramer, The competitive advantage of corporate philanthropy, *Harvard Business Review* 80, 12 (2002), 57–68; Strategy and society: The link between competitive advantage and corporate social responsibility, *Harvard Business Review* (December 2006), 2–15; Creating shared value, *Harvard Business Review* 89, 1/2 (2011), 62–77.

14. Evergreening is achieved by seeking extra patents on variations of the original drug—new forms of release, new dosages, new combinations, or new forms. The pharmaceutical companies call this practice "lifecycle management."

15. See, for example, F. Campbell, Executive Producer, *The Men Who Made Us Fat* (London: BBC, Fresh One Productions, 2012).

16. Food companies: Food for thought, *The Economist—Special Report, Obesity* (December 15, 2012), 9–12.

17. K. D. Elsbach and R. M. Kramer, Members' responses to organizational identity threats: Encountering and countering the Business Week rankings, *Administrative Science Quarterly* 41, 3 (1996), 442–76.

18. See www.reputationinstitute.com for this and similar claims about the general importance of a good corporate reputation.

19. M. E. Porter, *Competitive Strategy* (New York: Free Press, 1980); M. E. Porter, *Competitive Advantage* (New York: Free Press, 1985).

20. J. Robinson, How the Ritz-Carlton manages the mystique, *Gallup Business Journal* (undated) available at http://businessjournal.gallup.com/content/112906/How-Ritzcarlton.

21. H. Schultz, *Put Your Heart Into It* (New York: Hyperion, 1997), 131.

22. C. Lucier, Herb Kelleher, *Strategy+Business* (Summer 2004), 119–25.

23. Steven Covey notes that intent is one of the four main determinants of trustworthiness. The others are integrity, capabilities and results. See S. M. R. Covey with R. R. Merrill, *The Speed of Trust* (New York: Free Press, 2006).

24. Many senior managers were also financially rewarded based on the airline's profitability.

25. www.macquarie.com/about/companyprofile/what we stand for.

26. For many years including 2014 and 2015 it was voted by its peers as the top commercial law firm in the United States; see www.vault.com.

27. See G. Colvin, The trembling at News Corp has only begun, *Fortune* (July 19, 2011); Fazed and refused, *The Economist* (October 20, 2012).

28. www.qantas.com.au/ourcompany. Accessed April 5, 2015.

29. Qantas posted a $2.8 billion loss for the financial year ended June 30, 2014. The CEO's pay fell by 40 percent. A prominent business journalist suggested that he was Australia's most disliked chief executive. And during the next week the share price rose by 20 percent! Go figure?

Chapter 5

1. The last three are attributed to Joe Barton, chairman of the US House Energy Committee in 2004.

2. In February 2015 *Apple* became the first US company to record a stock market valuation of more than $700billion—which just exceeded the combined market value of *Google* and *Microsoft*.

3. See money.cnn.com/magazines/fortune/most_admired/.

4. ft.com/reports/global brands. Accessed May 27, 2015.

5. For an autobiographic description of this effect see D. Deephouse, From the colors of the rainbow to monochromatic grey: An $n = 1 + x$ analysis of Apple's corporate reputation, 1976–2013," *Socioeconomic Review* 12 (2014), 206–18.

6. W. Isaacson, *Steve Jobs* (Hachette Digital, 2011), p. 509.

7. P. Drucker, *Innovation and Entrepreneurship* (Oxford: Butterworth-Heinemann, 1985), p. 70.

8. See, for example, D. Zwerdling, Shattered myths, *Gourmet* (August 2004). Accessed from gourmet.com. What the shape of the glass probably does is to regulate how quickly people drink a glass of beer or wine; see Beer drinking: Shape up, *The Economist* (September 1, 2012), 66.

9. From the corporate website www.riedel.com/. Accessed June 12, 2014.

10. W. Isaacson, *Steve Jobs* (Hachette Digital, 2011).

11. From http://www.philips.com/about/company/ accessed June 12, 2014.

12. L. Kellaway, My brand new motto: Nomina rutrum rutrum, *Financial Times* (February 8, 2010), 12.

13. J. Laran, A. N. Dalton, and E. B. Andrade, The curious case of behavioral backlash: Why brands produce priming effects and slogans produce reverse priming effects, *Journal of Consumer Research* 37, April (2011), 999–1014.

14. The website boasts that the corporate re-branding from *Andersen Consulting* to *Accenture* was "one of the largest and most successful re-branding campaigns in corporate history." www.accenture.com/History. Accessed November 12, 2014.

Chapter 6

1. I was one of the people who waited for my defined benefit superannuation. As the last associate dean for research, one of the roles I gave myself in the new merged faculty was to protect the *AGSM* academics who decided to stay. Even though I was a bit pigheaded about this, graciously on my retirement a couple of years later, the university made me an emeritus professor.

2. There was an interesting conflict between being best at research and best at teaching in the *AGSM* and many other business schools. While best at teaching was something that was clearly valued by most stakeholders, being best at research had a more limited application. For example, students often didn't care about the research agenda of a faculty member and the faculty member's research seldom had a big impact on what they taught. Nor was research the principal driver of the school's *Financial Times* ranking. Paradoxically where research played its largest role was to drive the reputations of the faculty members, which in turn made them more marketable and more likely to be poached by another business school.

3. A. St. George, *Royal Navy Way of Leadership* (London: Preface Publishing, 2012).

4. H. Gardner, *Changing Minds* (Boston: Harvard Business School Press, 2004).

5. S. Denning, *The Springboard: How Storytelling Ignites Action in Knowledge-Era Organizations* (Boston: Butterworth Heinemann, 2000); *Squirrel Inc.: A Fable of Leadership through Storytelling* (San Francisco: Jossey-Bass, 2004); *The Leader's Guide to Storytelling* (San Francisco: Jossey-Bass, 2005). A. Simmons, *The Story Factor* (New York: Basic Books, 2006).

6. The others are concepts, theories, and skills.

7. Rebuilding the garage, *The Economist* (July 15, 2000), 59–61.

8. N. Mourkogiannis, The realist's guide to moral purpose, *Strategy + Business* (Winter, 2005), 42–53.

9. A new boss for Tata: From pupil to master, *The Economist* (December 1, 2012), 65–66.

10. From www.tata.com/aboutus/management.AccessedJune26, 2014.

11. Someone in *3M* chronicled the company's track record in a wonderful book—*A Century of Innovation: The 3M Story* (3M Company, 2002). I found this book only by accident.

12. 3m.com. Accessed April 11, 2015.

13. S. Denning, *The Leader's Guide to Storytelling* (San Francisco: Jossey-Bass, 2005).

14. J. Crown, Adding it up at IBM, *Chicago Booth Magazine* (Spring 2013), 20–24. See also R. Waters, Rometty's IBM overhaul becomes more urgent, *Financial Times* (October 24, 2014).

15. B. Lane, *Jacked Up: The Inside Story of How Jack Welch Talked GE into Becoming the World's Greatest Company* (New York: McGraw-Hill, 2008).

16. A. Crippen, Warren Buffett's "editor" retires after 60 years, *CNBC* (July 2, 2014) available at http://www.cnbc.com/id/101805642?

17. M. Barbaro, A new weapon for Wal-Mart: A war room, *New York Times* (November 1, 2005). J. Birchall and H. Yeager, Big-box politics: Wal-Mart takes the fight to its critics, *Financial Times* (August 17, 2006), 9.

18. P. Robinson, *Snapshots from Hell: The Making of an MBA* (New York: Warner Books, 1994).

19. G. R. Dowling, Journalists' evaluation of corporate reputations, *Corporate Reputation Review* 7, 2 (2004), 196–205.

Chapter 7

1. G. R. Dowling, *Creating Corporate Reputations* (Oxford: Oxford University Press, 2001).

2. Such as F. Partnoy, *Infectious Greed*; M. Lewis, *Liars Poker*; B. McLean and P. Elkind, *Enron: The Smartest Guys in the Room*; M. Benns, *The Men who Killed Qantas*.

3. He held this position until December 2012. He was also on the advisory board of the *Reputation Institute*.

4. Tribal Japan, *The Economist* (December 3, 2011), 38.

5. www.theaustralian.com.au. Accessed November 22, 2014.

6. From the About Us, Our History section of the corporate website. www.economist.com. Accessed November 22, 2014.

7. The foundation paper was R. K. Mitchell, B. R. Agle, and D. J. Wood, Toward a theory of stakeholder identification: Defining the principle of who and what really matters, *Academy of Management Review* 22, 4 (1997), 853–86.

8. This decision tree is derived from V. H. Vroom and P. W. Yetton, *Leadership and Decision Making* (Pittsburg: University of Pittsburg Press, 1973). Summaries of this model of leadership can still be found in most good textbooks on leadership.

9. Blame Qantas for grounding, *Essential Report* (November 7, 2011) at *Essential Media Communications* at essentialmedia.com.au.

10. See S. Janoff and M. Weisbord, *Future Search: An Action Guide to Finding Common Ground in Organizations and Committees* (Berrett-Koehler, 1995).

11. J. Useem, Business school, disrupted, *New York Times* (June 1, 2014), BU1.

12. A. Adkins, Consumers are still wary: Here's how to win them, *Gallup Business Journal* (undated) available at http://buinessjournal.gallup.com/content/171716/consumers-wary.

13. See for example, A. Chatterjee and D. C. Hambrick, It's all about me: Narcissistic chief executive officers and their effects on company strategy and performance, *Administrative Science Quarterly* 52, 3 (2007), 351–86. See also P. Elkind, The trouble with Steve Jobs, *Fortune* (March 17, 2008).

14. Schumpeter, The cult of the faceless boss, *The Economist* (November 14, 2009), 73.

15. It turned out that this was achieved by using some accounting tricks. *GE* was later fined for this.

16. Reported in T. S. Stewart, Why leadership matters, *Fortune* (March 2, 1998), 39–50.

17. *State of the Global Workforce* (Washington, DC: Gallup, 2013), available from www.gallup.com.

18. M. McNamee with A. Borrus, Out of control at Andersen, *Business Week* (April 8, 2002), 74–75. See also B. L. Garrett, *Too Big to Jail: How Prosecutors Compromise with Corporations* (Cambridge: Harvard University Press, 2014).

19. Recently the UK Corporate Governance Code has recognized that the "tone from the top" of a company is vital to its success. A. Hill, Outsiders will struggle to control hidden CEO risks, *Financial Times* (October 13, 2014).

20. Reported in S. M. R. Covey with R. R. Merrill, *The Speed of Trust* (New York: Free Press, 2006), 265.

21. Reported in S. Foley, Warren Buffett rolls out the Berkshire Hathaway brand, *Financial Times* (October 13, 2014).

22. Often, just after a sports person is lauded in the press, his performance falls off dramatically.

Chapter 8

1. See, for example, G. R. Dowling and N. A. Gardberg, Measuring corporate reputation, in T. Singer (ed.), *Sustainability Matters 2014* (New York: The Conference Board, 2014), 64–69.

2. See, for example, J. Louviere, I. Lings, T. Islam, S. Gudergan, and T. Flynn, An introduction to the application of (case 1) best–worst scaling in marketing research, *International Journal of Research in Marketing* 30, 2 (2013), 292–303.

3. There is often a trap with using customer satisfaction as a surrogate for reputation. If all competitors offer a similar level of service or similar quality products, then customers come to expect that this is the only thing on offer. Surveys will reveal that most of the customers will be satisfied with what they receive because there is no point in changing supplier. I have seen different surveys of the same people where, in one, they say they are satisfied with the products and service but, in the other, they say they do not hold the company in high regard.

4. G. R. Dowling and N. Gardberg, Keeping score: The challenges of measuring corporate reputation, in M. Barnet and T. Pollock (eds.), *Oxford Handbook of Corporate Reputations* (Oxford: Oxford University Press, 2012), 34–68. For another review, see S. L. Wartick, Measuring corporate reputation: Definition and data, *Business and Society* 41, 4 (2002), 371–92.

5. G. R. Dowling and W. Weeks, What the media is really telling you about your brand, MIT *Sloan Management Review* 49, 3 (2008), 28–34.

6. A. Schiffrin, The US press and the financial crisis, in A. Schiffrin (ed.), *Bad News: How America's Business Press Missed the Story of the Century* (New York: New Press, 2011), 1–21.

7. E. Steel, How Shell was hijacked by a new style of cyber protest, *Financial Times* (June 22, 2012), 10.

8. T. Bower, *Oil: Money, Politics and Power in the 21st Century* (New York: Grand Central Publishing, 2009).

9. L. Lee and P. Burrows, A bruise or two on Apple's reputation, *Business Week* (October 22, 2007), 81–83.

10. J. Gapper, Goldman's glory may be short-lived, *Financial Times* (December 6, 2007),

11. Hay Group (2013). See www.haygroup.com/ww/best_companies/index.aspx?id=155). Accessed November 1, 2014.

12. J. Jacoby. Consumer research: How valid and useful are all our consumer behavior research findings? A state of the art review, *Journal of Marketing* 42, 2 (1978), 87–95.

13. The one thing that potentially saves the integrity of the WMAC measure is that the people who are chosen to rate the companies are all managers and

company analysts. They presumably have a similar notion of what each of these attributes means, and they believe that these are the true underlying determinants of admiration or reputation.

14. The issue here is equivalent to determining what is called the gamma change between the measures of a variable. See G. R. Dowling, The alpha, beta, gamma change approach to measuring change and its use for interpreting the effectiveness of service quality, *Australian Journal of Management* 26, 1 (2001), 55–67.

15. S. Dolnicar and B. Grün, How constrained a response? A comparison of binary, ordinal and metric answer formats, *Journal of Retailing and Consumer Services* 14 (2007), 108–22; S. Dolnicar, Asking good survey questions, *Journal of Travel Research* 52, 5 (2013), 551–74.

16. When this happens, the random error part of the measure increases, and thus decreases the accuracy of the measure.

17. If this type of measure is adopted then a good way to introduce the SVP attribute is to state it as the center part of the SVP onion. For example, for *Riedel*'s customers this would be how their wine glasses help produce a better drinking experience.

18. As chapter 3 suggests, these people may also have a quite complex structured reputation of the company.

19. P. Auger, T. Devinney, G. Dowling, C. Eckert, and N. Lin, How much does a company's reputation matter in recruiting? *MIT Sloan Management Review* 54, 3 (2013), 79–88.

20. L. Muchnik, S. Aral, and S. J. Taylor, Social influence bias: A randomized experiment, *Science* 341 (August 9, 2013), 647–51.

Chapter 9

1. B. Garratt, *The Fish Rots from the Head* (London: Profile Books, 2010).

2. R. J. Thomas, M. Schrage, J. B. Bellin, and G. Marcotte, How boards can be better—A manifesto, *MIT Sloan Management Review* 50, 2 (2009), 69–74.

3. H. Mintzberg, *Managers Not MBAs* (San Francisco: Berrett-Koehler, 2004), 104–11.

4. M. Diamond, Woes for Johnson & Johnson, *USA Today* (November 20, 2011).

5. The research that came up with this idea was later found to be flawed because it focused only on those companies that survived. It was later discovered that being a fast follower is often the most successful strategy.

6. L. Heracleous and J. Wirtz, Singapore Airlines' balancing act, *Harvard Business Review* (July/August 2010), 145–49.

7. A. Edgecliffe-Johnson, A bid to get everyone on board, *Financial Times* (September 27, 2005), 8.

8. M. T. Hansen, H. Ibarra, and U. Peyer, The best-performing CEOs in the world, *Harvard Business Review*(January/February 2013), 81–95.

9. See, for example, J. A. Schumpeter, Fallen idols, *The Economist* (May 2, 2002).

10. See, for example, Corporate governance: Anything you can do, Ichan do better, *The Economist* (February 15, 2014), 55–56.

11. M. Edwards, *Small Change: Why Business Won't Save the World* (San Francisco: Berrett-Koehler, 2009).

12. Tsunami: The backlash, *The Age* (February 12, 2005). Sourced from http://www.theage.com.au/articles/2005/02/11/1108061871800.html.

13. D. Kocieniewski, GE's strategies let it avoid taxes altogether," *New York Times* (March 24, 2011).

14. Charlemagne, The flying taxman, *The Economist* 407, 8832 (2013), 51.

15. G. R. Dowling, The curious case of corporate tax avoidance: Is it socially irresponsible? *Journal of Business Ethics* 124, 1 (2014), 173–84.

16. A good example of this is the tax reports issued by Rio Tinto. See http://www.riotinto.com/ourcommitment/taxes-paid-in-2014-14598.aspx.

17. This list comes from the *MSCI KLD 400 Social Index* social investment fund.

18. The old saying that "half my advertising is wasted, but I don't know which half" has been attributed to both John Wanamaker (founder of a US department store) and Lord Leverhulme of the United Kingdom. Ad agencies respond that the half that is wasted is "the second half" by which they mean media placement. The media agencies response is that the first half is wasted, namely the creative execution of the advertisements.

19. M. H. Bazerman and M. D. Watkins, *Predictable Surprises* (Boston: Harvard Business School Press, 2008).

20. Reported in the *Reputation Institute*'s 2013 Annual Reputation Leaders Survey—Making the Grade when Stakeholders Rule. www.reputationinstitute.com. Downloaded 5/09/2013.

21. P. Del Vecchio, R. Laubacher, V. Ndou, and G. Passiante, Managing corporate reputation in the blogosphere: The case of Dell Computer, *Corporate Reputation Review* 14, 2 (2011), 133–44.

22. P. Midler, *Poorly Made in China: An Insider's Account of the China Production Game* (Hoboken, NJ: Wiley, 2009).

23. For an example of the opposite situation, see F. Hilmer with B. Dury, *The Fairfax Experience* (Sydney: Wiley Australia, 2007).

24. Schumpeter, The wolves of the web, *The Economist* (February 22, 2014), p. 60.

25. R. Chittum, Missing the moment, in A. Schiffrin (ed.), *Bad News: How America's Business Press Missed the Story of the Century* (New York: New Press, 2011), 71–93.

26. A. Ferguson and C. Vedelago, Targets, bonuses, trips—Inside the CBA boiler room, *Sydney Morning Herald* (June 22, 2013).

27. For example, the chair on an Australian Government Senate inquiry into the *Commonwealth Bank* stated that the bank's financial advisers' "unethical and

dishonest" treatment of "vulnerable trusting people" involved "a callous disregard for their clients." Performance of the Australian Securities and Investments Commission (ASIC) *Senate Economics References Committee* (June 26, 1014), www.aph.gov.au/Parliamentary_Business/Committees?Senate/Economies?ASIC.

28. B. Butler and A. Ferguson, CBA rewards bosses of scandal-ridden financial planning division, *Sydney Morning Herald* (August 19, 2014).

29. J. Useem, Business school, disrupted, *New York Times* (June 1, 2014), BU1.

Chapter 10

1. A few years later we inherited a small program in Asia from another part of the university. It took years to make this a viable venture.

2. See, for example, D. Deephouse and S. Carter, An examination of the differences between organizational legitimacy and organizational reputation, *Journal of Management Studies* 42, 2 (2005), 329–60.

3. S. Grene, Ethical investing: An understanding of grey areas is crucial for success in business, *Financial Times* (November 9, 2014).

4. M. T. Hansen, H. Ibarra, and U. Peyer, The best-performing CEOs in the world, *Harvard Business Review* (January/February 2013), 81–95.

5. M. Mazodier and A. Rezaee, Are sponsorship announcements good news for the shareholders? Evidence from international stock exchanges, *Journal of the Academy of Marketing Science* 41, 5 (2013), 586–600.

6. For a description of this type of company, see J. S. Hiller, The benefit corporation and corporate social responsibility, *Journal of Business Ethics* 118, 2 (2013), 287–301.

7. G. Page and H. Fearn, Corporate reputation: What do consumers really care about? *Journal of Advertising Research*(September 2005), 305–13.

8. T. J. Brown and P. A. Dacin, The company and the product: Corporate associations and consumer product responses, *Journal of Marketing* 61, 1 (1997), 68–84.

9. D. Vogel, *The Market for Virtue* (Washington, DC: Brookings Institute Press, 2005).

10. See also T. Devinney, P. Auger, and G. Eckhardt, *The Myth of the Ethical Consumer* (Cambridge UK: Cambridge University Press, 2010).

11. P. Auger, T. Devinney, G. Dowling, C. Eckert, and N. Lin, How much does a company's reputation matter in recruiting? *MIT Sloan Management Review* 54, 3 (2013), 79–88.

12. J. Chen, D. Patten, and R. Roberts, Corporate charitable contributions: A corporate social performance or legitimacy strategy, *Journal of Business Ethics* 82, 1 (2008), 131–44; D. Proir, J. Surroca, and J. Tribo, Are socially responsible managers really ethical? Exploring the relationship between earnings manipulation and corporate social responsibility, *Corporate Governance* 16, 3 (2008), 160–77.

13. E. E. Warner, What's a Cigarette Company to Do? *American Journal of Public Health* 92, 6 (2002), 897–900.

14. G. R. Dowling, How the tension between good and bad profits can wreak havoc with a company's reputation, *Business Strategy Series* 9, 6 (2006), 330–35. Also, at the time of writing, these banks were rated as some of the most profitable commercial banks in the world.

15. A. Sampson, The bank's exit fees can be hefty when you quit a home loan early, *Sydney Morning Herald* (March 31–April 1, 2007), p. 51.

16. D. Glance, Banking's huge profits almost ready for the taking, *The Conversation* (June 24, 2014) available at theconversation.com.

17. For example, a US parliamentary committee reported that *Apple* had avoided paying corporate tax on $44 billion of profits during the period 2009 to 2012 (Cook lightly grilled, *The Economist* (May 25, 2013), 59–60). See also N. Irwin, How to make $30 billion and pay no corporate income tax, the Apple way, *Washington Post* (May 20, 2013).

18. C. Fombrun and C. van Riel, *Fame and Fortune* (New York: FT Prentice Hall, 2004), ch. 9.

19. This attitude is captured in the old saying about bankers—that they believe in capitalism when it comes to pocketing the profits and socialism when it comes to paying for their losses.

20. The big engine that couldn't, *The Economist* (May 19, 2012), 27–29.

21. See, for example, K. Malik, *The Quest for a Moral Compass* (London: Atlantic Books, 2014). This book shows how social needs and political desires have shaped the moral thinking of different cultures.

22. M. Alexei, Business ethics, *Stanford Encyclopedia of Philosophy* (Fall 2008 edition), E. N. Zalta (ed.), http://plato.stanford.edu/archives/fall2008/entries/ethics-business/.

23. Y. L. Cheung, P. R. Rau, and A. Stouraitis, How much do firms pay as bribes and what benefits do they get? Evidence from corruption cases worldwide, NBER Working paper 17981 (April 2012).

24. For a discussion of the "everyone's doing it" moral justification see R. Green, When everyone's doing it, *Business and Ethics Quarterly* 1, 1 (1991), 75–93.

25. From Guidance Note 8 of the Australian Stock Exchange Listing Rules (January 2013).

26. For example, see the "our goals" section of the company website at www.seventhgeneration.com/.

27. Corporate storytelling, *The Economist* (November 4, 2004).

28. J. Freedman, Improving (not perfecting) tax legislation: Rules and principles revisited, *British Tax Review* 6 (2010), 717–36.

29. J. Finch, Be fair plea as tax loopholes targeted, *The Guardian* (March 18, 2004).

30. Financial Crisis Inquiry Commission, *The Financial Crisis Inquiry Report* (New York: Public Affairs, 2011).

31. An interesting description of the global financial crisis can be found in the various essays in A. Schiffrin (ed.), *Bad News: How America's Business Press Missed the Story of the Century* (New York: New Press, 2011). See also J. R. Barth, R. Levine, and G. Caprio, *Guardians of Finance: Making Regulators Work for Us* (Cambridge: MIT Press, 2012).

32. A. R. Sorkin, *Too Big to Fail* (London: Penguin, 2010).

33. B. L. Garrett, *Too Big to Jail: How Prosecutors Compromise with Corporations* (Cambridge: Harvard University Press, 2014).

34. M. L. Barnett and T. G. Pollock, Charting the landscape of corporate reputation research, in M. L. Barnett and T. G. Pollock (eds.), *The Oxford Handbook of Corporate Reputations* (Oxford: Oxford University Press, 2012), 1–15 at 12.

35. B. Wernerfelt, The resource based theory of the firm, *Strategic Management Journal* 5, 2 (1984), 171–80; J. B. Barney, Firm resources and sustained competitive advantage, *Journal of Management* 17, 1 (1991), 99–120; J. B. Barney, Looking inside for competitive advantage, *Academy of Management Perspective* 9, 4 (1995), 49–61; I. Dierickx and K. Cool, Asset stock accumulation and sustainability of competitive advantage, *Management Science* 35 (1989), 1504–11. C. J. Fombrun, *Reputation: Realizing Value from the Corporate Image* (Boston: Harvard Business School Press, 1996).

36. J. Davis and T. Devinney, *The Essence of Corporate Strategy* (Sydney: Allen and Unwin, 1997), 25–27.

37. B. Lev, *Intangibles* (Washington, DC: Brookings Institute Press, 2001).

38. F. Partnoy, Six shades of grey: A legal perspective on reputation, *Socioeconomic Review* 12 (2014), 195–200.

39. For one of the more confusing attempts to value corporate reputations, see N. Kossovsky, *Reputation, Stock Price, and You* (New York: Apress, 2012).

40. Schumpeter, Why companies should worry less about their reputations, *The Economist* (April 21, 2012), 73.

41. As also noted in *RI*'s Corporate Reputation Briefing, The pharma industry (2013). Accessed from the Reputation Institute website September 4, 2013.

42. H. Rao, The social construction of reputation: Certification contests, legitimization and the survival of organizations in the American automotive industry: 1895–1912,*Strategic Management Journal* 15 (Winter 1994), 29–44.

43. J. Surowiecki, *The Wisdom of Crowds* (London: Abacus, 2004).

44. R. G. Eccles, S. C. Newquist and R. Schatz, Reputation and its risks, *Harvard Business Review* 85, 2 (2007), 104–14.

45. See, for example, T. Devinney, G. Dowling, and N. Perm-Ajchariyawong, The *Financial Times* business schools ranking: What quality is this signal of quality, *European Management Review* 5, 4 (2008), 195–208.

Chapter 11

1. P. J. Firestein, Building and protecting corporate reputation, *Strategy and Leadership* 34, 4 (2006), 25–31.

2. G. Haigh, Who's afraid of Macquarie Bank? *The Monthly* (July 2007). Downloaded from http://www.themonthly.com.au/issue/2007/july/12409644771.

3. Flocks and shepherds, *The Economist* (March 9, 2013), 55–56; Schumpeter, Pope, CEO, *The Economist* (March 9, 2013), 65; The Francis effect: The Pope as a turnaround CEO, *The Economist* (April 19, 2014).

4. G. R. Dowling, The curious case of corporate tax avoidance: Is it socially irresponsible? *Journal of Business Ethics* 124, 1 (2014), 173–84.

5. G. Jackson and S. Brammer, Introducing grey areas: The unexpectedly weak link between corporate irresponsibility and reputation, *Socioeconomic Review* 12 (2014), 154–66.

6. D. Vogel, The private regulation of global corporate conduct, *Business and Society* 49, 1 (2010), 68–87; B. G. King, Reputational dynamics of private regulation, *Socioeconomic Review* 12 (2014), 200–206.

7. In the discipline of finance, the event study methodology has been used to study this kind of problem. If one could identify a number of public company crises that had reputation effects, then changes in share price data (abnormal returns) might throw some light on this question.

8. A. Zavyalova, Negative consequences of good reputation and positive outcomes of negative events, *Socioeconomic Review* 12 (2014), 181–86.

9. See, for example, D. Lange and N. T. Washburn, Understanding attributions of corporate social irresponsibility, *Academy of Management Review* 37, 2 (2012), 300–26.

10. L. N. Spiro, Dream team, *Business Week* (August 29, 1994), 48–52.

11. *LTCM*'s success and growing reputation allowed it to secure $3billion in investment funds and billions more in borrowings.

12. R. Lowenstein, *When Genius Failed: The Rise and Fall of Long-Term Capital Management* (New York: Random House, 2001).

13. For an explanation of how reputation and status combine to form such a signal of quality, see I. Stern, J. M. Dukerich, and E. Zajac, Unmixed signals: How reputation and status affect alliance formation, *Strategic Management Journal* 35, 4 (1014), 512–31.

14. L. Kellaway, Listening to your customers can be bad for business *Financial Times* (18 October 18, 2010), 12; Schumpeter, Logoland, *The Economist* (January 15, 2011), 66.

15. T. Spaeth, The identity recession, *Conference Board Review*, Report TCBR4 (January 2010).

16. T. Bower, *OIL: Money, Politics and Power in the 21st Century* (New York: Grand Central Publishing, 2009), p. 231.

17. At the time *Federal Express* (*FedEx*) was using the slogan "when it absolutely, positively has to be there overnight."

18. For an historical account of logos, see W. Olins, *Corporate Identity* (Boston: Harvard Business School Press, 1989).

19. See, for example, D. L. Kirp, *Shakespeare, Einstein and the Bottom Line* (Cambridge: Harvard University Press, 2003).

20. See the following paper and its references: L. Muchnik, S. Aral, and S. J. Taylor, Social influence bias: A randomized experiment, *Science* 341 (August 9, 2013), 647–51.

21. J. Useem, Business school, disrupted, *New York Times* (June 1, 2014), BU1.

22. For example, an interesting and easy to read treatise on such technology-based innovations is G. Moore, *Crossing the Chasm* (New York: Harper Business, 1991, 2006).

23. A. L. Penenberg, *Viral Loop: From Facebook to Twitter. How Today's Smartest Businesses Grow Themselves* (New York: Hyperion-HarperCollins, 2009).

24. See, for example, C. Dellarocas, Online reputation systems: How to design one that does what you need, *MIT Sloan Management Review* 51, 3 (2010), 33–38.

25. P. Del Vecchio, R. Laubacher, V. Ndou, and G. Passiante, Managing corporate reputation in the blogosphere: The case of Dell Computer, *Corporate Reputation Review* 14, 2 (2011), 133–44.

Epilogue

1. R. Florida, *The Rise of the Creative Class* (Melbourne: Pluto Press, 2003).

Appendix: How Much to Pay for a Customized Study of Corporate Reputation?

The answer to this question depends on how much a better reputation is worth, how much the study costs to do, and how accurate the study is likely to be. Some large companies do regular reputation monitoring research because they are convinced that some benefits will flow from having a better reputation than their competitors. This often takes the form of media monitoring and stakeholder surveys. However, given the relatively low costs of customized research relative to the size of a company's annual research budget, it is surprising to me that more customized studies are not done.

If, however, there is a squeeze on the research budget, a thought experiment might be used to determine if reputation research should be done. Then some back-of-the-envelope calculations might be all that is needed to convince the chief financial officer to free up some extra funds. For example, consider what it would it be worth to a company to conduct research to determine if say a once-off 2 percent improvement in its corporate reputation would be worth the cost. To keep the calculations simple, assume that the net financial benefit from a successful program will be $1 million and the costs of the program will be $100,000. Now it is worthwhile pausing here to think about this investment. In a world of certainty, spending $100,000 to make $1 million is an easy decision to make. So when the payoff is many times larger than the cost, our instincts tell us that this is probably a good investment. But we don't live in a world of certainty.

Thus any new initiative is not guaranteed to be successful. So assume that an expert's advice is that for companies like yours there is a 70 percent chance (0.7 probability) that your planned program will deliver a 2 percent improvement to the company's reputation. This means that we have a 70 percent chance of making $1 million. If this was a bet on a horse race, many rich people would take it. The expected value of the wager is 0.7 × $1 million = $700,000. So the intuition is still that it might be a good investment. But because there is a 30 percent chance of losing $100,000, the expected value of making a loss is 0.3 × –$100,000 = –$30,000. Here the manager faces a decision with two expected payoffs –$700,000 versus –$30,000. Hence many managers would like more information before making this investment.

The question facing the manager is how much should be paid for a research study to provide more clarity about this decision? Another way to frame this issue is how much should a manager pay to protect his or her reputation when they make this "go" or "no go" decision to conduct the reputation improvement program.[1] The answer to this question hinges on how accurate the research will be. Because it generally costs more to do better quality research, it would be good to know the maximum amount the company should be prepared to pay for a study that provides perfect information about the outcome of the program to improve the company's reputation. This is called the "value of perfect information." It would tell us if the project will succeed ($1 million) or fail (–$100,000). It also sets the upper limit on the amount the research firm should charge for a perfectly reliable study.

The way to answer this question is to structure the problem as a decision tree and then use a decision-making approach, called Bayesian inference, to calculate the maximum amount of money that should be spent on research.[2] Figure A.1 shows this approach.

The Bayesian decision inference approach requires that we calculate the following set of "expected values"—these are the probabilities multiplied by the dollar values in the decision tree.

1. Expected value of implementing this program
2. Expected value of not implementing the program

1. In the corporate world many such research studies are conducted in order to provide some protection for the decision maker.
2. If you have done coursework on decision analysis or statistics, you may recognize that I have formulated this as a Bayesian decision problem. Thomas Bayes was an eighteenth-century British mathematician and Presbyterian minister who developed a statistical method for incorporating a person's current knowledge into statistical decision making. Here I use a simplified version of his approach.

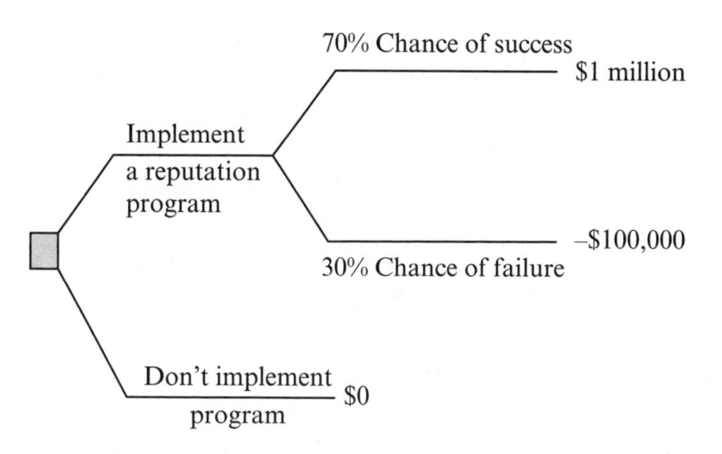

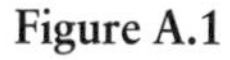

Figure A.1

Should we spend $100K to improve our reputation?

3. Overall expected value of both options
4. Expected value under certainty (i.e., of the best option)
5. Maximum amount we are prepared to pay for perfect information about the situation faced

Here are the calculations:

1. $\text{Expected value}_{\text{Introduce}} = (0.7 \times \$1\text{million}) + (0.3 \times -\$100{,}000)$

$= \$670{,}000$

2. $\text{Expected value}_{\text{Not introduce}} = 1.0 \times \$0$

$= \$0$

3. $\text{Expected value}_{\text{Overall}} = \$670{,}000 + \$0$

$= \$670{,}000$

4. $\text{Expected value}_{\text{Certainty}} = (0.7 \times \$1\text{million})$

$= \$700{,}000$

5. $\text{Expected value}_{\text{Perfect information}} = \text{Expected value}_{\text{Certainty}} - \text{Expected value}_{\text{Overall}}$

$= \$30{,}000$

These back-of-the envelope numbers suggest that the risk of losing $100,000 to gain a probable $1million is still a good decision. Its overall expected value is $670,000. The expected value of perfect information calculation also suggests that the company should spend up to $30,000 to clarify its thinking about this investment. Of course, any such calculation relies on the accuracy of the probabilities and the dollar costs and returns. In the situation noted above, you could halve the returns to $0.5 million and double the costs to $200,000 and it would still be a good investment because the overall expected value is positive. ($EV_{\text{Introduce}}$ = $290,000; $EV_{\text{Not introduce}}$ = $0; EV_{Overall} = $290,000; $EV_{\text{Certainty}}$ = $350,000; $EV_{\text{Perfect information}}$ = $60,000.) Notice that as the investment becomes more problematic, the value of perfect information and thus less-than-perfect market research increases. The actual value of a customized research study will depend on how well the research firm can model the effects of the reputation enhancement program on stakeholder outcomes such as engagement and loyalty. Only a detailed discussion with the research firm will uncover this.

These simple calculations guided by the wisdom of Thomas Bayes can be quite informative. The results often suggest that a company is underinvesting in its corporate reputation research. They may also suggest that market research firms underprice their research. Typically these firms base their price on their costs rather than the value of the research to the client. If this type of thought experiment seems informative, as the math becomes more complicated, there are personal computer packages to guide you through the assumptions in this decision technique and the formal calculations.

Index